Choices and Changes

Choices
and Changes

*Interest Groups in the
Electoral Process*

Michael M. Franz

TEMPLE UNIVERSITY PRESS
Philadelphia

TEMPLE UNIVERSITY PRESS
1601 North Broad Street
Philadelphia PA 19122
www.temple.edu/tempress

♾ The paper used in this publication meets the requirements of the American National Standard for Information Sciences—Permanence of Paper for Printed Library Materials, ANSI Z39.48-1992

Library of Congress Cataloging-in-Publication Data

Franz, Michael M., 1976–
Choices and Changes : Interest Groups in the Electoral Process / Michael M. Franz
     p. cm.
Includes bibliographical references (p.) and index.
ISBN-13: 978-1-59213-673-5   ISBN-10: 1-59213-673-7 (cloth : alk. paper)
ISBN-13: 978-1-59213-674-2   ISBN-10: 1-59213- 674-5 (pbk. : alk. paper)
1. Political science—political process.   2. American studies—perspectives in politics.   3. Politics—United States.   4. Political science—public policy.
ML3795.Y67 2007
780.89'95–dc22

2007018929

2 4 6 8 9 7 5 3 1

For Laura, Matt, Mom, and Dad

Contents

Acknowledgments

I n the spring of 2007 I taught a class at Bowdoin College called "Money and Politics." During one class session at the beginning of the semester, while discussing the dimensions of existing election laws, the conversation turned to legal loopholes. One student asked, "What happens if I leave a bunch of money on a candidate's doorstep? Can they claim to have 'found' it, thereby allowing me to avoid a contribution limit?" The class laughed, compelling other students to offer their own equally strange, but conceptually serious, alternatives. The bulk of the scenarios involved interest groups. What are the limits of the law relative to interest group electioneering? How and to what effect can candidates and their allies bend the rules to allow more money to enter the system? After class, I reflected on the experience and could not help but laugh. Loopholes are fun to find, but when you are actually participating in an election, where winning and losing is serious business, locating loopholes is more than an intellectual game; it's serious, risky, and consequential.

Indeed, the research for this book took place in the context of consequential debates over campaign finance reform. I first thought seriously about interest groups in the electoral process during the summer of 2000. As a research assistant for the University of Wisconsin Advertising Project, I witnessed the ad war firsthand (The Project coded every major political ad that year on dozens of different attributes). Interest groups and parties aired thousands of ads during the campaign, and almost none of the financing for those ads was reported to or tracked by the Federal Election Commission. Loopholes were being forced open, and millions of unregulated funds poured into the presidential race and dozens of congressional elections.

When the campaign ended, congressional debate in Washington, D.C., heated up over the consideration of major campaign finance reform. Advocates for reform wanted, among other things, new restrictions on the types of television ads that interest groups could air close to Election Day. They were successful in their efforts, and the Bipartisan Campaign Reform Act (BCRA) became law in 2002. Then, the Supreme Court in 2003 determined that much of BCRA was constitutional. For many, these developments were hard-fought victories— gaping loopholes in election law had been closed; the system was now safe from big money.

By the 2004 and 2006 elections, though, new loopholes emerged (quickly and efficiently, in fact). Swift Boat Veterans for Truth and MoveOn.org, for example, sponsored millions of dollars worth of television advertising, much of it in the weeks leading up to Election Day. Both groups claimed that these ads were not covered by the new law. No one knew quite how to react.

As I finish this project, the debate rages on. In the summer of 2007, the Supreme Court argued in *FEC v. Wisconsin Right to Life, Inc* that some of the new rules on interest group television ads had gone too far. The Court argued that interest groups should be permitted without regulation to discuss issues at any time during the campaign. The decision sent campaign finance reformers reeling, and as the 2008 presidential election season heats up, we are once again left with uncertainty as to the scope of existing regulations.

The story is always the same, it seems—Congress closes old loopholes and then new loopholes are found. This book is about that process relative to interest groups. It is not a book that offers an answer to what is the best election law system. People often always ask me whether campaign finance reform "worked," or whether I believe in certain reforms. No doubt, I started my experience with this project as a firm believer in finance reform. In carrying out this extensive research, however, these normative beliefs subsided. I can now argue both sides of the reform divide, and I find each to have very com-pelling arguments. My goals with this book are more systematic—to help readers understand the developments of campaign finance in the last generation (most especially as they relate to interest groups), and also to help them better predict and expect the yet unseen develop-ments of future election cycles. In other words, how did we get here and where we going?

At the 2007 meeting of the American Political Science Associa-tion, I was awarded the E.E. Schattschneider prize for the best disser-tation in the field of American government. My dissertation served as the first draft of this now revised and completed projected. I am particularly proud of that accomplishment, especially because Profes-sor Schattschneider's research on American politics (from the 1940s through the 1960s) was inspirational in developing my perspective on contemporary interest group politics. Some of my fondest intellectual memories in Madison, Wisconsin, involve reading the work of Pendle-ton Herring, Robert Dahl, and E.E. Schattschneider over countless cups of coffee on State Street. In particular, Schattschneider's discus-sion of the relationship between interest groups and parties was the theoretical motivation for the research in this book.

A number of people deserve considerable thanks; I would not be to this point without their help and encouragement. First, I am very grateful to David Canon, John Coleman, and Charles Franklin; their feedback on every chapter was influential in helping me sharpen and tighten the analysis. I am particularly appreciative for the hours spent talking with Charles about everything from politics to evolutionary bi-ology. Not only did he provide crucial empirical advice for the analysis in Chapter 4 but also I could always count on him to move me beyond a theoretical or empirical snag. I am thankful also to Byron Shafer and Laura Stoker. Byron's insights on American politics are truly first-rate, and I benefited immensely over the years from reading his work. Laura's close reading of the manuscript was helpful in highlighting as-pects of the analysis that were unclear.

I will always be indebted to Ken Goldstein. I spent four years as Ken's research assistant, but more important, I have spent years learn-ing from him. I have enjoyed both his good cheer and keen insights, and he was a wonderful advisor. As Ken well knows, I am hardly an as-set on the softball field, but I am very proud to have been part of his political science team. One of Ken's strengths is loyalty, and I have enjoyed working alongside him on numerous other projects.

I have made many good friends along the way, and each and every one of them has had a strong and unique impact on me (and on this project). Thanks to Travis Ridout, Paul Manna, Dave Parker, Patty Strach, Rudy Espino, Larry Markowitz, Alex Caviedes, Rachel De-Motts, Paul Schlomer, Travis Nelson, Dan Kapust, and Simanti Lahiri.

I also want to thank Alex Holzman and his colleagues at Temple University Press, including the anonymous reviewers of the manuscript. They have all helped streamline the analysis and advance the contribution, and I am very proud to have had the opportunity to work with Temple.

I also want to express my appreciation to the Government Department at Bowdoin College, in particular to Paul Franco, Christian Potholm, Richard Skinner, and Lynne Atkinson. In reworking and completing this project, I have benefited from their advice and encouragement. And as I mentioned already, the first-rate students of Bowdoin served as valuable sounding boards for the main ideas found herein.

Finally, my love and thanks to my family, to whom I dedicate this book. You inspire me every day with your love, affection, and hard work. I especially thank my wonderful wife Laura, who has cheerfully listened to far too many stories about soft money, political ads, campaign finance reform, and FEC advisory opinions. Chapter 1 is greatly improved because of her careful reading. I could never have completed this project without the love and support of her and the rest of my family.

1 The Puzzle of Interest Group Electioneering

October 11, 2000, was typical of most days in the final frantic weeks before the November elections. The *New York Times* reported in its "Campaign Briefing" that Congressman Clay Shaw was attacking his opponent Elaine Bloom on prescription drugs, that Ralph Nader had given a harsh speech the previous day on vehicle safety standards, and that, of the four candidates in the previous week's presidential and vice presidential debates, Joe Lieberman had used the "brainiest language."[1] The *Atlanta Journal-Constitution* reported on that day that Bush was campaigning in Tennessee and winning there in the latest poll and that Gore's Southern strategy was based on upsetting Bush in Florida.[2]

And on this very normal day, deep into the 2000 election, candidates, parties, and interest groups raised and spent campaign funds. The Walt Disney Corporation's Political Action Committee (PAC) in Washington, D.C., for example, made seven candidate contributions of $1,000 each, six to incumbent House Democrats and one to an incumbent Republican Congressman. The money used to pay for these contributions was raised in small amounts by Disney's PAC, and the PAC abided to an upper limit in the total amount given to each candidate for that election cycle. In other words, the PAC used "hard money." All told, almost 300 PACs contributed $1,966,344 in hard money that day.

On the same day, the nonfederal account of the Democratic National Committee (DNC) received a check for $80,000 from the Walt Disney Corporation in Burbank, California; the check exceeded the hard money upper limit on contributions to political parties *for an entire election cycle* by $65,000. Because Disney delivered the check to the DNC's nonfederal account, however, this contribution was "soft," meaning the source of the funds was neither regulated nor tracked. On October 11th, almost 300 groups of all types and sizes joined the Disney Corporation, contributing $2,784,148 in soft money to the Democratic and Republican parties. CSC Holdings in Woodbury, New York, for example, gave $250,000 to the Republican National State Election Committee; Collazo Enterprises in Huntsville, Alabama, contributed $10,000 to the DNC's nonfederal corporate account; and Walco Sheet Metal Inc. in Coralville, Iowa, contributed a modest $300 to the nonfederal account of the National Republican Congressional Campaign Committee (NRCC). Combined with hard money, interest groups contributed more than $4.7 million on that Wednesday in October—a substantial amount for only one day.

In many ways, the fund-raising activity of October 11th was not unique. The following Monday, five days after giving $80,000 to the DNC, Walt Disney contributed $50,000 to the NRCC. The Eastern Band of Cherokee Indians in Cherokee, North Carolina, gave $100,000 to the DNC, and the National Education Association contributed $20,000 to the DNC's nonfederal Building Fund. Indeed on October 16, 2000, 169 groups contributed $1,781,136 in soft money, adding to the $1.5 million in hard money contributions from interest groups that day.[3]

Most of this money, going straight into the accounts of candidates and parties, was spent by the recipients in the days and weeks that followed, but interest groups were also spending independently of federal candidates. Hard money funded some of this activity, but a lot was paid for with unregulated interest group soft money. Between October 23rd and November 6th, for example, the National Rifle Association's Political Victory Fund—a PAC registered with the Federal Election Commission (FEC)—aired a television ad in five presidential battleground states (Michigan, Pennsylvania, Virginia, Minnesota, and Washington). Actor and gun activist Charlton Heston narrated the ad. Looking directly into the camera, he explained to viewers:

Did you know Al Gore's Justice Department argued in Federal Court that the Second Amendment gives you no right to own any firearm? The Supreme Court could be next with new justices hand-picked by Al Gore if he wins. Think what Justice Hillary Clinton or Charlie Schumer would do to your gun rights. When Al Gore's Supreme Court agrees with Al Gore's Justice Department and bans ownership of firearms, what freedom is next?

Vote George W. Bush for President.

Between October 28th and November 4th, by comparison, the National Rifle Association aired another ad in two different media markets, one of them Memphis. This time executive vice president Wayne LaPiere narrated:

Did you know that right now, in Federal Court, Al Gore's Justice Department is arguing that the Second Amendment gives you no right to own any firearm? No handgun, no rifle, no shotgun. And when Al Gore's top government lawyers make it to the U.S. Supreme Court to argue their point, they could have three new judges, hand-picked by Al Gore if he wins this election. Imagine what would Supreme Court Justice's Hillary Clinton, Charlie Schumer, and Diane Feinstein do to your gun rights? There would nothing you can do. What you think wouldn't matter anymore because the Supreme Court is the final interpreter of the Constitution. And when Al Gore's Supreme Court agrees with Al Gore's Justice Department and bans ownership of firearms, that's the end of your Second Amendment rights.

So, please call this number now to join the NRA or just find out how you can help. Thank you.

Both Heston and LaPiere make the case that Gore's election would result in a more liberal Supreme Court (even positing Hillary Clinton as a future justice), one that would threaten gun ownership. While the Heston advertisement was paid for with regulated hard money, raised in small amounts and reported to the FEC as an independent expenditure (the term for hard money spent on behalf of a candidate but uncoordinated with the candidate), the LaPiere ad went unreported to the FEC and was classified as unregulated issue advocacy (the term for public communications that focus on public policies and avoid expressly calling for the election or defeat of a candidate). The only distinguishing characteristic of these similar ads was the presence of "vote for" in the former ad and the absence of such an explicit exhortation in the latter.

Indeed, in 2000 the presence or absence of so-called magic words—of which there are eight—*"vote for," "elect," "support," "cast your ballot for," "Smith for Congress," "vote against," "defeat," or "reject"*—was the legal bright-line test between issue advocacy and independent expenditures. All told, interest groups in 2000 aired 77,687 television advertisements that mentioned or pictured federal candidates, and 78 percent of them (60,623 ads) aired within 60 days of the November elections. Further still, only 1,157 of interest group ads aired within 60 days used "magic words"; that's only 2 percent.

Stories about magic words and soft money abound from the federal elections of 1996–2002. Before campaign finance reform went into effect in 2002, parties and interest groups were allowed to build unlimited war chests—in source and amount—of nonfederal soft money (which the FEC and Congress sanctioned in 1979), and they could spend these war chests on advertisements and other public communications as long as they avoided those call-to-action magic words (which the Supreme Court elucidated in 1976 in *Buckley v. Valeo*). The soft money allowance was intended to give parties leeway in mobilizing a partisan electorate and to allow both interest groups and parties the opportunity to help nonfederal candidates. Furthermore, the magic word distinction was designed to leave issue-based and nonfederal speech unregulated by federal election law.

Still, by avoiding the magic words in party-building activities, get-out-the-vote (GOTV) efforts, nonfederal electioneering, and issue-based advocacy, groups and parties could by implication spend millions of dollars in unregulated money in ways that aided or hurt federal candidates, prompting many to refer to these allowances as massive "loopholes" in election law. Indeed, the *Washington Post* editorialized that parties in the 1990s had become "addicted" to soft money in a campaign finance regime that increasingly "smelled bad."[4]

The examples above make the *Post's* assessment seem credible.

The unregulated anti-Gore ad by the NRA aired in a competitive market days before the election, and in a must-win state for Gore. (Indeed, Gore lost the state, and President Bill Clinton hypothesized that the NRA may have made the difference [Clinton 2004, p. 928]). And the Democrats and Republicans were free to use the soft money contributed on October 11th and 16th to fund advertising efforts in competitive Senate and House races. All of this activity occurred in an electoral context in which partisan control of the White House, the Senate, and the House of Representatives was highly contested. In 1996, for example, the Democrats needed 13 seats in the House and 3 in the Senate to regain majority control; in 1998 it was 10 in the House and 5 in the Senate; and in 2000 it was only 6 and 5, respectively. By the elections of 2002, only six seats in the House separated the Democrats and Republicans, and the Democrats held a slim one-seat control of the Senate.

While the campaign finance activity in the fall of 2000 might look similar to any typical campaign day between 1996 and 2002, it was atypical when compared to earlier elections. If we had similar comprehensive data on soft money contributions or advertising logs for every election cycle back to the early 1970s, we would see important differences.[5] On October 11, 1992, or October 11, 1988, or October 11, 1982, we would see much smaller soft money contributions to the Democratic and Republican parties from very few contributors (and almost no soft money in the late 1970s and early 1980s). There would be fewer advertisements sponsored by interest groups and almost none that mentioned candidates or were funded with unregulated money; even the (in)famous Willie Horton ad, an interest-group-sponsored attack on presidential candidate Michael Dukakis that many believed was racist, was paid for with hard money.

And while this is not to say that groups avoided aggressively engaging elections during this time—indeed some groups spent millions in the 1980s with the goal of aiding or defeating candidates—it was in the mid-1990s when interest groups and parties began spending hundreds of millions in soft money and on public communications that specifically avoided FEC regulation (Herrnson 1998a, Magleby 2001, 2002, 2003). Noted one early analysis of issue advocacy in the 1996 elections, "This is unprecedented, and represents an important change in the culture of campaigns" (Beck, et al., 1997).

These developments, however, are puzzling. If the distinction between unregulated and regulated money is so clear (simply avoid the use of magic words), the implications obvious (millions more for electioneering), and the loopholes old (a consequence of statutes passed and court cases decided in the 1970s), why did most interest groups and political parties wait until 1995 and 1996 to use these tactics in such high numbers? What happened to make them so common? Indeed, as Parker and Coleman (2004, p. 244) note, "As far as we can discern, none of these [issue advocacy and independent expenditure] activities were prohibited at any time following the Progressive era. In theory, PACs, private persuasion efforts, and independent expenditures were every bit as legal in the 1920s as in the 1990s."

I start with this puzzle and focus on the campaign finance regime beginning in 1974, which was part of the major governmental reforms following Watergate.[6] I use the puzzle of the 1990s as a launching point to answer a broader question, however: *Under what conditions do interest groups adopt or change election strategies?*

Interest groups participate in elections for a variety of reasons, which scholars of PACs have debated for more than two decades. Most studies, however, examine the determinants of contributions to or expenditures for individual candidates in one or a few elections; furthermore, the key causal variables are too often static (i.e., does party, seniority, committee assignment, or district characteristics predict a contribution?). For the most part, we are left wanting a theoretical understanding of these big changes in campaign finance—that is, the dynamics of why tactics shift, expand, or emerge over time.

More broadly, in answering the larger question I advance important debates about the power of interest groups in American politics and the relationship between interest groups and political parties. Scholars traditionally assume that interest groups are concerned with narrow issue agendas, while political parties are the province of majoritarianism (Baer and Bositis 1993). In the late 1990s, however, after the Republican gains in the 1994 elections, the number of highly competitive House and Senate seats regularly exceeded the number of seats needed to shift control of each chamber. With such an electoral environment, the participation of groups and parties in a handful of races had the potential to drastically shift the policymaking environment.

Consider the electoral context of 2002. In June 2001 Vermont Senator James Jeffords—a Republican—switched parties to become an independent. Because the Senate was split 50-50 between Democrats and Republicans (with Cheney as president of the Senate), Jeffords' switch gave the Democrats a slim 50-49-1 majority. But why was party control important? After all, if we look at the median voter in the Senate, little changed because of Jeffords' actions. According to one assessment, Jeffords became slightly more liberal after switching parties, but the ideology of the rest of the chamber remained stable.[7]

However, although nothing may have changed in this ideological sense, everything changed in the partisan sense. Senator Olympia J. Snowe, a Maine Republican, summarized it best when she said, "You're talking about control of the agenda."[8] After Jeffords became an independent, for example, Robert C. Byrd (D-West Virginia) replaced Ted Stevens (R-Alaska) as chair of Appropriations; Patrick Leahy (D-Vermont) replaced Orrin G. Hatch (R-Utah) as chair of Judiciary; Max Baucus (D-Montana) replaced Charles E. Grassley (R-Iowa) as chair of Finance; Joseph R. Biden Jr. (D-Delaware) replaced Jesse Helms (R-North Carolina) as chair of Foreign Relations; and Thomas Daschle (D-South Dakota) replaced Trent Lott (R-Mississippi) as Majority Leader. Indeed, everything changed in June 2001, the consequence of one Senator's party switch.

Because of this context, I show that many interest groups found reason to cast their lot with the electoral hopes of party entrepreneurs. These groups understood that, by helping party leaders retain or regain control of the House or Senate, policymaking rewards would follow, and perhaps to a degree far exceeding the politics of gaining access to individual legislators.

In the fall of 2002, the *Washington Post* made this pre-election assessment on the stakes of the upcoming mid-term elections:

Shifting Senate control to the GOP [in the 2002 elections] could secure priorities such as a permanent repeal of the estate tax, bigger tax deductions for business investments, elimination of the corporate alternative minimum tax and curbs on legal liability judgments. Conversely, [business groups] say, Democratic control of the House could mean higher corporate tax rates to finance Social Security and a prescription drug benefit for Medicare, and could jeopardize the tax cut that business groups helped secure last year.[9]

Such perceptions were not unique to 2002, however. In a 1998 plea to members of the Brotherhood of Locomotive Engineers and Trainmen, Congressman Patrick Kennedy said,

> We need you to remind people what's at stake in the fall elections: Do we continue to let the Republican majority cut backroom deals that sell out our nation's workers and threaten our way of life, or do we elect a Democratic majority that is committed to making right-wing extremism a thing of the past and putting working families first? Make sure that they know what a Democratically-controlled Congress would stop cold: saying "no" to bogus comp time bills; saying "no" to unfair striker replacement bills; and saying "no" to paycheck reduction efforts. Make sure they know just what a Democratically-controlled Congress would make happen: creating smaller class sizes and safer schools for our children; offering better access to quality child care and affordable health care for families; ensuring equal pay for equal work; and providing a secure retirement and improved long-term care for our seniors.[10]

Two years later, the president of the National Education Association wrote, in a post on the association's Web site: "A lot is up for grabs in Election 2000. The White House. The Congress. The Supreme Court. We stand to make a crucial difference."[11] And in 2004, the Club for Growth urged its members to take action in the presidential and congressional elections, saying: *"There's a lot at stake in the 2004 elections.* Control of the White House, Senate and House of Representatives is all up for grabs. The House and Senate Republican majority—slim as it is—must be defended. We can't afford to lose that controlling stake the GOP now enjoys in Washington. We can't let Democrats like Minority Leaders Nancy Pelosi and Tom Daschle take the gavel, and control the flow of all legislation in the Congress."[12]

Indeed, recent controversies about Tom Delay's fund-raising strike at the very heart of the importance of majority status. Delay, former Republican House Majority Leader, was indicted in 2005 on charges of funneling corporate contributions during the 2002 elections through his own Texans for a Republican Majority PAC (TRM-PAC) to the Republican National Committee (RNC). The RNC in turn sent contributions to Texas statehouse candidates, leading to the charge of money laundering, as corporate contributions to state candidates are prohibited under Texas election law. Those Republican candidates, whose electoral victories were presumably aided by the RNC money, delivered control of the state legislature to the Republican Party in 2002, which redrew the state's federal House districts before the 2004 elections. Court documents demonstrate that Delay's fund-raising for TRMPAC was motivated to elect Republicans and had the explicit goal of redistricting.[13] The resulting district map helped shore up Republican control in Washington, D.C., by boosting the number of Republicans from Texas by six. Delay's actions reflect a strategy of enticing corporate and individual support under a plan of ensuring long-term Republican majorities in Washington. Indeed, when majority status is at stake (and when its meaning is impactful and significant), it seems that political necessity is the mother of electioneering innovation.

The Argument

To answer the question—under what conditions do interest groups adopt or change election strategies?—my dependent variable is the observed tactics of interest groups; for example, patterns of hard money contributions, independent expenditures, voter mobilization, issue advocacy, and soft money donations. *The central argument is that to understand how interest groups engage elections in these varying ways, and to understand how this engagement has changed over time, we must comprehend how changing political and legal contexts create both opportunities and impediments for certain forms of electoral participation.*

My argument proceeds as follows. First, we know that tactical choices follow the strategic goals of interest groups (Goldstein 1999). If an interest group seeks to help elect or defeat candidates for office, it will select tactics appropriate to such a goal. We know less, however, about the source of interest group goals. Why would an interest group seek to help elect candidates? When are interest groups concerned more with seeking access to candidates than with helping with their actual election or defeat? I argue that an interest group's position in two crucial political contexts—ideological and partisan—will significantly determine the goals it sets for its electoral participation. Liberal interest groups faced with a conservative policymaking environment (the ideological context), for example, should pursue electoral politics designed to elect new (more liberal) members. Groups that favor one party should invest more heavily in that party when partisanship drives policymaking (the partisan context). On this latter point, the elections of 1994 and the electoral stakes in each election since form the crux of this argument. Why did interest groups wait so long to adopt soft money and issue advocacy? I argue that the polarized party politics of the late 1990s was a crucial motivating factor, compelling interest groups to mobilize in alliance with party agendas.

Additionally, I argue that tactical choices are determined by interest group capacity to support or utilize certain tactics. We know, for example, that an interest group's size and political experience have a powerful influence on its tactical selection (Cyert and March 1963, Masters and Keim 1985, Walker 1991). We know less, however, about how regulatory restrictions on certain tactics limit the capacity of a group to act in certain ways and at certain times (the regulatory context). In a sense, the point is obvious; pundits and journalists often note the manner in which political actors seek to "evade" campaign finance law. Senator Mitch McConnell (R-Kentucky), a vocal opponent of campaign finance reform, compared trying to limit money in politics to "putting a rock on jello," in that "You can squeeze it down, but it just goes in different directions"; this is similar to the more common metaphor that money in politics is like water on rock—it always finds the cracks.[14] I broaden that point beyond the anecdotal, arguing that political actors generally and interest groups specifically not only "learn" about regulatory boundaries but also adopt or change tactics at moments when the regulatory community appears most willing to permit those tactics. Why did interest groups wait so long to employ issue advocacy and soft money contributions? I argue that the regulatory context simply did not give the same leeway to innovative tactics in the 1980s as it did in the mid-1990s and that this too was a motivating factor.

All told, I argue that the political demand for funds coming from this extremely partisan and polarized political context combined with increased regulatory openness to create a "perfect storm" necessary to allow this "explosion" in interest group electioneering.

Data and Definitions

I bring to bear a diverse and unique set of data on my question. For example, I examine all soft money contributions to parties by interest groups from 1991–2002, using data from the FEC and the Center for Responsive Politics (CRP). Soft money has been largely ignored by scholars of interest groups, mostly because of data accessibility challenges, but in the six election cycles between 1992 and 2002, interest groups contributed a total of about $1 billion to the parties' nonfederal accounts.[15]

Second, I examine money given to and spent by Section 527 groups for political purposes from 2002–2004, using data from the Internal Revenue Service (IRS). These data have only become available in recent years, after Congress in 2000 passed an amendment to the Internal Revenue Code requiring 527s to disclose their contributions and expenditures. Section 527 groups are IRS-classified political organizations, a category that includes parties and PACs. Not all 527s are regulated by the FEC, however; most notably political organizations that operate below the federal level or only raise and spend soft money. In the elections of the mid-1990s, before passage of the Bipartisan Campaign Reform Act (BCRA) in 2002, 527s became a principal organizational vehicle for issue advocacy and soft money. After BCRA, high-profile 527s (such as the Media Fund, MoveOn.org, and the Swift Boat Veterans) continue to raise and spend soft money, much to the ire of campaign finance reformers; indeed, in the 2004 election, partisan 527s spent nearly $500 million.

Third, I investigate political advertisements aired by interest groups and parties from 2000–2004, using data from the Wisconsin Advertising Project. These data are the most comprehensive available for use in tracking the most visible public communications from interest groups and parties; analyzing these data remains one of the only ways to track expenditures on issue advocacy. The Wisconsin Advertising Project has not only tracked when ads air but has also coded each unique advertisement on content and tone. Since 2000, candidates, parties, and interest groups have sponsored more than 3 million ad spots meant to influence federal elections.

Fourth, I build a number of unique datasets measuring the nature of the regulatory context. I code more than 1,200 requests from 1977–2003 made by parties, candidates, and interest groups to the FEC asking for clarification in existing campaign finance law. I code more than 300 major campaign finance court cases during the same time span, and I track more than 100 changes in regulations as mandated by Congress and as modified by the FEC. These data are an invaluable source of qualitative and quantitative information on how political actors view the regulatory context and interpret the boundaries of permissible election activity.

In addition to these rich data sources, I also examine PAC contributions to candidates and parties from 1983–2002, a time span covering 10 elections. There have been numerous studies of PAC contribution behavior, but I critique the PAC literature as suffering longitudinally—that is, in explaining disparities in contribution patterns over time and across groups. I test hypotheses about aggregate PAC behavior for each election cycle. The value of this analysis comes in lending better theory to the literature on PACs, in addition to covering a number of election cycles under different electoral conditions.

Finally, I conduct individual, semi-structured interviews with political elites at the forefront of campaign finance. Because political actors participate in a campaign finance system that is complicated legally, many interview subjects preferred to remain anonymous or on background, especially concerning questions of the regulatory context. Nonetheless, these interviews serve both to clarify my other findings and to better situate the actions of interest groups in the changing political and legal contexts.

It is also important, before proceeding, to make clear my universe, as well as my conceptualization of interest groups. Because the principal focus of this study is on election-related tactics and how interest groups choose to engage electoral politics, I am interested in all interest groups that make at least some minimal electoral investments. My question then relates to why groups in this population choose some tactics over others. By implication, such tactics include some lobbying behavior. Indeed, some election-related tactics—such as contributing to safe seat incumbents—are chiefly designed to facilitate access to policymakers. As such, my empirical investigation of money raised and spent around elections is aimed at distinguishing election tactics designed to move votes from those election tactics meant to aid lobbying. I exclude from my analysis those groups that care not about elections, but care only about the writing and debating of policy (even choosing to avoid electoral politics as a lobbying tactic).[16]

As such, I make limited reference to what some have called the "K Street Project," a Republican plan to reinforce the lobbying corps in Washington with Republican operatives. According to Grover Norquist, president of Americans for Tax Reform, the Project was designed to identify "how many R's [Republicans] and D's [Democrats] are being hired by trade associations or companies," with the goal of giving more consistent access to those represented by pro-Republican lobbyists.[17] In many ways, a study of the K Street Project would demonstrate clearly the partisan environment in Washington and the development of that environment post-1994. With that said, my empirical investigation of elections proves a much harder test of the motivating force of the partisan context.

As a final point, I define interest groups as organizations involved in electoral politics that are neither individuals (using their own name as the source of the action) nor political parties. Therefore, law firms contributing soft money and corporations funding issue advocacy are identified as interest groups. Although my universe is large and my conceptualization of interest groups broad, I do not track all interest group electoral activity, nor do I list a universe of groups active in elections.[18] For example, I do not systematically track the ground war— mailings, phone banks, and door-to-door mobilization (although I include some of these efforts with my analysis of 527s). To do so would be overwhelmingly time consuming, and to the extent that others have done this, it is as part of a larger project involving dozens of scholars (Magleby 2001). I am confident, however, that these ground war tactics are motivated by the same factors that compel groups to act in ways that I am able to track.

Book Preview

In Chapter 2, I lay out three major changes in the political landscape of the last 30 years. First, I outline the expansion in interest group electoral tactics, focusing on soft money contributions, issue advocacy expenditures, and 527s. Second, I review partisan changes in Congress over the last three decades, most noticeably the Republican gains in 1994. Finally, I track the evolution of campaign finance law since the 1970s, namely the hundreds of court cases and regulatory changes, the dozens of minor (and a handful of major) amendments to existing statutes, and more than 1,200 opinions issued by the FEC. This chapter is a crucial primer for the empirical investigations that follow.

In Chapter 3, I build my theoretical argument, asserting the partisan and legal changes identified above as the driving causal forces in shifting interest group electoral tactics. In Chapter 4 I begin my empirical analysis by investigating how PACs respond to the ideological and partisan context. Chapter 5 analyzes the partisan context relative to soft money contributions. Although BCRA essentially banned soft money contributions to parties, this analysis is a crucial study of how groups respond to the partisan environment. I switch to an analysis of 527s and interest group television ads in Chapter 6. Chapter 7 concludes the empirical analysis with an investigation of interest groups and the regulatory environment.

Finally, I conclude in Chapter 8 with a discussion of the implications of my findings. For example, concerns about campaign finance have consistently focused on the potential corrupting influence of money in elections. In many ways, aggressive electoral activity may be less of a normative concern than the potential quid pro quo of money for specific votes on bills in Congress. More specifically, if a group engages the electoral process with the goal of moving votes—that is, convincing voters to cast their ballot for a specific candidate—one might assume this approach to be more satisfying and acceptable than the more hidden politics of access. Nonetheless, when that activity is designed to tip the balance of power in Congress as a whole, we are faced then with a community of interest groups invested in majoritarian outcomes, a concern that stems all the way back to the drafting of the Constitution.

2 Election Law and Electoral Politics Between FECA and BCRA

n April 1989, speaking on the floor of the Senate, Harry Reid (D-Nevada) implored his colleagues to take action and pass campaign finance reform:

> Mr. President, [in] the 1988 Senate race in the State of Nevada . . . there was a mass advertising campaign directed against the present Senator Richard Bryan, who was then the Governor. This money that was spent, more than one-half million dollars, was spent by foreign auto dealers. Now, you would think they would be spending their money to talk about stands that Governor Bryan had taken relative to commerce or trade. But, no; the foreign auto dealers were spending money on Social Security issues. The people in the State of Nevada had no way of knowing that it was the foreign auto dealers who were spending these huge sums of money on Social Security ads.
>
> I think that the voters have a right to know who is sponsoring the political advertisements and the literature designed to sway their choice. I think it is also important to note, Mr. President, that this is not a partisan issue. In the State of Nevada, the money was spent, over one-half million dollars against a Democrat, but there is nothing to prevent independent expenditures,

and they have been made in the past, against a Republican. I
see in the coming election in 1990 huge amounts of money being spent against Republicans and against Democrats (accessed
from the *Congressional Record*, http://thomas.loc.gov/).

Reid's predictions about the 1990 elections were not borne out.
While groups spent $21 million on independent expenditures in all
campaigns in 1988, they spent only $5.5 million on such expenditures
in 1990. Reid also slightly exaggerated his point. The "foreign auto
dealer" ads were sponsored by the Auto Dealers and Drivers for Free
Trade PAC, a group registered with the FEC. It did spend more than
$540,000 against Bryan and for his opponent during the campaign, but
the *Washington Post* in early November 1988 had reported on such activity, noting specifically that the PAC also spent money in other elections and on advertisements about Social Security issues.[1] In this
sense, Reid's assertion that the advertisements were hidden and that
voters were duped overstated the case.

Reid's concerns were not unfounded, however. In the 1980s, the
National Conservative Political Action Committee (NCPAC) spent
millions on independent expenditures in a number of crucial Senate
races, claiming to have defeated six liberal Democrats and causing a
stir similar to Reid's reaction over the Auto Dealers PAC (Sabato
1984). Still, while the actions of NCPAC and the "foreign auto dealers" in Nevada mobilized many to consider campaign finance reform in
the 1980s, as Reid did, major reform did not pass until 2002. And it
was in the mid-1990s when interest group money in elections "exploded" in the form of soft money and issue advocacy (Herrnson
1998a, Magleby 2001, 2002, 2003). To wit, by passing the Bipartisan
Campaign Reform Act (BCRA) in 2002, many proponents of campaign finance reform actually *supported* regulated independent expenditures (of the kind Reid warned about). Said Congressman
Gerald Kleczka (D-WI) in the 2002 House debate over BCRA:

> Some of my colleagues claim that [BCRA] would violate the
> freedom of speech guaranteed by the First Amendment. That
> is simply untrue. Corporations, labor unions, and other organi-
> zations would still be permitted to use any funds they have to
> run ads that discuss issues of legislation, so long as they do not

specifically refer to a candidate for federal office. If they do mention a candidate by name, all they have to do is to use hard money, which is regulated, subject to contribution limits and disclosure laws. These groups may also fund advertisements that do attack or support a specific candidate, the only requirement being that they do so through the established regulated process using hard money donations to their political action committees (accessed from the *Congressional Record*, http://thomas.loc.gov/).

It is curious that supporters of campaign finance reform in the late 1980s (i.e., Reid) could oppose regulated independent expenditures, while reformers in the late 1990s (i.e., Kleczka) could defend them. What happened in between? In this chapter, I highlight three major changes in American electoral politics over the last 30 years. First, I review the expansion in the size and scope of interest group electoral tactics in the mid-1990s—*the dependent variable*. More specifically, I review how interest groups in a variety of forms (527s, 501c nonprofits, labor unions, and corporations) learned to spend millions in unregulated soft money and issue advocacy.

Following this review, I identify two factors as the driving forces in this tactical expansion—*the chief independent variables*. The first concerns the partisan shifts in Congress since the 1970s (namely, more ideologically polarized and more cohesive parties-in-government, along with slimmer majority control of each chamber), and the second relates to legal changes in campaign finance made between the 1974 amendments to the Federal Election Campaign Act (FECA) and the passage of BCRA in 2002 (namely, an evolving regulatory environment that reduced barriers to more money in elections). In Chapter 3, I lay out an interest-group-level model of tactical selection, using this discussion as the foundation.

PACs and Hard Money

Before outlining the ways interest groups expanded their presence in campaigns, I begin with a brief discussion of one stable feature of interest group electoral involvement—PACs and hard money. When Congress passed campaign finance reform in the early and mid-1970s (the specifics of which are discussed later in the chapter), it legitimized a way for corporations, unions, and other interests to engage federal electoral politics in ways that were limited, regulated, and observable. They did so through political action committees (PACs), organizations that register with the Federal Election Commission, report receipts and expenditures in a regular fashion, and conform to standards in the raising and spending of money.

Any labor union, corporation, or trade association wanting to give money to federal candidates or to spend on their behalf is mandated to form a PAC (also called a Separate Segregated Fund, or "connected" PAC) and conduct any electioneering activity separate from its general treasury. These PACs are split into different categories depending on their sponsor: labor union, corporation, trade/health/membership association, cooperative, and corporation without stock. For example, Miller Brewing Company sponsors a corporate PAC with an office in Milwaukee, Wisconsin. The trade association that advocates for beer wholesalers has a PAC with an office in Alexandria, Virginia. And beer workers at the Miller Brewery are represented by a Milwaukee branch of the United Auto Workers, which has its main PAC headquarters in Detroit, Michigan.

Any other interest group seeking to influence federal elections, but without a sponsor, is also required to form a PAC. These "nonconnected" groups are often called ideological PACs because they organize to advocate for specific issue agendas. For example, the Women's Alliance for Israel PAC donates to federal candidates that the organization believes will facilitate better U.S.-Israeli relations. The Black America's PAC (BAMPAC) supports predominantly black candidates and advocates for a range of issues of concern to African Americans.

There are extensive regulations concerning how both connected and nonconnected PACs can raise hard money. For instance, connected PACs can only raise funds from their "restricted class." This means that corporations can only solicit contributions from executive and administrative personnel, as well as from stockholders; labor can only solicit from dues-paying members. In contrast, nonconnected PACs can solicit from anyone.

There are also limits on a PAC's contributions—$5,000 to a candidate per election and $15,000 to a national party committee per year.[2] All PACs, however, can spend unlimited amounts on independent expenditures (like the Charlton Heston ad described in Chapter 1), but they must raise those funds in hard dollars and cannot coordinate the production or distribution of the campaign message with candidates.

Unlike the electioneering tactics discussed later in this chapter, PACs have had a consistent presence in campaigns since the late 1970s. Indeed, political action committees were once described as the "Precincts of the '80s," implying that hard money PAC donations were replacing grassroots advocacy as the primary vehicle of interest group electoral involvement (Elliot 1980, Wright 1989). The top left panel of Figure 2.1 shows the number of corporate, labor, trade association, and nonconnected PACs registered with the FEC between 1974 and 2002. Of particular note is the incredible increase in the number of corporate PACs from 1974—when there were almost none—to about 1986, when there were almost 2,000 (Schlozman 1984). In contrast, the number of labor and trade association PACs rose slowly, from about 200 labor and 300 trade PACs in 1974 to about 300 and 800, respectively, in 2002. Interestingly, the number of nonconnected PACs exploded from 1974 to 1986 (at a similar pace to corporate PAC growth), but plummeted from more than 1,000 in 1986 to fewer than 300 in 2002.[3]

Figure 2.1 also shows the total money contributed by each PAC type in the election cycles between 1979 and 2002 (all dollar values are in constant 2002 dollars).[4] It should be noted that contribution totals for cooperatives and corporations without stock are not included here because they account for a small percentage of all PACs and their participation in campaigns is limited. For example, cooperative PACs contributed (in total) only about $2.5 million in any given election cycle between 1980 and 2002. Contribution figures for corporations without stock were a bit higher (about $4 million for any cycle), but they remained much lower than all other PAC categories.

This figure makes clear that PAC hard money contributions represent a powerful and stable force in electoral politics. Contribution totals from all PACs do track slightly upward between 1984 and 2002, but at a modest pace. For example, labor PACs contributed just under $50 million in 1984, but just more than $50 million in 2002. Trade associations contributed about $50 million in 1984 and about $60 million in 2002. Corporate PACs accounted for about $70 million in 1984 and close to $100 million by 2002. Finally, nonconnected PAC contributions

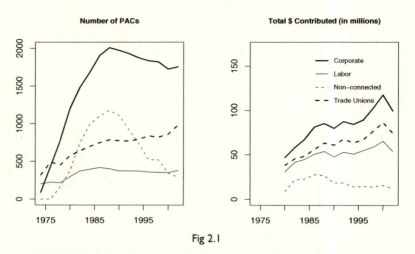

Fig 2.1

The Stability of PACs in Elections. (*Source:* Federal Election Commission. Dollar amounts are in constant 2002 dollars. I do not include three other PAC types—Corporations without Stock, Cooperatives, and Nonclassified PACs. PAC—Political Action Committee.)

actually declined slightly in this time frame.

All told, the presence of hard money in federal elections remains highly relevant. For example, although individual candidates can only accept $5,000 per election from a PAC, collectively PACs can leverage considerable influence on what happens in federal elections. Furthermore, PAC contribution limits remain higher than individual donor limits ($5,000 vs. $2,000), which is attractive to candidates seeking to raise large amounts of campaign funds.[5]

Finally, although hard money went largely unnoticed in the era of soft money, many have returned to PACs and hard money in the wake of BCRA's passage. For instance, in July 2004, the *New York Times* reported on a group of artists who were working to raise money for the Downtown for Democracy PAC. Although they were not traditionally interested in politics or elections, they felt compelled to mobilize against George Bush in the presidential election. (Said one organizer: "It's 'fashionable' to hate George Bush right now.") To facilitate their activism, they sponsored an event called "Art Works for Hard Money," with the goal of raising $1 million.[6] Because PACs are so important to understanding interest group electioneering in contemporary American politics (and have been for over a generation), it is important to consider them along with the development of soft money, issue advocacy, and 527s.

Soft Money

In Chapter 1, I noted Walt Disney's soft money contributions to the Democrats and Republicans. During the entire 1999–2000 election cycle, Walt Disney contributed $690,291 in 26 soft money contributions, compared to $290,571 in 219 hard money contributions. Disney was not alone in such endeavors. In the 2000 election cycle, 560 interest groups gave more than $100,000 each to Democratic and Republican nonfederal accounts. This number was up from 321 such groups in 1998, 379 in 1996, 124 in 1994, and 115 in 1992. In 2002, the last year of party soft money, 509 interest groups contributed at least $100,000 each in nonfederal funds.

To show the rise of soft money, Figure 2.2 tracks the number of hard and soft money contributors over time, as well as the total amount contributed (in constant 2002 dollars). The hard money data (in the figure) go back to the 1983–1984 election cycle, and I show PAC contributions to candidates and parties as well as independent expenditures by PACs. The soft money figures go back only to 1991, when the FEC first mandated that parties report soft money receipts. (By interest group soft money contributions, I mean any contribution not given in the name of an individual. Thus, soft money contributions from all corporations, unions, law firms, nonprofits, and so forth are subsumed into this total.) Although we do not have the data on soft money from the 1980s, the consensus is that the amount raised and spent by parties then was significantly lower (Drew 1983, Dwyre and Kolodny 2002); one FEC report, for example, noted that one national party committee raised only $3.7 million in soft money in 1984.

The graphs in Figure 2.2 illustrate a powerful point. Between 1983 and 2002, the number of PAC hard money contributions ranged between 150,000 and 200,000, while the frequency of independent expenditures stayed fairly constant and very low. Between 1991 and 2002, however, the number of soft money contributions rose steadily, from about 11,000 in the 1992 cycle to nearly 50,000 in 2002 (an increase of

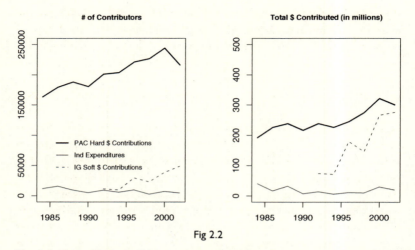

Fig 2.2

The Soft Money "Explosion." (*Source*: Federal Election Commission. Dollar amounts are in constant 2002 dollars. Data on soft money start in 1991 and exclude contributions from individuals.)

424 percent). In terms of total amount contributed (the right panel), interest group soft money contributions nearly equaled all hard money PAC contributions in 2000 and 2002—a striking trend given that the number of PAC contributions was still more than four times greater than the number of soft money donations. Note, also, that independent expenditures (which caused Harry Reid considerable consternation in 1989) never approached the hard and soft money totals in this period.

Despite arguably being the "Precincts of the '90s," though, soft money had its roots in both FEC and congressional actions in the late 1970s. First, the FEC ruled in the late 1970s and early 1980s that state, local, and federal parties could raise soft money from prohibited sources if that money was used for activity in state and local races. Party committees had to abide by state law in the raising of such non-federal money, but many states had far looser restrictions on the source of party funds (compared to federal law). Parties also had to maintain separate federal and nonfederal accounts and pay for any federal electioneering with hard funds. All told, the FEC considered 20 separate legal requests between 1977 and 1984 (called "advisory opinions," which are discussed later in this chapter) from Democratic and Republican party committees exploring the potential of raising and spending nonfederal money for various party functions.

A handful of important opinions were issued in 1978. For example, the Republican State Committee of Kansas (in Advisory Opinion 1978-10) asked the FEC in February that year if it could allocate some nonfederal resources for get-out-the-vote (GOTV) efforts; this request was controversial because Republican federal candidates in Kansas stood to benefit from the party's mobilization.[7] The FEC permitted such action and even left the decision of how to allocate funds (that is, how much would be paid for with hard and soft dollars) to the party committee.[8] A few months later, the Michigan Democratic Party asked a similar question (in Advisory Opinion 1978-50), and the FEC again affirmed the ability of party committees to spend nonfederal resources on voter turnout efforts.

In addition, Congress amended federal election law in 1979, and one important component allowed state and local parties to spend un-limited hard money funds on grassroots campaigning, slate cards and sample ballots, GOTV efforts, and voter registration. In other words, the law did not count those expenditures as limited in-kind contributions to federal candidates. Campaign finance expert Anthony Corrado notes that the amended law did not completely create or directly sanction the concept of soft money, but it did pave the way for parties to infuse larger amounts into the electoral process (Corrado 2005, p. 26).

It took nearly 15 years, but by the 1990s, federal party committees were raising soft money with increasing levels of sophistication. This is evident when one examines the number of party committees raising soft money. The Democrats, for example, maintained specific nonfederal accounts associated with their major national committees—the Democratic National Committee, the Democratic Congressional Campaign Committee, and the Democratic Senatorial Campaign Committee. The same was true for Republicans, who raised nonfederal funds through the Republican National Committee, the National Republican Congressional Committee, and the National Republican Senatorial Committee. The parties, however, also established a number of other nonfederal accounts. These included Democratic and Republican "building funds," Republican House and Senate "Dinner" committees, and Democratic "Max PAC," "Labor," and "Corporation" committees. Both Republicans and Democrats increased the number of nonfederal accounts between 1992 and 2002, from about 20 for the Democrats and 12 for the GOP in 1992 to nearly 50 and 30, respectively, in 2002.

Both parties also developed a number of "state-specific" party committees, which are nonfederal accounts named after states or federal candidates—for example, the Ashcroft Victory Committee or the DSCC Nonfederal-Minnesota account. Proponents of campaign finance reform often noted the presence of these committees (especially the candidate Victory funds) as a sign that soft money had become increasingly specialized and obviously meant to influence federal elections (Herrnson and Patterson 2002, Magleby 2002). As a specific example, one of the most-noted Victory funds—the nonfederal Giuliani Victory Committee—raised $292,500 in interest group soft money funds in 2000.

In the context of this growing soft money presence, one must ask this question: What are interest groups after in contributing large soft money dollars to party committees (Apollonio and La Raja 2004, Clawson, Neustadl and Weller 1998, Dwyre 2002)? In principle, as mentioned, these nonfederal funds were purportedly contributed to help state and local candidates, but by the late 1990s much of the parties' soft money was being spent by party entrepreneurs to air non-magic word advertisements in federal races. McCarty and Rothenberg (2000) note the potential benefit for interest groups: "the use of so-called 'soft money' contributions [has enhanced] the role of the party as an intermediary between groups and candidates: Interest groups [had] an incentive to channel large amounts of money to party organizations so it could be funneled into accounts where it could be spent directly on favored candidates" (292).

At the same time, however, fund-raisers and party officials also acknowledged that soft money was used to purchase access to party leaders and federal policymakers. According to former Senator Dale Bumpers, in his 2003 affidavit for *McConnell v. FEC*:

> I believe that, in many instances, there is an expectation of reciprocation where donations to the party are made. . . . I do not think the tobacco industry gives the Republican Party a million and a half or two million dollars because they expect

them to take a very objective view on tobacco issues. I think the tobacco industry got what they expected when, after they had given scads of money to both the Republican National Committee and the National Republican Senatorial Committee, a majority of Republicans killed the tobacco bill (accessed from Key Documents section of www.democracy21.net).

As such, soft money became an important avenue by which interest groups bolstered their presence in federal politics and in federal campaigns. The presence of soft money allowed interest groups to contribute to parties with the goal of helping candidates in close races and to signal their loyalty to a party agenda.

Issue Advocacy and Political Advertisements

In addition to contributing directly to candidates and parties, many interest groups also spend independently on behalf of candidates. By the late 1990s, hard money ads such as the Heston spot from Chapter 1 were not nearly as abundant as issue advocacy spots like the LaPierre example. The vigorous debate over issue advocacy really began in 1993 and 1994 when the Health Insurance Association of America aired its famous "Harry and Louise" ads, which opposed the Clinton health care plan (Goldstein 1999, p. 74). In the 1996 elections, the AFL-CIO shocked the political world, though, by spending an unprecedented $35 million on television "issue advertisements" that attacked 32 Republican freshman members of Congress (Magleby 2001).

Such spots, in avoiding magic words, were considered unregulated, and thus, interest groups were free to raise and spend unlimited amounts. As mentioned in Chapter 1, these magic words are "vote for," "elect," "support," "cast your ballot for," "Smith for Congress," "vote against," "defeat," or "reject." Such a distinction was particularly important for labor unions and corporations who could use general treasury funds to pay for nonmagic-word advertisements. Recall the quote from Chapter 1, which noted that the explosion of issue advocacy was "unprecedented, and represent[ed] an important change in the culture of campaigns" (Beck et al. 1997).

Table 2.1 lists the groups that spent more than $100,000 in advertisements mentioning a federal candidate within 60 days of the

2000 general election. The biggest spender, Citizens for Better Medicare, spent more than $6.6 million on almost 11,000 ads. That total is greater than all hard money independent expenditures by labor and nonconnected PACs in 2000. Even groups spending comparatively less, such as the Campaign for a Progressive Future, still spent more than $400,000 in the last eight weeks of the campaign—equivalent to making 80 candidate contributions of $5,000 each. And groups like the Coalition for Future American Workers, Citizens for Better America, and Clean Air Project, all of which sponsored fewer than 200 ads in the final 60 days, spent more than $100,000 in that period.[9]

The table also shows that the vast majority of these ads did not employ magic words. Only 4 of the 22 groups used magic words in some of their ads, and only one group, the National Education Association, used them in any significant proportion (31 percent of their 511

TABLE 2.1 INTEREST GROUPS MENTIONING FEDERAL CANDIDATES IN ADVERTISEMENTS WITHIN 60 DAYS OF 2000 ELECTION

Organization	Total Spent	# of Spots	% w/ Magic Words
Citizens for Better Medicare	$6,615,826	10,753	7%
Chamber of Commerce	$5,480,846	7,574	0%
Plan Parenthood	$5,340,506	5,916	0%
AFL-CIO	$5,142,962	9,779	0%
Women Voters: A Project of Emily's List	$3,635,178	2,645	0%
Americans for Job Security	$2,826,989	5,007	0%
Business Round Table	$2,685,977	4,571	0%
Handgun Control	$1,793,938	2,887	2%
Sierra Club	$1,112,387	1,707	0%
League of Conservation Voters	$900,601	1,705	0%
Americans for Quality Nursing Home Care	$803,195	980	0%
Right to Life Committee	$707,660	601	0%
Voters for Choice	$699,024	683	0%
American Medical Association	$477,077	543	0%
Emily's List	$443,120	800	0%
Campaign for a Progressive Future	$410,983	863	0%
Coalition for Future American Workers	$241,001	172	0%
NAACP	$212,106	461	0%
National Rifle Association	$205,609	333	11%
Citizens for Better America	$137,337	72	0%
National Education Association	$179,601	511	31%
Clean Air Project	$127,602	191	0%

Source: Courtesy of Wisconsin Advertising Project
*This table does not include unidentified ad sponsors or groups spending less than $100,000, and these are numbers for groups airing advertisements in the top 75 media markets.

ads). In general, of the 77,687 interest-group-sponsored ads in 2000 that mentioned or pictured a federal candidate, only 1,561·(2 percent) used one of the eight magic words.

Like soft money, however, although issue advocacy became popular in the mid- to late 1990s, its legality was debated far earlier. For example, in his classic book on campaigning—*The Advance Man*—Jerry Bruno (a veteran of John Kennedy's presidential campaign in 1960) notes the clever ways incumbents in the 1960s used the franking privilege (free mailings to constituents) to advance their electoral chances; he cites specifically the avoidance of certain words, like "Vote for Me," in campaign communications (Bruno and Greenfield 1971, p. 24).

It was not until *Buckley v. Valeo* in 1976 that the Supreme Court first enunciated—in footnote 52 of its opinion—the "magic word" test of express advocacy. Justifiably, the Court was worried about the boundary between election speech (which they were willing to regulate) and issue speech (which they were not). They listed the eight words and phrases that—in their minds—clearly demarcated express from issue advocacy. Bradley Smith (2001, pp. 180–188) notes that a close reading of the Court's decision in this area shows that the justices were well aware of the potential loophole a magic word distinction might create. For example, in striking down Congress's attempt to limit express advocacy, the Court said in *Buckley*: "[Such a ban] would naively underestimate the ingenuity and resourcefulness of persons and groups desiring to buy influence to believe that they would have much difficulty devising expenditures that skirted the restrictions on express advocacy of election or defeat but nevertheless benefited the candidate's campaign" (quoted from Smith 2001, p.183).

Of course, the famous footnote 52 only established the *possibility* of distinguishing issue from express advocacy. It did not end the debate. After *Buckley*, interest group and party entrepreneurs sought advice from the FEC in defining and understanding the standard for express advocacy. Between 1977 and 1980, the FEC considered 29 legal requests about whether proposed activity was election or issue speech.

For example, in November 1979, the LTV Corporation Active Citizenship Campaign (LTV/ACC) asked the FEC (in Advisory Opinion 1979-70) if it could compile the issue stances of the two major presidential candidates that year (with the candidates' approval) and distribute the information to the general public (mostly through print advertise-ments). LTV/ACC asked specifically if it could pay for the effort di-rectly from its corporate account; since the effort did not directly advocate for a candidate, the corporation believed it was performing a public service. The FEC responded, however, that the activity was an in-kind contribution to the candidates because it represented some-thing of value to them, and it was permissible only if paid for with hard money. In making this decision, the FEC did not reference the magic word test and footnote 52.

In contrast, in January 1980 Arizonans for Life sought advice on the permissibility of a public mailer linking Senator Edward Kennedy (D-Mass.)—then a candidate for president—with the abortion debate (Advisory Opinion 1980-9). The mailer noted that if "Senator Kennedy becomes President he can make or break us on the abortion front." The group asked whether the mailer, which did not use magic words, was considered a hard money express advocacy communication or unregulated issue speech. In this decision the FEC concluded that because the communication avoided magic words it was unregulated.

BCRA's passage in 2002 altered the landscape by expanding a magic word bright-line test to include a "candidate mention" test. The BCRA standard works as follows. If an interest group airs a television or radio ad that mentions or pictures a federal candidate within 60 days of a general election or 30 days of a primary (and is aimed at 50,000 or more members of the electorate), the ad is classified as an "electioneering communication." For labor unions and corporations, electioneering communications must be funded with hard dollars (that is, through their PACs). Unions and corporations can, however, still use soft money to fund nonmagic-word candidate-mention ads outside the 60- or 30-day windows. Furthermore, the expanded test excludes ads aimed at fewer than 50,000 viewers.[10]

In many ways, interest groups' attempts to avoid federal election-eering regulations mirror the debate over pharmaceutical companies and their direct-to-consumer (DTC) advertising. In the last 20 years the Food and Drug Administration has altered regulations governing the television, radio, and print ads of drug companies. For example, the FDA issued rules in the 1980s that seemed to restrict what pharmaceu-tical companies could put in their advertisements (forcing companies to include information on possible health risks, for example), but relaxed the rules in 1997. In the wake of the 1997 ruling, which permitted pharmaceutical ads to refer viewers to other media for health risk information (such as on the Internet), television DTC ads in particular skyrocketed, from 13.5 percent of all DTC advertising in 1994 to 63.8 percent by 2000 (Bradford and Kleit 2006).

Opponents argue that such weakened regulations enable the pharmaceutical companies to evade restrictions on truth-in-advertising, but supporters of the trend argue that free speech rights trump all. This is precisely the same debate scholars, politicians, and citizens have been having for years in the realm of election and issue advocacy.

527s and 501(c)s

One of the most controversial questions surrounding the 2004 election was the continued presence of unregulated, interest group candidate ads in the final two months of the campaign; most of these ads were sponsored by the Swift Boat Veterans for Truth, the Media Fund, MoveOn.org, and Progress for America Voter Fund. For many, the prevalence of these ads after September 4 (the 60-day cutoff) flouted the law—for did not BCRA force all interest groups that air federal candidate ads within 60 days of the election to fund them with hard money? The answer is technically yes, except when those ads are funded by interest groups operating under specific exemptions applying to certain nonprofits.[11]

Much has been made in recent years of Section 527 groups, a classification drawn from the U.S. tax code. All PACs and parties are considered 527 groups (for tax purposes), but not all 527 groups are registered with the FEC. According to IRS regulations, a 527 does not need to register with the FEC if it actively attempts to influence elections but does not expressly advocate on behalf of any specific candidate.[12]

For proponents of campaign finance reform, 527s represent the latest significant loophole in the campaign finance system. Before the passage of BCRA, 527s were popular in the 2000 election because they could raise soft money funds with no disclosure requirements, meaning donors to these groups were not made public. The 527s could then spend these unlimited donations on election-related activities that avoided magic words. The most-famous 527 from 2000 (at least from the standpoint of media coverage) was Republicans for Clean Air, a 527 that aired advertisements against John McCain in the Republican primaries.[13]

In July 2000, however, Congress passed an amendment to the Internal Revenue Code requiring 527s to report receipts and expenditures to the IRS and to notify the IRS within 24 hours of their creation.[14] In addition, BCRA mandated that any electioneering communication, including those sponsored by 527s, be disclosed to the FEC. In October 2002 Congress further mandated that any 527 raising or spending $50,000 file all forms to the IRS electronically.

Figure 2.3 shows reported expenditures by 527s over a 24-month period starting in January 2003 and ending in December 2004. The graph shows a sharp increase during the 2004 election cycle, with expenditures reaching more than $150 million in the month before the 2004 elections. As noted, much of this activity was aimed at helping or hurting federal candidates. For example, according to FEC records on electioneering communications, 527s spent more than $82 million in October 2004 on television and radio ads that featured federal candidates. They spent nearly $18 million in September. The Swift Boat Veterans for Truth reported ad buys on October 14, 15, 22, 27, and 29 totaling more than $22 million. The Progress for America Voter Fund reported electioneering communications on nine separate days in the final two weeks of October totaling more than $17 million. And the Media Fund reported spending nearly $7 million between October 14 and the end of the month.

The question remains: How is it possible for these groups to spend so much money but remain beyond the scope of existing election law? Further still, how is this possible in the wake of BCRA? There are two explanations. First, the Supreme Court has long allowed individuals to pay for political advertisements with their own money. Individuals can fund any type of political ad they desire, without having to raise regulated hard money funds. Further still, a collection of individuals can form a group and use their shared resources to air ads. The only condition is that individuals use only their own money and remain unincorporated (Potter 2005, p. 79). The Swift Boat Veterans for Truth is one example of such an organization.

A second exemption, however, lies with the Supreme Court's decision in *FEC v. Massachusetts Citizens for Life*. In September 1978 a

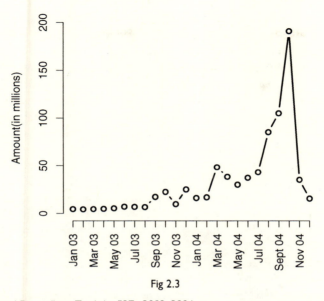

Fig 2.3

Reported Expenditure Totals by 527s, 2003–2004. (*Source:* Form 8872 in IRS political organization database. IRS—Internal Revenue Service.)

group called Massachusetts Citizens for Life (MCFL)—a nonprofit corporation without members—printed and distributed tens of thousands of flyers to the general public (some were sent directly to the group's contributors) that contained abortion-related issue positions of federal and state candidates and an exhortation to "vote pro-life." The FEC filed suit in district court charging that the group had violated the FECA's ban on corporate expenditures relating to federal elections. After district and appeals court rulings in 1984 and 1985 (both of which affirmed MCFL's stance on slightly different grounds), the Supreme Court ended the debate in December 1986 by declaring that the voter guides as printed were unregulated issue advocacy.

In so ruling, the Court carved out a specific exemption under existing federal election laws that allowed nonprofit groups like MCFL to use soft money to pay for express and issue advocacy without having to report to the FEC. The exemption applied to groups that met three criteria: first, the group must be organized for the explicit purpose of promoting political ideas and cannot engage in any business activity;

second, the organization must have no shareholders; and third, the group cannot be established by any corporation or labor union and must have a policy of accepting contributions mostly from individuals.

Before BCRA's passage, the MCFL case was important but not salient, as the magic word test was considered the accepted bright line between express and issue advocacy. By avoiding magic words, labor unions and for-profit corporations were allowed to fund issue advocacy with general treasury money. After BCRA, however, the MCFL test resurfaced. Interest groups asserted that, if they met the above criteria, the 30- and 60-day windows did not apply.[15] This was particularly important for 527s in 2004 because the FEC failed to establish rules for them in the run-up to the fall campaign season. As such, 527s were free to act under their own interpretation of the law (and defend themselves by noting that the FEC had not provided clear guidance).[16]

Indeed, in years to come, defining which groups fall under the MCFL exemption is likely to be one of the major focal points of contention at the FEC and in election law litigation. In December 2006, for example, the FEC completed a review of these 527s' activity in the 2004 campaign and ruled that MoveOn.org, the Swift Boat Veterans, and the League of Conservation Voters had violated the law by focusing almost exclusively on candidate advocacy (as opposed to noncandidate issue advocacy). Although the three groups accepted the judgment of the FEC commissioners and agreed to pay more than $600,000 in fines, they did not concede that they had broken the law.

The controversy is not limited to 527s, however. In the earliest days after the 2000 IRS amendment, some predicted that 527s would disappear in favor of 501(c) groups, which are nonprofit organizations that are not allowed to fund election-related activity and whose principal purpose is considered issue advocacy (Rozell and Wilcox 1999). Some examples of 501(c) groups include Handgun Control, Inc (which advocates for gun control and most often opposes the NRA) and the Christian Action Network.

There are two main categories of 501(c) groups distinguished by whether contributions to them are tax deductible. The 501(c)(3) groups, for which contributions are tax deductible, can engage in very limited issue advocacy—developing and distributing voter guides, for example. Their 501(c)(3) status is at risk, however, if they engage in advocacy deemed too partisan. Indeed, the Christian Coalition lost its tax-exempt status in 1999 because the IRS judged its activities to be too close to those of the Republican Party.[17] The 501(c)(4) groups can advocate political positions more freely than their 501(c)(3) counterparts, but such political activity cannot be their sole purpose; contributions to these groups are not tax deductible.

In recent years, the IRS has attempted to clarify the acceptable boundaries between legitimate 501(c) issue advocacy and prohibited election advocacy. As usual, the distinction is contested and often unclear. Some 501(c)s consider the MCFL exemption to apply to them exclusively, and not to 527s. The FEC appeared to agree with this assessment in drafting regulations after the passage of BCRA. In addition, the IRS has tended to define prohibited electioneering more broadly. In a February 2006 press release, for example, the IRS detailed 21 very specific examples of permitted and prohibited political activity; some of these examples of prohibited activity might be deemed acceptable by commissioners at the FEC (who have their own perspectives on the boundaries of election law).

Questions over what constitutes a political organization, however, are not unique to recent elections. For example, in 1986 the National Conservative Foundation, a 501(c)(3), sought to raise and spend corporate money to pay for an issues-based convention at which Republican presidential candidates would appear. The group asked the FEC for advice on this activity (notably in the same year in which the MCFL case was being considered by the Supreme Court), and the Commission responded by preventing the group from sponsoring the event. The Commission believed the function was electioneering activity (Democratic candidates were not invited), from which the Foundation—as a nonprofit—was prohibited in engaging.[18]

All told, then, as with party soft money and magic words, the debate over organizational form is not new.[19] The MCFL case specifically demonstrates that election law is unclear as to which groups can or cannot sponsor certain campaign-related activities. In this case alone, justices at multiple levels were conflicted over the reach of campaign finance laws. Indeed, as the examples in the previous sections have illustrated, interest groups and parties have for years attempted to understand the limits of existing regulations. But why did these tactics finally explode onto the political scene in the late 1990s? In the remainder of the chapter I describe the driving forces for their eventual widespread adoption—the changing political landscape and the evolving regulatory environment.

The Changing Political Landscape

One of the most powerful and fundamental changes in American politics over the last 20 years has been the resurgence of political parties (Herrnson 1998b, Maisel 2002), coming only years after many bemoaned their decline and long-term fate (Fiorina 1980, Pomper 1977, Wilson 1981). Indeed, party politics has proved to be compelling drama. First, Republicans won control of the Senate in 1980, before losing the chamber to the Democrats in 1986. Then, 50 years of Democratic dominance in the House was shattered with the 1994 elections, with the House remaining in Republican control until 2006. The GOP regained control of the Senate in 1994, lost it in 2001 with the unexpected party switch of James Jeffords, re-won a small majority in the 2002 mid-term elections, and lost it again in the 2006 midterms. Finally, the presidential election of 2000 was quite literally evenly split between Gore and Bush, with the winner being declared only after 30 days of vote recounts in Florida and a 5-4 Supreme Court decision.

In the last two decades, party politics in Congress has been embodied in increased ideological polarization between the Democrats and Republicans (Bond and Fleisher 2000, Coleman 1997), as well as in more disciplined party organizations (Aldrich 1995, Aldrich and Rohde 2000a, Bibby 1998). There is considerable scholarship on the nature of party politics. Overall the party divisions became particularly extreme around the 104th Congress, which began in January 1995 (Aldrich and Rohde 2000b).

In Figure 2.4, I show party cohesion scores and party fluidity scores between 1974 and 2002. The scores are from Cooper and Young (2002),[20] and the four panels show scores for Democrats and Republicans in the House and Senate. Party cohesion is defined as "the average absolute percentage of Democrats (Republicans) voting yes subtracted from Democrats (Republicans) voting no." For example, in a case where 90 percent of Democrats voted yes on a bill and 10 percent voted no, the cohesion score on that vote would be 80. Higher

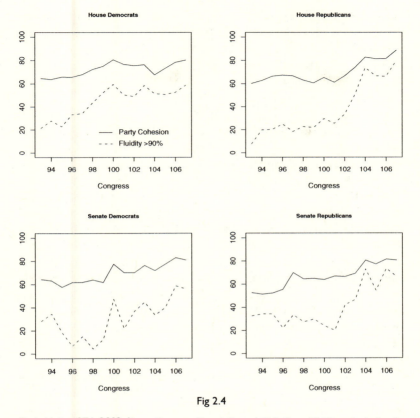

Fig 2.4

Party Unity, 1974–2002. (*Source:* Courtesy of Joseph Cooper). Definitions of fluidity and cohesion discussed in text.

average scores, then, indicate more unity in the party. Fluidity is defined as "the percentage of Democrats (Republicans) who supported the party on at least 90 percent of all party votes," in which party votes are those roll call votes with at least 50 percent of Democrats opposing 50 percent of Republicans. Higher fluidity scores indicate that the Democrats or Republicans have a higher number of core supporters.

Party cohesion tracks slightly upward over the time series, from about 60 percent for all House and Senate Democrats and Republicans to about 80 percent in 2002, a relative improvement of about 33 percent. All told, these trends are modest, while changes in party fluidity are far stronger. For example, only 20 percent of House Democrats (and only 10 percent of House Republicans) in 1974 supported the party on at least 90 percent of party votes. That number rose to nearly 60 percent for House Democrats (a 300 percent increase) and nearly 80 percent for House Republicans (an 800 percent increase) by 2002. In the Senate, fluidity reached a low for Democrats in the 98th Congress (about 5 percent), rising to more than 50 percent in 2000 (a relative increase of 1,000 percent). Republicans reached their low point in the 101st Congress (about 20 percent), but fluidity more than tripled by 2000 and 2002.

Taken alone, more cohesive and more polarized parties-in-government might not explain the dramatic rise in interest group electioneering in the mid-1990s.[21] Distinctive to the mid-1990s, however, was the perception that control of each chamber was up for grabs in each congressional election. Figure 2.5 illustrates this dynamic, showing in each election back to 1978 the number of House and Senate seats needed to shift control to the other party and the number of "competitive" seats, defined as races "too-close-to-call" by *Congressional Quarterly (CQ)*. In the electoral environments of the 1980s and early 1990s, the number of seats needed to shift control almost always exceeded the number of competitive seats. Even in the years in which Senate control changed (1980 and 1986), competitive seats matched but did not exceed the number needed to shift control. And in only one House election, 1982, was majority control at risk. Consider the elections of 1978, when the Democrats held a 75-seat advantage and only 25 races were thought "too close to call."

This trend reversed in the second half of the 1990s. In every House and Senate election except two between 1996 and 2004 (one House cycle and one Senate cycle), the number of too-close-to-call seats exceeded the number of seats needed to change control. The first exception is the Senate in 2000, but even in that case, *CQ*'s ranking had the Michigan and Virginia Senate races—both of which turned out to be two of the most contested Senate seats that year—as "leaning" and not "competitive." In the other case—the 2004 House—the number of competitive elections was 6, but the Republicans held a firm 13-seat majority. As such, only in the latter case can we say that the majority party was safe. All told, House and Senate elections looked a lot different in the late 1990s than they did in the late 1970s, the 1980s, and the early 1990s.[22]

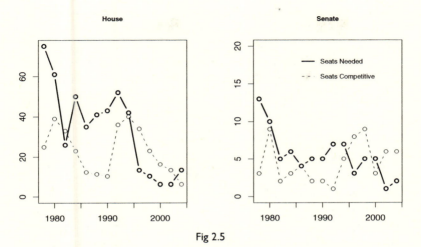

Fig 2.5

Party Balance in Congress Compared to the Number of Competitive Elections, 1978–2004. (*Source:* Competitive scores are from *Congressional Quarterly* ratings; the trend reported is the number of "too-close-to-call" races. Party balance numbers are from www.house.gov.)

A quick glance at *CQ's* pre-election analysis is also instructive. In 1984, for example, it described Republican chances of winning control of the House as "historically unlikely," in that it would require "an intense psychological reaction" against Democrats in a year when a Republican president was cruising to re-election. They predicted, at most, slight Democratic gains in the Senate but not enough to wrest control from the GOP. In 1990, *CQ* predicted the Democratic majority in the Senate to be secure, with only two Democratic seats seriously at risk, and it said nothing about control of the House, except to predict that Democrats would end up with more than 250 seats (over 30 seats more than needed for control of the chamber).

By 1996, however, the Senate was described as "anybody's call," and *CQ* argued that Democrats were "likely to gain seats in the House, if not control of the chamber itself." And in 2000, the entire election forecast was focused on the battle for control. According to Bob Benenson at *Congressional Quarterly*, "The congressional landscape has changed dramatically since 1994. . . . Both the Democratic and Republican parties are locked in a desperate and expensive battle for power this election year. Control of the White House is up for grabs, and every leadership position and committee chairmanship in Congress ultimately will be decided by the difference of a dozen House and Senate races."[23]

In Figure 2.6 I show the amount of stories from varied media outlets between 1978 and 2002 that mention "control of Congress," "control of the Senate," or "control of the House." I track these stories in the *Washington Post* and the Associated Press between 1978 and 2002; in ABC News Transcripts and the *New York Times* between 1980 and 2002; and in *Hotline* (from 1988) and *Roll Call* (from 1990).[24] The trend lines in the graph show increased "chatter" in 1986 and in the late 1990s, with a small decline in 1998. Associated Press stories show a similar pattern—note the small increase in 1986—but there is no decline in 1998.

These patterns tend to reflect the party balance numbers shown in Figure 2.5. For example, in 1986—the year the Democrats regained control of the Senate—the number of competitive seats equaled the number of seats needed to alter majority control. Given that the Republican gains in 1980 had given the GOP control of the Senate for the first time in nearly 30 years, the rise in "chatter" surrounding the 1986 elections makes sense. All told, we see a higher number of stories about control of Congress in the late 1990s.

As I make clear in Chapter 3, these trends are important in explaining the dramatic rise of interest group electioneering. In 1988, for example, political scientist Thomas Mann noted that, given the dominance of Democrats in the House, "Business PACs have learned they can live in a body dominated by liberals."[25] By 1996 and later, this perception was no longer held—indeed, a handful of competitive elections during this time had the potential to shift the entire policymaking environment.

This is only half the story, however. Although contested partisan politics may have compelled interest groups to funnel more money into the electoral arena (the empirical chapters that follow look for specific evidence of this activity), elections are the most watched and regulated democratic activity. Interest group and party entrepreneurs cannot ignore statutory restrictions on electioneering. I turn now to a review of the evolution of election law post-FECA, and I assert that because interest groups are embedded in an evolving regulatory environment, only after learning the dimensions of election law and only

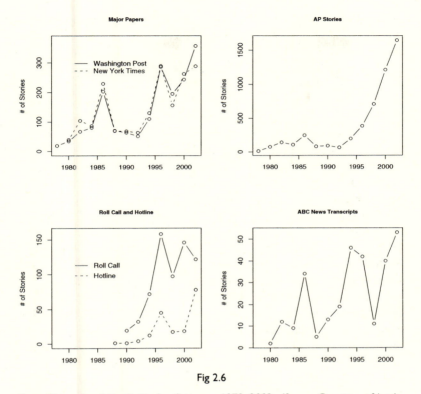

Fig 2.6

Press Coverage of the Battle for Congress, 1978–2002. (*Source*: Courtesy of Lexis-Nexis;)

after convincing the enforcers of such law did they innovate or employ untested tactics.

The Evolving Regulatory Environment

When Congress passed the Bipartisan Campaign Reform Act of 2002, it attempted to bring campaign finance law into line with the intentions of those who passed major reform in 1974. In other words, as supporters argued, BCRA was less a fundamental change than an attempt to "correct" for the exposed loopholes in existing campaign finance law. And yet, although no major campaign finance reform passed Congress in the 28 years separating the 1974 reforms and the 2002 BCRA reforms, it would be wrong to assume that election law was static.

David Tell uses extreme language to make that point, arguing as follows in *The Weekly Standard*[26]:

> Federal campaign law is a freakish mess—a 1974 omnibus statute, gutted and rendered only semi-coherent by the Buckley decision in 1976; the scars then plastered over with a quarter-century's worth of regulatory microscopia and equally gnostic judicial edicts; next, McCain-Feingold, a second omnibus statue barnacled onto the first; and finally, [2003's] "landmark" Supreme Court look-back at the whole, decades long lost weekend.

While Tell offers a skeptical view of the evolution of election law, his larger point is the relevant issue. Although many argue that money in elections is like water on pavement, always seeking out and finding cracks, if one were to expand the metaphor (and include the notion that election law can change), it would be that the crevices of campaign finance are never fixed. Indeed, they often close up to prevent money's passage or widen to facilitate it.

Campaign finance law is not unique to the last 30 years, however (Alexander 1972, Heard 1960), nor is the concern over money's influence in politics. One need only read Henry Adams' *Democracy*—published in 1880—to recognize the prevailing sense that politicians are susceptible to bribes and corruption. And while it has been said that the campaign finance reform effort of the 1970s "marked the end of an informal but historic division of labor in which parties had mobilized support in elections and interest groups brought influence to bear on officials already elected" (Sorauf 1996, p. 123), this is only partly true.

Congress curtailed electoral participation by corporations in 1907 with the Tillman Act, which put a ban on direct expenditures to candidates, and placed similar restrictions on labor unions in 1946 with the Taft-Hartley Act. Indeed, after Taft-Hartley some unions formed the first PACs, which would serve as the model for their legitimization under FECA. Other major congressional legislation includes the Federal

Corrupt Practices Act of 1910, which required party committees to report receipts and expenditures for House races. This act was amended in 1911 and 1925, expanding reporting requirements and imposing controversial limits on what candidates could spend in House and Senate campaigns. Congress also passed the Clean Politics Act, known as the Hatch Act, in 1939, which put limits on which public workers could be solicited for campaign contributions. All told, as Corrado (2005) notes, early campaign finance legislation was easily circumvented because of poor enforcement mechanisms and broad loopholes.[27]

In the next few sections I focus on how election law has evolved since the early 1970s. First, Congress has amended or changed existing legislation. Second, the FEC has issued regulations and advisory opinions that have altered the application of election law. Finally, the courts have ruled on the legality of FEC and congressional actions. Understanding interest groups as embedded in this shifting environment gives insight to how and when interest groups adopt or change election strategies.

Changes Mandated by Congress

When Congress passed the Federal Election Campaign Act of 1971, it contained three major provisions. First, it set limits on what candidates could contribute to their own campaigns, which added to existing laws already prohibiting labor unions and corporations from directly contributing to candidates. Second, it limited what candidates could spend on media, including restricting candidates to spending only 60 percent of their media budget on television and radio ads. Finally, FECA mandated candidates to disclose receipts and expenditures to the Clerk of the House (for House candidates), the Secretary of the Senate (for Senate candidates), or the General Accounting Office (for presidential candidates).

Congress passed major amendments to FECA in 1974, 1976, and 1979. In fact, on January 2, 1975, the *New York Times* reported, "The most sweeping political campaign reforms in the nation's history took effect today. The changes [the 1974 amendments], a direct result of Watergate, are considered certain to revolutionize campaigns for federal office."[28] The 1974 amendments to FECA established the Federal

Election Commission (which strengthened disclosure mandates), instituted expenditure limits (which replaced the media provisions in FECA), and expanded contribution limits (including limits on what individuals and PACs could contribute).

Although PACs had existed before the 1970s (Epstein 1980a), the 1971 Act gave them legal standing, and the 1974 FECA amendments mandated that organizations making political contributions or expenditures register with the FEC and abide by limits and regulations in the raising, contributing, and spending of money. Interestingly, the legal uncertainty surrounding PACs was clarified during this time as a result of two strategic errors made by organized labor. It was the AFL-CIO that pressured Congress in 1971 to include the amendment that legally allowed for PACs, and it was the AFL-CIO that lobbied in 1974 for the elimination of a provision that prohibited campaign contributions by government contractors (Epstein 1980a, pp. 112–113). Both changes, inspired by labor's lobbying, spawned corporate PAC growth (see again the top left panel of Figure 2.1).

After *Buckley v. Valeo* in 1976 ruled some aspects of FECA and the 1974 amendments unconstitutional (such as spending limits and contribution limits by candidates to their own campaign), the 1976 revisions implemented the Court mandates, including expanding contribution limits to political parties. Finally, the 1979 changes exempted certain grassroots, registration, and voter drives, as well as generic party-building activities, from hard money spending limits (as mentioned earlier see p. 23). They also no longer allowed candidates to convert excess campaign funds into personal funds.

Beyond this, Congress has also amended FECA in every congressional session but two since 1975, as I show in Table 2.2. On balance, these amendments are very minor. For example, in 1993, Congress tripled the tax check-off for the presidential public funding program from $1 to $3. In 1995, Congress permitted candidates, parties, and interest groups to file reports to the FEC electronically, and in 2000 Congress mandated that all candidates and committees file reports electronically.[29]

Finally, Congress passed BCRA in March 2002, and it became law following the mid-term elections of that year. The *New York Times* called it "the biggest election reform in a generation."[30] First, with

TABLE 2.2 AMENDMENTS TO FECA, 1974–2002

	Congress	Amendment to FECA?	Major Focus
93	(1973–1974)	Yes	1974 Amendments°
94	(1975–1976)	Yes	1976 Buckley Amendments°
95	(1977–1978)	Yes	Candidate honoraria
96	(1979–1980)	Yes	1979 Amendments°
97	(1981–1982)	Yes	Honoraria
98	(1983–1984)	Yes	Honoraria; Matching funds for Pres Cands
99	(1985–1986)	No	
100	(1987–1988)	Yes	Judicial Review of FEC
101	(1989–1990)	Yes	Honoraria, Cand use of campaign funds
102	(1991–1992)	Yes	Honoraria
103	(1993–1994)	Yes	Matching funds
104	(1995–1996)	Yes	Reporting Requirements
105	(1997–1998)	No	
106	(1999–2000)	Yes	Internet, Reporting Requirements
107	(2001–2002)	Yes	BCRA amendments°

Source: Courtesy of Thomas online
°The 1974, 1976, 1979, and 2002 Amendments were key shifts in campaign finance law and are described in more detail in the text.

one small exception, BCRA banned national parties from raising and spending soft money. That exception—known as the Levin amendment (for the amendment's sponsor, Senator Carl Levin of Michigan)—allows soft money contributors to give up to $10,000 dollars to any state or local party committee. That money must be used for voter registration or GOTV materials, however, neither of which can mention nor picture a federal candidate. Second, as mentioned earlier, BCRA redefined the boundaries between regulated and unregulated political communications to the general public, with the mention or depiction of a candidate replacing the magic word test.

There were a number of other major changes as well. For example, BCRA doubled individual contribution limits from $1,000 to $2,000 and indexed those limits to inflation. Also, the "millionaires' amendment" increased contribution limits to candidates facing a wealthy opponent who expects to use a large amount of personal funds in the campaign. This was intended to level the playing field between wealthy and nonwealthy candidates. In addition, BCRA mandated that candidates announce on-screen that their ad was approved by their campaign (known as the "stand by your ad" provision).

BCRA also outlawed contributions from individuals 17 years old or younger.

Regulatory Changes Instituted by the FEC

The Federal Election Commission has undergone its own evolution. As created by the 1974 FECA amendments, it was made up of six voting members (two appointed by the president and four by the House and Senate) and two nonvoting ex officio members (the Clerk of the House and the Secretary of the Senate). The commission was to be balanced by having three voting Democratic members and three voting Republicans, but it had few enforcement powers and no authority to levy penalties against election law violators.

Buckley v. Valeo ruled unconstitutional the process of joint presidential-congressional appointment, and Congress responded in its 1976 FECA amendments by giving the president power to appoint all six commissioners, with advice and consent from the Senate. Congress also gave commissioners stronger enforcement powers, but mandated that any action be approved by four of the six commissioners. In 1993, the D.C. Appeals Court in *FEC v. NRA Political Victory Fund* ruled that the presence of two nonvoting ex officio members (the Clerk of the House and the Secretary of the Senate) was unconstitutional.

The FEC has altered and clarified the regulatory context in two principal fashions—through regulation changes and through advisory opinions. In Figure 2.7, I show the number of changes made in FEC regulations since 1980. The FEC initiates these changes to reflect mandates from Congress (i.e., in the case of amendments to FECA), to reflect changes in the nature of politics (i.e., electronic filing or the use of the Internet), or to address consistent concerns with the clarity or applicability of certain provisions of the law. Regulatory changes are the result of the rule-making process in which the FEC Commissioners hold public hearings and gather information. If a change is accepted, it goes before Congress for 30 legislative days before becoming effective. Before the Supreme Court ruled legislative vetoes unconstitutional in 1983, either chamber could overrule an FEC regulation change. With no legislative veto, Congress must now pass legislation to overturn new FEC rules.

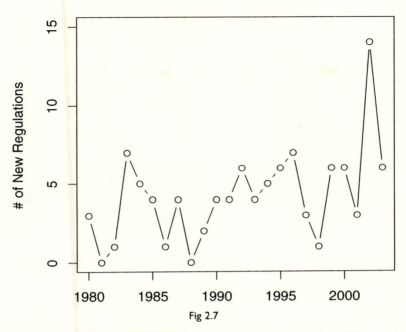

Fig 2.7

FEC Regulation Changes, 1980–2003. (*Source:* Federal Register. The large spike in 2002 is caused by the FEC's implementation of the BCRA. FEC—Federal Election Commission. BCRA—Bipartisan Campaign Reform Act.)

As an example, the FEC issued a regulation change in 1985 that prohibited potential candidates from accepting excessive or prohibited funds under the "testing the waters" exemption. Prior to the change, candidates who had not yet formally declared their candidacy could accept such funds, provided they were returned on making the decision to run. Many were concerned that candidates were using such prohibited or excessive funds to build a base of support prior to the initial campaign. The FEC, at the behest of those concerned, held public hearings and invited feedback, eventually finding cause for a change in the regulations.

The FEC also responds to inquiries from candidates, parties, interest groups, or individuals about permissible campaign activity. These responses come in the form of advisory opinions (AOs), and there were more than 1,200 AOs between 1977 and 2003. (I have referenced a number of them already in this chapter.) Election law mandates the FEC to consider and rule on these requests, which must relate to specific (and not hypothetical) activity directly relating to the person making the requests. These opinions have covered a whole range of issues, including soft money and issue advocacy (as noted earlier); what constitutes membership for purposes of solicitation; the way a group, party, or candidate can form or organize; how petitioners can handle loans or debts; what candidates can do with war chests when they leave office; and how to organize a campaign after a candidate dies.

In 1975, for example, the Federal Election Commission clarified the parameters of PAC political activity by establishing differences between connected PACs and nonconnected PACs. More specifically, the opinion allowed connected PACs to have overhead costs paid for by their parent organization. Nonconnected PACs can solicit from anyone, but must pay for the overhead costs on their own.

Figure 2.8 shows, first, that the number of AOs has declined over time. In the early years after the passage of FECA and its major amendments, the FEC considered on average two AOs a week. Throughout the 1980s and 1990s, however, those numbers slowly moved downward, with small election-year spikes. Perhaps as interesting, however, are the changing characteristics of AOs. Even as their frequency decreased, issued opinions got longer (in terms of total words) and more complex (in terms of the Commission's reference to previously decided AOs).

These changing characteristics make some sense. In the early years after FECA was passed and amended, there were thousands of potential questions, some that sound trivial today. For example, in 1977 Congressman John Duncan asked the FEC if he could transfer his 1976 campaign war chest to his 1978 campaign committee; he also asked if contributors from his 1976 campaign could begin making contributions in 1977 to his next election (Advisory Opinion 1977-24). By all accounts, these are basic questions that are now well understood. Over time, the AO process became more of an avenue for complicated and innovative questions; in that sense, the regulatory environment has become denser.

Indeed, the data on regulatory changes and advisory opinions demonstrate not only the kinds of questions being asked or considered (and when) but also how the FEC interprets election law and how this

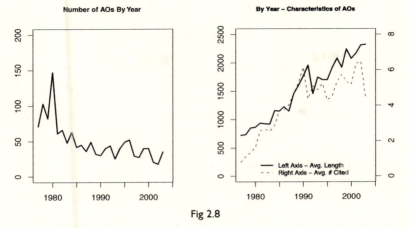

Fig 2.8

Advisory Opinions to Federal Election Commission, 1977–2003. (*Source:* Federal Election Commission. Length is the average number of words in each Advisory Opinion.)

interpretation varies or changes over time. The FEC is not a passive participant in these matters. Commissioners have strong opinions on the FEC's role in interpreting election law, and in the reach and scope of existing statutes. Thus, interest groups are embedded in a regulatory environment that has two principal features relative to the FEC. First, it is an environment that does change; regulatory changes and advisory opinions can directly alter what the law proscribes. This creates a dynamic in which interest groups learn about election law as it changes. Second, the enforcers of election law have orientations toward and perspectives on the law, which can also change. This creates a dynamic where interest groups face obstacles to learning.

Changes Coming From the Courts

Finally, changes in the scope of election law have come from the courts. First, as mentioned earlier, two Supreme Court cases dealt with the constitutionality of FECA and BCRA: *Buckley v. Valeo* in 1976 and *McConnell v. FEC* in 2003. Second, the courts have ruled a number of times on the applicability of magic words in determining the boundary between regulated and unregulated public communications.

There have been more than a dozen such cases at the circuit and district court level, but only one, *FEC v. Furgatch* in 1987, that extended express advocacy beyond magic words. The Ninth Circuit in this case established that the context of the communication might deem it express advocacy, even without the use of such words. The majority of cases affirming the magic word bright-line test were decided after 1991 (Smith 2001, p. 183).

There have been hundreds of other court cases pertaining to election law, however. Using a list of more than 300 cases compiled by the Federal Election Commission, I coded each case on its major purpose, the year it was decided, the final court in which it was heard, and the identity of the plaintiff and defendant. The upper left panel of Figure 2.9 shows the number of election law cases decided in each year between 1976 and 2004. The drop-off in the final years of the time series is the result of a number of cases still pending or on appeal (at the time of the coding), but the highest number of cases were decided in 1996.

The upper right panel shows the frequency with which candidates, parties, interest groups, and the Federal Election Commission were plaintiffs or defendants in these cases. The FEC was the plaintiff or defendant in the most number of cases (in about 125 and 175, respectively). Interest groups were the second most common defendants, but the third most common plaintiffs (behind candidates). Interestingly, parties have been the plaintiff or defendant the fewest times.

The FEC has been the defendant most often because plaintiffs regularly challenge FEC actions or inaction on a plaintiff's complaint. For example, in *NRA v. FEC*—a case decided by the D.C. Circuit Court of Appeals in 1988—the National Rifle Association claimed that the FEC had acted improperly by dismissing an administrative complaint concerning the status of Handgun Control (a pro-gun control group) as a membership organization. The D.C. Court ruled in favor of the FEC.

In the bottom left panel, we can see that only about one-third of the included cases have life beyond the district courts, and far fewer were decided by the Supreme Court. Of the almost 300 court cases heard at the district court level, over half were heard in D.C. district court. And over half of the cases heard in appeals court were decided

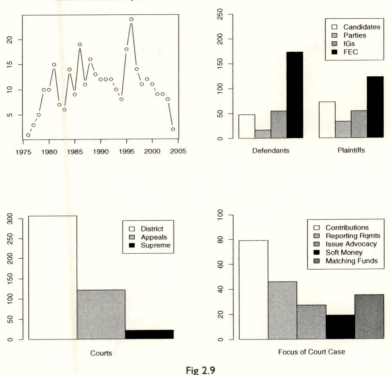

Fig 2.9

Elation Law Court Cases, 1975–2005. (*Source:* Federal Election Commission.)
y-axes represent the number of relevant cases.

in the D.C. Circuit. The second most common appeals court is the 9th Circuit, but with less than 10 percent of the cases.

Finally, the bottom right panel shows the number of court cases pertaining to contributions, reporting requirements, issue advocacy, soft money, and presidential matching funds; this is only a partial list of potential issues covered by these cases. There were almost 80 cases pertaining to contributions (in relation either to how to make them or how to receive them), and more than 40 cases about FEC reporting requirements.

Conclusion

Both the size and scope of interest group electoral tactics have expanded in recent years. This expansion included soft money contributions to parties and issue advocacy communications to the general public, and organizations external to political action committees often funded both expenditures.

In February 2002, when Congress was debating BCRA, the *Denver Post* editorialized, "The last time Congress adopted meaningful campaign finance reform, the Berlin Wall still stood and the words 'AIDS' and 'Internet' hadn't been invented. The 1974 reforms adopted in the Watergate scandal's wake brought some accountability to American politics by forcing disclosure of many campaign contributions. But in the last three decades, special interests found new ways to manipulate the system and block further, needed reforms."[31] As made clear here, however, it was the timing of this tactical expansion that is particularly puzzling. The "explosion" of soft money and issue advocacy occurred long *after* the words "AIDS" and "Internet" had been invented and close to 10 years after the Berlin Wall fell. What happened to make interest group leaders in the mid-1990s so eager to expand beyond the boundaries of regulated hard money?

I argue in the next chapter that the two major factors explaining the timing of this emergence are the ones outlined and reviewed here—the partisan polarization and parity in Congress post-1994 and the shifting regulatory environment. In the next chapter, I build a more complete and general theoretical argument, stating more clearly how these factors affect tactical selection for interest groups.

3 A Theory of Emergent and Changing Interest Group Tactics

Under what conditions do interest groups adopt or change election strategies? I argue that to understand how interest groups engage elections and to understand how this process changes over time, we must comprehend how shifting political and legal contexts (described in Chapter 2) create both opportunities and impediments for certain forms of electoral participation. As Petracca (1992, p. 23) argues, "When we ask why the interest group system has changed, we are really asking what aspects of American politics changed to transform the interest group system."

In this chapter, I review the literature on interest group electioneering, taking care to highlight the importance of these larger contextual factors in models of electoral participation. Failing to do so limits what we can say about the dynamics of interest group electoral tactics. Thomas Mann (2003, p. 78) writes, "These relatively new developments in campaign-finance practice [i.e., soft money and issue advocacy] provided much of the policy rationale and constitutional justification for [BCRA]. For the most part, however, political scientists have not done research that directly addresses these issues. Findings based entirely on hard-money PAC contributions to individual members shed little light on the policy consequences of these developments."

I begin with a brief review of the initial model, which focuses on the concepts of interest group goals and capacity. I follow with a longer treatment of the importance of political context in understanding the structure of interest group electioneering, namely how politics can help shape goals. I conclude with an overview of the regulatory context and a discussion of how the nature of this context can structure an interest group's capacity to act on its goals.

Set-Up

Interest group tactical choices are principally a function of two dynamics: their goals and capacity. If T is the observed tactic of an interest group in an election (contributions, political advertisements, voter mobilization), it is a function of the group's goal (G), its tactical capacity (C), and some error (e). Because interest groups can make mistakes and miscalculations and because they also pick tactics idiosyncratically (Sabato 1984, p. 80), I assume at the outset that interest groups are rational actors with imperfect information (hence the concept of error):

$$T = f\ (G, C, e)$$

To elaborate, goals are the most crucial element in the determination of interest group electoral action (Goldstein 1999, Hojnacki and Kimball 1998). That is, interest groups act in elections in accordance with their desired ends. These ends are quite diverse and can include gaining access to policymakers, helping elect or defeat friends or foes, or making issue agendas salient with the voting public. As goals vary or change across groups and time, so also should tactics vary. Goldstein asserts this relationship in the lobbying realm: "different strategic objectives demand different tactical choices" (1999, p. 52).

Goals only partly determine tactics, however. The capacity to support or use tactics is also important. Tactical capacity weights the translation of goals to tactics. For example, if a group wants to help a candidate who is in electoral trouble (its goal), the tactic it selects will be one it can support financially, legally, and/or politically. As capacity increases, the translation of goals to tactics is enhanced. As capacity is reduced, groups have less opportunity to act on goals.

Therefore,

$$T = f\,[(G^{\circ}C) + e]$$

All told, as goals change or as capacity changes, so too should tactics. If we are interested in changing electoral tactics, then we should assume at the outset that goals or capacity or both have changed at the group level.

To be sure, this is a simplified initial model. I have deliberately left out a number of additional factors that are surely relevant, though not in conflict with the above specification. First, leadership is an important component of any interest group decision-making process. Hrebenar and Scott (1997, pp. 36–58) review the rich literature on leadership in the realm of interest group lobbying. Furthermore, in his study of the AFL-CIO, Francia (2006) makes clear how the leadership style of John Sweeney in the late 1990s was a determining factor in the style of political action undertaken by the union. Indeed, major leadership changes can dramatically alter an interest group's tactical repertoire. But leadership effects can be seen at any point in the above model. Leaders can force goal changes, for example; strong or weak leaders can strengthen or weaken the group's capacity (i.e., by being good or bad fund-raisers); and leaders can also make mistakes in understanding which tactics are important or influential.

Second, implicit in a direct, goals-to-tactic relationship is the notion that groups make some evaluation as to whether a tactic is working. That is, if the goal is access, groups will be unlikely to employ tactics perceived to be ineffective. Indeed, in the 2002 elections many groups perceived political advertising to be less effective than grassroots voter mobilization (see *New York Times*, A1, 9/5/02), and the same was said about the 2004 contest (see *New York Times*, A1, 4/6/04).[1] Groups might evaluate tactical effectiveness using internal polling and focus groups, for example; other groups might assume a tactic works if supported candidates win their election. There is almost no research on how groups evaluate tactical effectiveness, but it makes sense to assume that groups weigh this factor in the selection of tactics that match their electoral goals. In other words, effectiveness may help determine the *specific* tactic selected, conditional on established goals.

Finally, the spread of tactics may follow an arms race dynamic, in which interest groups copy competitors in the adoption of election tactics (Gray and Lowery 1997, Lowery and Gray 1995). As such, tactics emerge or disappear as the community of interest groups responds to what allies or competitors are doing. However, this dynamic assumes that the arms race is a function of perceived tactical success/failure or a sense that its legality has been clarified. Put simply, as interest groups employ a tactic, others come to assess their capacity to utilize it as enhanced.

Having said that, I first explore the relationship between goals and tactics. We can understand goals as coming predominantly from the political contexts surrounding each election, and I posit that changes in these contexts, as described specifically in Chapter 2, compelled groups to change goals. I follow with a discussion of the relationship between capacity and tactics, arguing that the literature has ignored the role of the regulatory context in defining capacity. As such, I posit that the changing regulatory environment (as exemplified in Chapter 2) affected the capacity to act.

The Relationship Between Goals and Tactics

The interest group literature focuses predominantly on two electoral goals, which are most often applied to the allocation of PAC money: access or replacement (Sabato 1984). These are alternatively called pragmatic or ideological goals (Evans 1988).[2] Access goals are derived from the monetary needs of candidates running for office. Many interest groups, in recognizing these needs, seek access by alleviating the fund-raising requirements of relevant office seekers, thus demonstrating loyalty through campaign contributions (Austen-Smith 1995). It is hoped that this loyalty will result in some ability to influence how members of Congress design policies.[3]

Elections, however, are more than symbolic moments during which organized interests can attempt to form bonds with politicians. Elections can be used to create more directly a policymaking environment that reflects the desires of participating interests. That is, while one use of elections is the formation of closer bonds, another is the direct election of more favorable candidates (or the defense of vulnerable ones). In this sense, contributions or other electioneering efforts are designed to move votes at the ballot box.[4]

Consider the following example of a conscious shift from the goal of access to that of replacement. In 1981 the National Association of Retired Federal Employees (NARFE) asked the Federal Election Commission for advice on a planned strategy to contribute to members of Congress. NARFE had spent considerable time and energy seeking access to sympathetic legislators. According to one solicitation from the group to its members, "NARFE's national office is working very hard on establishing a good working relationship with all the members of Congress." The group was frustrated in its efforts, however, and sought to alter its tactics. As such, NARFE "now believes that an essential element of protecting its interests in maintaining the Federal Retirement System separate and apart from the Social Security System is by electing individuals whose views are sympathetic to [the group]." NARFE sought advice from the FEC on how to use already existing funds to that effect (Advisory Opinion 1981-34).

For the most part, however, we rarely know the explicit goal of interest group electoral participation; we usually infer it from their observed activity. For example, we know interest groups consider voting record and institutional position (relevant committee, party leadership role, for example) in deciding whom to support, and we assume contributions in this context are most likely designed to secure policymaking access (Gopoian 1984, Grenzke 1989, Poole, Romer and Rosenthal 1987, Romer and Snyder 1994). There is also evidence that interest groups consider district-level characteristics (percent unionized, per capita income, for example) when seeking access to members representing relevant constituencies (Davis 1992, Wright 1985). For example, labor surely wants access to legislators who represent constituencies with a high number of union workers.

On the other hand, we know that a member's party, ideology, and electoral vulnerability often predict the receipt of hard money contributions (Endersby and Munger 1992, Evans 1988, Herndon 1982, Malbin 1980, Nelson 1998). We often assume to that effect that interest groups contribute to competitive candidates because the marginal impact of those dollars on the electoral outcome is greatest. Replacement-inspired contributions only make sense in such races.

One should be cautious, however, in dichotomizing access and replacement. Evans (1988, p. 1050) makes this point: "Just as ideological, electoral change-oriented PACs are likely to target close races, seeking to protect ideologically compatible and defeat incompatible members, pragmatic, access-oriented PACs might believe that the more the members need the contributions, the more likely they are to respond gratefully later on. Thus, both types of PACs may contribute in close races and marginality may not differentiate between them."

Therefore, it might be better to understand groups as on a tactical continuum, from favoring pure access to pure replacement, in contrast to treating each contribution decision as the dependent variable. When we look at electoral activity at the interest group level, we should see that groups tending toward access will, on balance, contribute more to safe seat incumbents, to members on important committees, and to legislative friends and ideological allies. In contrast, groups tending toward replacement will, on balance, contribute more to competitive candidates or to candidates in open seats.

This conceptualization does not preclude interest groups from engaging in both access and replacement politics, however, or from making candidate-to-candidate assessments and supporting friends and allies for even idiosyncratic reasons—what Gopoian (1984) refers to as "parochial issue concerns." As groups tend to favor one goal over the other, however, we should see disparities in spending at the aggregate group level, and as that preference changes, so too should the pattern of spending.

What drives a group to favor access over replacement, however? Or vice versa? The standard approach is to examine differences across group types. Labor groups and nonconnected PACs are considered more ideological and therefore more likely to invest in open seats, competitive races, and so forth. Corporations are seen as more pragmatic and therefore more likely to give to both parties in hopes of gaining access.

This approach may be too static, however. What about labor makes them more ideological, and what makes corporations more pragmatic? Are these orientations always true? Further still, are there not important differences within group types (i.e., not all labor unions have the same viewpoints)? Indeed, one of the most undeveloped questions in the literature on interest groups electoral politics concerns the origin of these goals.

One answer is to assume that groups have different viewpoints on the persuadability of candidates. More specifically, replacement groups view legislator preferences as fixed (hence the need to elect new ones), while access groups do not (Apollonio and La Raja 2004). But this argument also suffers; what drives an interest group to make this very different judgment about policymakers?

Alternatively, I assert that all interest groups have some orientation to both the *ideological* and *partisan* make-up of Congress. On balance, while corporations may be more conservative and favor the Republican Party, and labor may be more liberal and pro-Democratic, it is certainly possible for some corporations to be more liberal than some conservative unions, and for unions and corporations to vary their participation on the basis of who is in power and the likelihood that one party or ideology will retain or gain control of the policymaking environment. As ideological and partisan conditions change, then so too should the group's evaluation of how to participate in elections.

The idea that larger contextual factors drive the political participation of interest groups is not new. Indeed, one consistent story of American political development is the manner in which organized interests have historically responded to dominant power dynamics, both by conforming to the manner in which policy is created at the time or by moving beyond (and challenging) constraining institutional relationships (i.e., strong parties; Archer 1998, Coleman 1996, Harvey 1996, Parker and Coleman 2004). For example, both Clemens (1997) and Hansen (1991) investigate the relationship between interest groups and parties in the early and mid-20th century.

Do interest groups only react to existing political contexts, however? Do not groups play some independent role in shaping this context? For example, when we note that politics in America is more polarized in recent years and that interest groups respond to that characteristic, are we precluding the likelihood that interest groups had some role in bringing to life such polarization? Indeed, we should not deny this possibility; prior behavior may make the current political context for interest groups more favorable (or even ideal). Because each new election is in a sense an independent game, however, interest groups must defend that context or work harder to change it. In other words, as a new election season dawns, interest groups respond to the current conditions—regardless of previous behavior.[5]

Ideological Context

I argue first that interest groups have some ideological ideal point that is a powerful predictor of aggregate campaign activity. Just as candidates can be aligned on a continuum from liberal to conservative, we can imagine a similar arrangement of interest groups. Consider a liberal interest group faced with a legislature filled with conservative incumbents. Such a group may have incentives to become marginally involved in competitive contests in which conservative opponents have a relatively high chance of losing. In this sense, replacement politics may be the most optimal strategy for some groups (ideological outcasts, for example; Gaddie and Regens 1997, p. 350). That is, interest groups seeking policy benefits with a legislature far afield from the group's own position might see pragmatic investments in sympathetic members as yielding less policy pay-off than engaging in more risky electoral—that is, replacement—strategies.

Furthermore, ideal points should not be synonymous with organizational type. In other words, a liberal labor union might have the same or similar grievances as a liberal nonconnected PAC. Some work has shown, in fact, that corporations can be as ideological in their giving patterns as single-issue groups (Evans 1988). On that end, Gopoian (1984) writes, "Generic treatments of 'labor' and 'corporate' PACs mask the diverse orientation of individual PACs" (259).

This ideological dynamic has some foundation in the early PAC literature (Kau, Keenan and Rubin 1982, Poole and Romer 1985, Saltzman 1987, Welch 1980). McCarty and Rothenberg (1993) and Poole and Romer (1985) estimated ideology scores for large PACs, using them successfully in various models of PAC contributions. Most of the theoretical and empirical work in this area, however, tests the assumption that "a political action committee's contributions are positively related to the extent to which its ideology matches that of the legislator" (Poole and McCarty 1993 in Austen-Smith 1995, p. 567) or, more specifically, that an ideological match between the group and the candidate predicts a contribution.

But if interest groups have ideal points, there may be more to the story. Austen-Smith (1995) theorizes that PACs use contributions to signal their ideal point, which is assumed to be unknown to the member. He premises this on the (obvious) incentives that legislators have to seek out groups that are "like" them; these groups can in turn alleviate the informational needs of developing sound public policy. Yet this dynamic also implies that groups will be motivated to elect a set of members who are "like" them. After all, "interest groups prefer legislatures consisting of more people with preferences close to their own to legislatures with fewer such people; therefore, groups give money to candidates who are relatively like themselves to increase the probability of such legislatures arising" (Austen-Smith 1995, p. 575). And this dynamic need not relate only to the position of the median voter. In 1973, for example, the president of the AFL-CIO, George Meany, claimed that labor's electoral participation was motivated to produce "a veto-proof Congress" (Holloway 1979, p. 117).

As such, I offer the **ideological distance hypotheses**, one of several relevant empirical hypotheses that are the focus of the chapters to follow. The ideological distance hypothesis asserts that PACs more satisfied in the existing policy environment—that is, those with ideological closeness to the House and Senate floor median—will give less to competitive candidates and more to safe seat incumbents. The floor median represents the ideology of the most moderate member in each chamber. Participation in competitive races is high risk for these satisfied PACs (favored competitive candidates are more likely to lose) for only small gain (the PAC is already satisfied with the existing distribution of members).

Conversely, groups less satisfied in the existing policy environment—those with ideological distance from the floor median—are more likely to contribute in ways designed to help candidates win elections. I expect these groups to give more to competitive candidates. Although, "in the aggregate [such activity] might affect the organization's political support within Congress by only a member or two" (Hall and Wayman 1990, p. 799), participation by these groups in these ways is low risk (if the PAC is unsuccessful in helping candidates win, you return to the status quo) for high gain (victory has pleasing aggregate effects of shifting the policy environment in a preferable direction).[6] Put simply, although most of the literature explores "candidate-picking," the ideological distance hypothesis explores "legislature-picking."

I make an assumption at the outset that interest groups respond to competitiveness more so than they make a race competitive. In a sense, this is a smaller scale issue of the one noted earlier—about whether interest groups respond to or shape the larger political context. In this case, it is certainly possible for interest group electioneering to force a race to be competitive; indeed, this might be the goal of some interest group participation. On the other hand, making a race competitive is much harder to do on a larger scale; very few interest groups can invest enough resources in potentially competitive races to force scores of candidates into electoral trouble. As such, it seems far more efficient for an interest group to respond to the electoral environment instead of trying wholesale to shape it.

Finally, it is important to consider the larger theoretical issue of a PAC ideal point. Can organizations have ideal points in the same way candidates or other individuals (i.e., Supreme Court justices) can? Indeed, we often talk about the behavior of corporations or labor groups, asserting the organization as supporting or opposing certain policy positions. For example, "don't use Mobil Oil. It opposes environmental protections on oil drilling." Or, "the AFL-CIO is really liberal; it opposes free trade." Recent work by Groseclose and Milyo (2005) has estimated the ideology of news outlets, finding that most mainstream media tend to be more liberal than the average voter. But are organizational ideal points the aggregation of individual preferences in the organization, or are they independent of those individuals? Put differently, how does an organization become liberal or conservative?

I make no definitive claims here, but only make note of the uncertainty. I treat PAC ideal points as the preference point for the organization, and I make almost no reference to the individuals running the PAC. Nonetheless, there can be no doubt that individual conflicts within the organization can have significant effects on the behavior of the PAC (Wright 1985), which might in turn influence what we infer is the PAC ideology. To that effect, these conflicts likely also affect the group's tactical capacity (more on that later).

Partisan Context

An ideological context is only part of the political dynamics that structure policymaking, however. Consider again the changing partisan context described in Chapter 2. I argue that this (shifting) partisan context (one more polarized) has had powerful effects on the electoral goals of many interest groups. Said Bernadette Budde, senior vice president for the Business-Industry Political Action Committee, in moderating a 2002 discussion on BCRA, "There is something about the nature of the majority in the legislature or the consensus building within the parties that motivates [some interest groups] to be involved" (Breaux Symposium 2002, p. 29).

More than two decades ago, Gopoian (1984, p. 262) argued, "The conventional wisdom holds that corporations are inclined towards bipartisanship in their PAC activity for a variety of reasons, including the likelihood of having to deal with a Democratic-controlled House, and the sharp ideological schism in the ranks of the Democrats which renders many conservative Democratic candidates palatable to corporation interests." Jackson (1990b) recounts the story of how Tony Coelho, former chairman of the Democratic Congressional Campaign Committee (and later Al Gore's campaign manager in 2000), convinced many corporate PACs in the 1980s to contribute to Democrats under the assumption of long-term Democratic control of the House. In 1988, the partisan context compelled Evans to agree: "If oil PACs had their druthers, Congress would be Republican," but they have had "to accommodate themselves to the reality of Democratic dominance of the House" (1988, p.1056).

Clearly, as noted in Chapter 2, this situation changed in the 1990s. Parties in the late 1990s grew more ideologically polarized and homogeneous, and majority control of each chamber became a primary focus of congressional elections. With such changes in the partisan context, we might expect a change in the electoral tactics of groups like the ones noted by Evans and Gopoian. Said one interview respondent: "In the Senate, 51 seats gets you the agenda. For interest groups today, it's easier [than in years past]. We're good; their bad. And to win, it's on the fringes, moving 3–4 percentage points."[7]

Some scholars have already noted the importance of changing partisan contexts in relation to interest group electoral participation. Eismeier and Pollock (1985), for example, examine tactical shifts between the 1980 and 1982 congressional elections, noting the "election-specific partisan forces" that inspired observed disparities in spending.[8] Cox and Magar (1999) ask, "How much is majority status worth in Congress," noting that the Republican gains of 1994 caused changes in contribution patterns that benefited members of the new majority party. And Taylor (2003) finds evidence that stronger congressional parties cause PACs to give less to members on relevant committees and more to majority party members and members in party-important positions.

The importance of majority control lies in all the "hidden" factors affecting policy development—committee control, agenda setting, bill scheduling, and so forth. Malbin (2004, p. 178) writes, "Nothing focuses a politician's mind more clearly than being on the edge of control—whether he or she is out of power looking up, or in power and feeling threatened." The same can be said for interest groups. Quite simply, many interest groups should understand that the policy gains that come from a particular party controlling Congress are more valuable than the policy gains of ensuring increased committee participation by individual members. When the policy environment is in play, in other words, the potential gains from aggressive electoral activity present an opportunity too good to pass up.

As such, I offer the **partisan hypothesis** about how interest groups contribute hard and soft money and spend independently on behalf of candidates. *For hard money*, the partisan hypothesis says that PACs with extreme ideal points (that is, groups more liberal than the Democratic median or more conservative than the Republican median) should be more likely to invest their competitive contributions in candidates from their preferred party. More importantly, as chamber control becomes more uncertain, these partisan PACs should invest competitive money more exclusively in candidates from their preferred party. To hedge their bets against losing control of the chamber, however, they should also increase their investments in safe seat candidates from the other party. In election cycles where control is less likely to change, these partisan PACs should be freer to invest in competitive candidates of the opposing party (presumably elevating issue stances of candidates over party affiliation). All told, the hypothesis predicts the use of highly partisan replacement tactics to increase when party is an important dimension of a congressional cycle.

With respect to *soft money*, we should observe a similar pattern: groups with a partisan preference should close ranks around their preferred party in years when chamber control is up for grabs, giving more soft money (than in other years) and more exclusively to one party. Such groups should be more bipartisan in years when control is more certain. As such, we should see evidence that interest groups pursue both replacement and access goals with soft money contributions.

Initial evidence suggests that soft money contributors pursued goals of both access and replacement. Recall from Chapter 2 the comment by former Senator Dale Bumpers that soft money had an access purpose. In contrast, former Congressman Timothy Wirth noted in a 1997 affidavit for *Federal Election Commission v. Colorado Republican Federal Campaign Committee* that soft money was solicited for electoral reasons. He said,

> When I solicited contributions for the state party, in effect I solicited funds for my election campaign. I understood that solicitees who made contributions to the party almost always did so because they expected that the contributions would support my campaign one way or another. . . . In this fund-raising, I often solicited contributions to the DSCC [Democratic Senatorial Campaign Committee] from individuals or Political Action Committees (PACs) who had already "maxed out" (contributed to my campaign committee the maximum amount allowed by federal law).[9]

At the outset, it seems reasonable to assume that a donor giving most or all of its soft money to Democrats and Republicans signals a more explicit electoral goal than a donor who splits donations between parties. The Supreme Court said in *McConnell*: "Particularly telling is the fact that, in 1996 and 2000, more than half of the top 50 soft money donors gave substantial sums to both major national parties, *leaving room for no other conclusion but that these donors were seeking influence, or avoiding retaliation, rather than promoting any particular ideology.*"[10]

The Court also cited one CEO, who makes clear the potential access risks of giving only to one party:

> [I]f you're giving a lot of soft money to one side, the other side knows. For many economically oriented donors, there is a risk in giving to only one side, because the other side may read

through FEC reports and have staff or a friendly lobbyist call
and indicate that someone with interests before a certain committee has had their contributions to the other side noticed.
They'll get a message that basically asks: Are you sure you want
to be giving only to one side? Don't you want to have friends
on both sides of the aisle? If your interests are subject to anger
from the other side of the aisle, you need to fear that you may
suffer a penalty if you don't give. . . . [D]uring the 1990s, it became more and more acceptable to call someone, saying you
saw he gave to this person, so he should also give to you or the
person's opponent . . . [11]

Reinforcing both points is this comment by soft money donor
Wade Randlett, CEO for Dashboard Technology: "If you want to enhance your chances of getting your issues paid attention to and favorably reviewed by members of Congress, bipartisanship is the right way
to go. Giving lots of soft money to both sides is the right way to go
from the most pragmatic perspective" (Corrado, Mann and Potter
2003, p. 305).

To reiterate, I expect groups with a partisan preference to be more
exclusive in their soft money contributions; groups with centrist issues
should be more likely to split their soft money. Second, and more important, as party balance in the House and Senate tightens (1992 and
1994 vs. 2000 and 2002, for example), investment in one party should
go up for partisan groups and down for centrist groups.

In addition to these partisan expectations, I offer the **competitiveness hypothesis** about the timing and geographical source of soft
money contributions. I expect interest groups in competitive states to
give more and to give closer to Election Day than contributors in states
with no competitive federal elections. Put differently, I expect interest
group donors surrounded by a competitive election to help parties facilitate replacement with bigger donations closer to Election Day.

Both hypotheses are also relevant for *independent spending* from
interest groups. In that regard, the partisan hypothesis predicts that
electioneering issue advocacy (ads without magic words but that mention or picture candidates) will be overwhelmingly partisan. In that regard, interest groups should almost never advocate in television ads for
candidates of both parties. The competitive hypothesis expects inter-

est groups to invest more heavily in competitive races and to expend almost no issue advocacy resources in races where the outcome is obvious.

Such predictions are not obvious, however. After all, many practitioners of issue advocacy maintain that their primary interest is promoting an issue agenda. In her testimony for *McConnell v. FEC*, Denise Mitchell, Special Assistant for Public Affairs at the AFL-CIO, argued as follows:

> I realize that AFL-CIO advertising could affect how citizens vote. If our advertisements succeed in educating the public about working families issues, and influence the actions, votes, positions and policy commitments of legislators and candidates, they may in some cases have an indirect effect on election outcomes, just as virtually every legislative and other activity undertaken by the AFL-CIO on behalf of workers that is conveyed to the public may have such an effect. This, however, has never been the point of our broadcast advertising program, within or outside the 30- and 60-day periods.[12]

Of course, others have dismissed this charge, arguing that interest group political advertising has the single goal of moving votes. According to Tanya Metaksa, former executive director of the National Rifle Association's Institute for Legislative Action, "It is foolish to believe there is any practical difference between issue advocacy and advocacy of a political candidate. What separates issue advocacy and political advocacy is a line in the sand drawn on a windy day."[13] In 1999, Sierra Club spokesman Daniel Weiss echoed the point: "In the old days, you had to have a fence between a campaign and issue advocacy groups. . . . Now all you have to have is a chalk line."[14] And as one interview respondent—an organizer of a nonconnected PAC—told me, "527s have changed [Washington, D.C.]. Politicians are terrified. PAC money doesn't buy them what they want anymore; they want to knock someone out."[15] As such, in line with these observations, both hypotheses expect interest groups to be motivated to help parties over candidates, and elections over issues.

Keep in mind, also, that the development of 527s and uncoordinated issue advocacy are tactics that might even *damage* a group's access on the Hill. In her testimony for BCRA, for example, Denise Mitchell noted that advertising decisions sometimes run at odds to the express wishes of candidates:

> The AFL-CIO has also declined as a matter of policy to desist from broadcast issue advocacy where candidates have called on groups not to engage in it while they are campaigning. This is because we make an independent judgment as to whether it is necessary or advisable for the AFL-CIO to run broadcasts, and we scrupulously avoid collaboration with officeholders in their capacities as candidates concerning our broadcast efforts, including whether or not to broadcast at all.[16]

In this sense, if interest groups air partisan ads in competitive elections, as both hypotheses predict, and if doing so can potentially anger candidates, it makes far more sense to infer these tactics as being motivated by replacement.

All told, both the partisan and competitive hypotheses make clear the observable implications of an interest group community's response to changes in the partisan context. The draw of the partisan context in the 1990s also counters a traditional assumption in the literature about the relationship between parties and groups. Schattschneider (1942) asserted that when parties are strong, interest groups lose influence, but when groups gain power, party dynamics weaken. Reiter (1993, p.155) calls this the "see-saw" relationship between parties and groups.

The evidence appeared to bear this out in the early years after FECA, when PACs blossomed but party leaders did not have decisive control over their members (Wilson 1981). Indeed, other empirical work of the time seemed to suggest a zero-sum power relationship between parties and groups. For example, Morehouse (1981) and Mayhew (1986) found that in states with strong parties, interest groups tended to be weak; in states with weak party organizations, interest groups held more power. Wattenberg (1984) also demonstrated that interest group campaign contributions were largest in states with weak party organizations.

The see-saw metaphor may have lost some relevancy, however. Interest groups can help parties alleviate the challenges of fund-raising for elections, in addition to independently advocating for candidates. After all, Aldrich (1995, p. 273) notes that as parties lost influence among the electorate over the course of the 20th century, they evolved from institutions "in control" of candidates to ones "in service" of them. Lowi, Ginsberg, and Shepsle (2006, p. 292) describe this as a shift from labor-intensive elections to capital-intensive ones. With such changes, interest groups are well suited to help with the service functions of parties. And when parties become more relevant for policymaking, it makes sense for many interest groups to care deeply about party control. This is exactly what I expect to find in the empirical evidence.

At the same time, the notion of a consequential, polarized, and charged partisan environment has consequences for how we understand the concept of "vanishing marginals," a trend noted by David Mayhew about the declining number of competitive congressional seats (Herrera and Yawn 1999, Mayhew 1974). The trends shown in Figure 2.5 from Chapter 2 make the point persuasively. Indeed, in both the House and Senate, the number of competitive seats continues to decline. This decline is oft noted and oft lamented. Nonetheless, whereas competitiveness has declined at the individual level in the last 20 years (meaning fewer citizens vote in elections that are close), competitiveness has increased at the macro, institutional level (meaning polarized parties fight aggressively in a handful of races for majorities in Congress and control of the policymaking agenda in Washington).

The Relationship Between Capacity and Tactics

While the goals of interest groups drive their participation in elections, their capacity to act affects how they can translate those goals into action. The literature on interest groups is insightful on this point. Groups with more resources are expected to participate more often and in diverse ways (Masters and Keim 1985), as are groups with extensive political experience (Cyert and March 1963). PACs sponsored by corporations or unions are expected to have more opportunity to participate with contributions (as opposed to PACs without a parent organization), because all solicited funds can be applied to electoral activity (Davis 1992). Wright (1985) demonstrates, however, that the exigencies and style of fund-raising can sometimes result in less efficient giving patterns for groups, dampening their capacity to act.

Indeed, the increase in issue advocacy rather than independent expenditures and the proliferation of soft money donations to parties are partly explained by the simple point that these tactics are easier to employ. Consider bundling, in which interest groups serve as a conduit for individual contributions to candidates. EMILY's List is a good example of a group made famous by its bundling techniques. Bundling is rare, however, because it requires an incredible amount of organization and skill to coordinate a significant and effective campaign. Or consider independent expenditures. If a group wishes to air advertisements using these funds, it has to raise regulated hard money.

In contrast, issue advocacy and soft money donations are easy to employ. One reason why a group uses issue advocacy more in one election than another is explained partly by the group's ability to raise large donations from wealthy benefactors (Malbin, Wilcox, Rozell and Skinner 2002). Apollonio and La Raja (2004) find that soft money tactics are more common in younger firms, something we might expect given it is one of the easiest tactics to use (i.e., writing a check without regard to the source of the funds).

The extensive literature on organizational innovation and diffusion is insightful in helping clarify the factors that affect a group's tactical capacity. This literature focuses on two major sets of independent variables in organizational innovativeness (Rogers 1983). First, individual leader characteristics (for example, a leader's attitude toward change) and the internal characteristics of organizational structure (for example, centralization, complexity, size, and available resources) are important determinants of innovation (Wilson 1995). We know this is true for interest groups in the PAC realm. Sabato (1984) highlights how PAC participation in elections is often a function of who is making the decisions and in what form (i.e., one individual vs. a board).

The second independent variable concerns the external characteristics of the organization, such as system openness, defined as "the degree to which the members of a system are linked to others who are external to the system. An open system exchanges information across its boundaries" (Rogers 1983, p. 356): as the system becomes more open, innovation and diffusion accelerate. A corollary of this is the concept of issue networks or policy networks, in which diffusion and innovation are hampered or hindered by the connectedness of organization entrepreneurs (Heclo 1978, Kingdon 1994, Mintrom and Vergari 1998).

Astley and Fombrun (1983) argue, however, that such environmental factors can often impede organizational action. They write, "Traditional business policy conceptions of the organization-environment relationship merely reinforce the view that environmental forces predominate over managerial choices as determinants of organizational action. The environment is typically regarded as more or less intractable externally, a predefined context that ultimately establishes what is feasible in operational terms" (576). Clemens (1997) relates this effect of environment to interest groups in the political realm (focusing on the labor, farmer, and women's movements in the early 20th century), arguing that interest groups are bound by the "logics of appropriateness" (which she means to be a set of norms) in their political activity. As group actions diverge from a set of acceptable behavior, defined exogenously, interest groups can be punished for their actions.

As such, external pressures vary in intensity, whereby more constraining external pressures hamper innovation. At the same time, organizations can respond by either lobbying to expand existing "logics" or by learning more about the scope and reach of these external pressures. This means that organizations should interact with and respond to changes in their environment (Cyert and March 1963, Martin 1995, Suarez 2000). Incidentally, such external constraints on political action—in acting as a weight in the translation of goals into tactics—complicate traditional assertions that all political action is explained by self-interested behavior under perfect information.

I argue that the regulatory context—the reach and scope of existing election law—is one component of system openness, acting as a variable that determines the group's capacity to act in campaigns. In a sense, the regulatory context post-FECA is an institutionalization of the "logics of appropriateness" dynamic.

Regulatory Context

The importance of the regulatory environment relates to how regulatory clarity affects the capacity to act. When the regulatory environment is unclear about a potential electoral tactic, capacity is low. This should compel political actors to seek out clarification and in the process expand capacity. For example, imagine an interest group with the goal of helping a handful of candidates in competitive races and with the resources and experience to act in accordance with such goals. As the group considers more innovative or untested tactics, we should expect it to factor the tactic's legality into its calculation. After all, violating campaign finance law can result in significant criminal, civil, and political costs. In justifying his opposition to BCRA, James Norell of the National Rifle Association argued, "Any [violation] could mean prison terms for officials of organizations such as the NRA and their employees simply for attempting to exercise the groups' collective First Amendment rights. . . . And running an unapproved ad could mean criminal prosecution and heavy fines under the Brave New World of John McCain and Russ Feingold."[17] According to one interest group leader: "We pay scrupulous, scrupulous, scrupulous attention" to election law; "the stakes are too high and the costs suicidal."[18]

As a tactic's legal uncertainty decreases, however, we should expect the likelihood of that tactic being employed to go up. Alternatively, when the regulatory environment spells out exactly the boundaries of participation (contribution limits, for example, which are well known), legal capacity is high and questions unnecessary. In theory, the regulatory context matters to all interest groups, although most groups employ tactics with relatively high legal certainty (such as contributions).

Pundits and scholars have articulated two hypotheses about the importance of the regulatory environment to interest groups, although neither has been tested with a significant amount of data. First, many assert the emergence of aggressive electioneering by interest groups and parties as the consequence of political learning, where the boundaries of election law are explored over time (Magleby 2003, Rozell and Wilcox 1999). Green (2002, p. 71) writes, for example, "After twenty years, political operatives, lobbyists, and election lawyers had mastered the loopholes in the Watergate reforms." How might we observe such learning, however? With the **political learning hypothesis**, I expect that the frequency of advisory opinions in certain issue areas (issue advocacy, soft money, solicitation, etc) will go up after the law has changed—i.e., where there is a recent regulatory change. As noted in Chapter 2, I tracked both regulatory changes and advisory opinions, coding both on content. If learning takes place, it should happen at moments when the law is most unclear.

Second, the FEC is often criticized for being lax enforcers of election law (Jackson 1990a). After the election of 1996, for example, many criticized the FEC's handling of alleged campaign finance violations by the Democrats (Magleby 2002). Even more, the FEC is often criticized as being overly partisan and as tied to the interests of incumbent politicians. Said John McCain, the FEC is "a corrupt, enabling organization stacked with political hacks."[19] This point is reinforced by one official at a leading campaign finance reform center: "The FEC is useless and has been for 20 years. Congress set it up to be useless."[20]

In the context of a lenient FEC, then, one might expect political learning to occur rapidly. The assertion of an FEC unable to control innovation, however, should be considered a hypothesis that can be tested, as opposed to a normative charge that is merely leveled. Lochner and Cain (1999) find evidence that the FEC "unintentionally enforces the law in a skewed manner" by leveling low fines and weak sanctions, and by relying heavily on third-party enforcement. On the other hand, Smith and Hoersting (2002) argue the FEC's real problem lies in over-enforcement, taking too strong a stand on the scope of the law.

Note that the constraints of the regulatory environment can be measured in two arenas: an evaluation of proposed action and a response to the action taken. On the former, constraints relate to advisory opinions (where political actors ask for advice on electioneering proposals); on the latter, they relate to court cases or administrative actions (such as levying fines as a result of tactics previously utilized). The FEC is most often criticized for the way it levies fines and enforces the law through litigation, but I explore the FEC's response to proposed activity.

To investigate the **lenient FEC hypothesis**, I examine how successful interest groups, candidates, and parties are on their advisory opinion requests (both across issue type and over time), to see if the FEC has, in fact, allowed these political actors to freely find and exploit loopholes in election law. I expect to find evidence that the FEC has not freely opened the door to issue advocacy and interest group electioneering, but has maintained some role in stemming its emergence.

Resource Context

Finally, many assert that the rise in unregulated money is a function of the increasing cost of campaigns. That is, since PAC hard money limits are not adjusted for inflation, groups have needed to find alternative methods of infusing money into elections. According to James Bopp of the National Right to Life Committee, "It has become increasingly difficult for people who want to influence the process to do it directly, by contributing to candidates, so they look for other avenues."[21] Sahr (2004) demonstrates, for example, the possibility that inflation can dampen the impact of contributions; he notes that the $5,000 PAC limit on contributions to candidates would have to be raised to $17,500 to count the same in 2004 as in 1974.

I have said little on this issue up to now, but the resource context is best understood as part of a group's tactical capacity. In other words, when resources are limited, capacity is diminished. When there are new avenues for acting on goals, capacity is enhanced. There is evidence that the resource context structures the actions of political parties and interest groups across different periods of American political development (Parker 2005), and this should also be true in contemporary American politics.

I have two expectations. First, the **hard-to-soft hypothesis** predicts that the most active hard money givers were also very active soft money contributors. As the capacity to achieve goals weakened with hard dollars that were devalued by inflation, I expect to find evidence that soft money was an attractive means to enhance tactical capacity. If so, we can safely assert that soft money was not a qualitatively different form of election funding, but simply an extension of hard money.

At the outset, this assertion was not obviously true. It could be that more active hard money PACs avoided soft money, while smaller PACs (that might have trouble raising the requisite hard funds to make a lot of contributions) found it easier to raise and spend unregulated soft money funds. Steven Kirsch, a soft money donor and the CEO of Propel Software Corporation, reinforced the hard-to-soft hypothesis in

his deposition for *McConnell*. He wrote, "The national party committees and the federal candidates who raise money for them prefer that
major donors first 'max-out' in hard money contributions . . . before
making soft money donations" (Corrado, Mann and Potter 2003,
p. 315).

Second, I offer the **soft-to-soft hypothesis**, which suggests that, in
the wake of BCRA and the ban on party soft money, former large soft
money donors are also the largest donors to 527s. According to one
early assessment in April 2004, 527s had the potential to become ex-
tensions of party soft money: "The speculation . . . is that all the party's
old soft money fat cats will redirect their money into the shadow
party's [pro-Democratic 527s] coffers. If they do so, these groups
could raise hundreds of millions of Democratic dollars."[22] Indeed,
many former party entrepreneurs went on to run some of the most
partisan 527s (i.e., America Coming Together and Progress for America Voter Fund; Skinner 2005).[23] On the other hand, this dynamic is
not obvious either. Donors might be wary of signing over large funds
to nonparty committees, and there was some initial skepticism that
527s could seriously function as "shadow" party committees.[24]

Both hypotheses test the dynamic first explained in Chapter 1—
that money in politics is like water on rock, always finding the cracks.

Conclusion

I have argued that understanding interest group tactical changes implies understanding goal changes and/or capacity changes. As such, I
have asserted two factors that might change interest group goals—the
ideological and political contexts that surround elections—and two
factors that might change tactical capacity—the regulatory and resource contexts. Most of the literature on interest group electoral politics focuses on PACs and in a relatively static framework. It is my goal
to integrate the continued presence of PAC politics with the developments of the last 10 years and offer a coherent representation of how
and why interest groups choose to engage elections in diverse and varied forms.

To summarize, I offer seven governing hypotheses. The first three
relate to interest group responses to the political context. The fourth and
fifth relate to interest group interaction with the regulatory context. The

final two concern the response of interest groups to the resource context.

1. **Ideological Distance Hypothesis** for PACS
2. **Partisan Hypothesis** for PACs, soft money, and issue advocacy
3. **Competitive Hypothesis** for soft money and issue advocacy
4. **Political Learning Hypothesis** for the frequency of advisory opinions
5. **Lenient FEC Hypothesis** for the evaluation of advisory opinions
6. **Hard-to-Soft Hypothesis** for PACs
7. **Soft-to-Soft Hypothesis** for 527s

I add a few final points here as caveats and conclusions. In many ways, the model as specified is unique to interest groups. With few exceptions, all candidates in American politics should have only the goal of "replacement," or winning elections; and in American politics the two major parties should be motivated predominantly by the goal of winning seats. As such, the goal component of the equation should not vary for these political actors, making most tactical innovations and diffusions for candidates and parties a function of capacity. Herrnson (1986), for example, notes the prevalence of the use by federal candidates of consultants for legal compliance issues, including advice on the dimensions of campaign finance laws and help on filing FEC reports.

Note, though, that three additional factors mentioned earlier are likely crucial for understanding the emergence of tactics among candidates and parties: leadership decisions, assessments of tactical effectiveness, and an arms race dynamic. To reiterate, I do not examine these in this book, and they remain important topics for future research on interest group electoral behavior. I turn now to an investigation of PACs.

4 Putting PACs in (Political) Context(s)

Speaking on the floor of the Senate on May 8, 1990, Democratic Senator David Boren (from Oklahoma) said,

> We have a cancer that is eating away at the heart of the political process. That cancer is composed of two main elements: Too much money being pumped into the election process, and too much of it coming from special interest groups. Mr. President, we have a serious national problem. We do not need to nibble away at it. We do not need to try to piecemeal it. . . . We need a comprehensive plan that will in essence do away with the influence of all political action committees, that will end undue influence by all special interest money in politics, and will get overall spending under control in the process.

Boren's remarks came nearly a year after Republican President George H.W. Bush proposed legislation to eliminate corporate, union, and trade association PACs and reduce the candidate contribution limit of ideological PACs from $5,000 to $2,500. PACs targeted under Bush's proposed reform were justifiably concerned. According to Steven Stockmeyer of the National Association of Business, "We're completely distressed about what [Bush] proposes."[1] Ultimately, the plan did not have enough support, and it was never seriously considered by Congress.

Not everyone during this time, however, saw PACs in such negative ways. Donald Foye—who in 1986 was the executive vice president of the Medical Society of New York—wrote a letter to the editor of the *New York Times* defending the expansion of PACs. He wrote, "To say that special interests govern the Congress assumes special interests are a monolith, but today there are more than 4,000 PACs. In the long run, the best defense against political action committees is more political action committees. The more of them there are, the harder it will be for any one, five or ten to have any undue influence."[2]

The tension between the views of Boren and Bush on the one hand and Foye on the other represent a fundamental conflict in democratic theory over the success of pluralist politics: is it really true that more input diffuses influence? In his famous Federalist Paper No. 10, which argued in favor of ratifying the American Constitution, James Madison proposed a political society in which competing factions would balance the undue influence of any single faction (Rossiter 1961, p. 83). A society in which such factional conflicts were abundant and vigorous was self-regulating, according to Madison. Such a perspective is what motivated Donald Foye (and others) to support the proliferation of PACs.

Of course, the realization of such a society has long been contested, and in the aftermath of reform in the 1970s, PACs drew the brunt of the criticism. It is for this reason and because of their consistent presence in American elections that I begin the empirical investigation with PACs. Whether PACs respond to the ideological and partisan environments is somewhat of an open question given that PAC contributions to candidates have a regulated upper limit and unlimited independent expenditures must be raised in small amounts. If we find that PACs disburse these funds in ways that respond to political conditions, we should have strong reason to believe that analyses in later chapters, which explore the distribution of unregulated funds, follow the same pattern.

I argue that traditional analysis of political action committees suffer in two respects. First, in limiting empirical investigations to differences across PAC types, we lose diversity within type. Second, in limiting empirical investigations to differences within one or two election cycles, we lose diversity across time. In this chapter I test both the **ideological distance** and **partisan hypotheses** with PAC contribution behavior from 1984 to 2002, covering 10 election cycles with significant variation in external political conditions.

Ideological Context

The ideological distance hypothesis predicts that PACs with ideal points close to the House and Senate floor medians will give less to competitive candidates and more to safe seat incumbents. Conversely, as distance from the floor median grows, PACs will invest greater resources in competitive candidates and fewer resources in safe seat candidates. While most of the literature explores "candidate-picking," this dynamic predicts "legislature-picking."

The crucial variable in this analysis is the PAC's liberal-conservative ideal point. There is no existing measure of each PAC's ideology, however, so the first task is to estimate one for relevant PACs. Almost 12,000 unique interest group PACs have registered with the FEC since 1983. More than half of these have contributed very little money to federal candidates in the last 20 years. As mentioned in Chapter 1, I am uninterested in PACs (and other interest groups) that make only minor investments in federal electoral politics. Therefore, I start with an inclusion criterion of the top 500 PACs, as defined by total expenditures in each election cycle. Thus, for a PAC to enter my sample, it must have been in the top 500 for at least one election cycle between 1984 and 2000. This sampling frame produced a list of 1,061 PACs, and I was able to estimate ideology scores for 927 (see the Appendix for a discussion of this reduction). The sampling frame accounts for more than 80 percent of all federal PAC money in the last 20 years.[3]

The estimation technique leverages PAC donations to individual members of Congress to compute the PAC ideal point. In brief, the estimation works as follows. We know the ideology of incumbent members of Congress because scholars and advocacy groups have been estimating incumbents' ideal points for years. We also know who PACs contribute to and how much they contribute. Under the assumption that PACs contribute to members with similar ideologies, we can infer the location of the PAC by observing the pattern of PAC contributions to incumbents.

For example, if a PAC contributes to a cluster of liberal incumbents, it seems reasonable to assume the PAC is liberal. If a PAC spreads its contributions among members across the ideological spectrum, however, the PAC is arguably more moderate. The Appendix describes the estimation in more detail, including how I control for other factors beyond incumbent ideology that might prompt a PAC to contribute. In addition, I use only PAC contributions to incumbents in the House to estimate ideology.

The estimated PAC ideology scores range between about −3 and 3, although the vast majority ranges between −1 and 1. Scores are scaled in this way because I used Poole and Rosenthal (1997)'s scores of incumbent members of Congress (which are scaled from −1 to 1) to identify the ideology of incumbents. Negative values indicate a liberal PAC and positive values indicate a more conservative committee. In Figure 4.1, I show histogram plots of the ideology scores by the four main PAC categories, and I overlay each with a kernel-density curve. The results are encouraging, in that most corporate PACs are conservative, most labor PACs are liberal, and trade association and nonconnected PACs have significant overlap above and below zero. But there is also incredible diversity within each PAC, which is exactly the point in estimating them. Although knowing the PAC type can give us a rough approximation of how liberal or conservative the PAC is, more information is always preferable.

Consider the following examples. J.C. Penney's estimated corporate PAC score is 1.118, indicating that among the universe of these PACs, the organization is quite conservative. The PAC for Kerr-McGee Corporation is 0.8810, also conservative. In contrast, the Chemical Bank PAC is moderate at 0.0479, and the New York Telephone PAC is more liberal, with an estimated score of −0.6738. There is also considerable diversity in labor PACs. The location of the Service Employees International Union is farther to the left with a score of −1.2355, as is the Nurses Coalition for Action in Politics (−0.8079). But not all labor PACs are far to the left. The PAC for Local 825 of the International Union of Operating Engineers is at −0.1107,

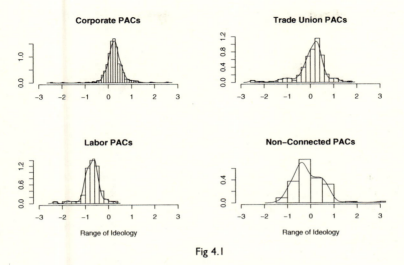

Fig 4.1

Ideology by PAC Type. PAC—Political Action Committee.

and the ideal point for the Midwest Region Laborers' Political League is −0.0909.

There are two initial caveats. I constrain the PAC ideology to be constant over time. In so doing I assume that PAC ideology is stable throughout the time period under analysis. Such an assumption makes sense, however, as most candidate ideology scores remain fairly fixed (Ansolabehere, Snyder, and Stewart 2001, Poole and Rosenthal 1997). Second, in the analyses that follow, I use estimated PAC ideology scores to predict the contribution patterns of the PAC in different election cycles. But because the ideology score is itself determined by PAC contributions to House incumbents, what sort of endogeneity am I introducing?

There is some concern about this, but I offer the following defense. First, I used contribution behavior over nearly 20 years to estimate the ideology scores; that is, I combined a PAC's contribution behavior to incumbent House members over as many election cycles as possible. This minimizes the endogeneity between the estimated scores and their aggregate activity in any one cycle. Second, the estimated ideology scores are completely exogenous from the Senate models, as I used no Senate contribution data in the ideology estimation. If the results are similar across the House and Senate models, I take this as evidence that endogeneity issues do not cloud the findings.

To test the ideological distance hypothesis, I estimated multivariate models of general election expenditures by PACs in House and Senate safe seat and competitive (too-close-to-call) races. These are races identified by the fall election issue of the *Congressional Quarterly*.[4] The unit of analysis is a PAC in each election cycle from 1984 through 2002. Each of the 927 PACs was included for each election cycle in which it spent money; thus some PACs were included for all 10 election cycles, whereas some were included for only one. The dependent variable combines all general election expenditures by PACs in this realm, including contributions, independent expenditures, and in-kind gifts.[5]

The principal explanatory variables are the PAC's ideal point and its distance from the House or Senate floor median. For example, in 1984 the House floor median was −0.1120. For a group like the National Restaurant Association, whose ideology is 0.3854, their ideological distance from the House median is 0.4974. Compare this to the PAC for Hallmark Company (the maker of greeting cards), whose estimated ideal point is −0.1076. This is nearly identical to the floor median. In 2000, after GOP gains in the mid-1990s, the floor median shifted right to 0.213. The ideological distance of both groups then changed. Hallmark was now 0.3206 from the floor median, but the National Restaurant Association was far closer, with only 0.1724 difference. Such a change in the ideological context should produce a shift in the pattern of contributions.

Of course, there are a number of factors that should predict how a PAC allocates its competitive and safe seat expenditures, and we should be careful to account for these. I am not claiming that the ideological context drives everything a PAC does, only that it is relevant above and beyond other factors. Most important, I control for PAC type—whether it is a corporate, labor, trade association, and nonconnected PAC. By including these variables as controls, I can isolate the true effect of a PAC's ideological distance.[6]

I also included several variables that tap different characteristics of the PAC—for example, whether the PAC listed its chief address as

Washington, D.C., and the total expenditures by the PAC in that election cycle (that is, all money spent in House, Senate, and presidential races).[7] The former variable helps account for differences in the contribution behavior of PACs situated inside the beltway, and the latter measure acts as a control for large PACs that can spend more by virtue of having more.[8] I also controlled for the number of years the PAC was repeated in the sample (this can range from one election to all 10), acting as a proxy for the political experience of the group.

A final set of variables tapped the political environment. For example, I included the year of each election cycle and a variable for whether the election year was a mid-term election. I also included a variable for whether the PAC was included in the sample after 1994; this was intended to control for shifts in contributions patterns (or increased expenditures in general) that came as a consequence of Republican gains in 1994. Finally, I controlled for the balance of power in each chamber, measured as the number of competitive seats minus the number of seats needed to shift partisan control of the chamber.

This final variable deserves some attention. Recall from Figure 2.5 that I showed how the number of seats needed to shift control of the House and Senate tended to exceed the number of very competitive elections for most of the 1980s and early 1990s. This trend changed after the elections of 1994, producing a political environment in which competitive elections had huge consequences for chamber control. The measure included here combines both trends (by simply subtracting the number of needed seats from the number of competitive races) to assess the relative importance of each congressional cycle to securing partisan control. Positive numbers indicate that the number of competitive elections exceeds the number needed to shift control; negative numbers mean that control is likely secure with more seats needed than are in play. The numbers tell the story of the changing partisan environment. In the House, for example, the balance measure is −27 in 1984; in 2002 it is 7. In the Senate, the measure is −3 in 1984; in 2002, it is 5. For this analysis, the measure is included as a control variable, but it is more central to the story in the next section.[9]

Tables 4.1 and 4.2 report the coefficient estimates for the independent variables in the House and Senate models.[10] In reading the tables, the direction of the coefficient and its significance level indicate the variable's importance. For example, if a coefficient estimate is positive, this indicates that as the independent variable goes up, the dependent variable is predicted to go up as well. Negative coefficients indicate that as the independent variable increases, the dependent variable is predicted to decline. If the coefficient has a significance indicator next to it, this means that the relationship is statistically significant. It should be noted that this simple advice on interpretation can be applied to all of the statistical models in the book.

As the results demonstrate, I find evidence that supports the ideological distance hypothesis. In the House models, PAC distance from the median voter predicts a significantly higher investment in competitive races (the positive and significant coefficient in the right column of Table 4.1), but no more or less investment in safe seat races (no significance indicator in the left column). The pattern is more distinct in the Senate (Table 4.2). Distance from the median voter results in lower investments in safe seat candidates, but significantly higher resources aimed at competitive candidates.

In addition, traditional PAC categories behave as we might expect, and this is true after we control for PAC ideology. Corporate and trade association PACs invest mostly for access reasons. More specifically,

TABLE 4.1 PAC INVESTMENTS IN HOUSE RACES, 1984–2002

Variable	Safe Seats	Competitive
PAC Ideology	−10438.1(3651.5)**	3261.1(883.6)**
Distance from floor median	1374.2(4711.7)	9392.1(1136.3)**
Corporate PAC	21659.9(7425.2)**	−6230.7(1801.0)**
Labor PAC	79673.8(9618.2)**	12718.6(2320.0)**
Trade Association PAC	60237.5(8037.9)**	8.7(1942.5)
Non-Connected PAC	−25151.3(8827.0)**	1694.1(2144.1)
DC office	−3600.4(4607.0)	2229.0(1110.9)*
Total expenditures	95193.3(1622.9)**	19742.8(432.3)**
Years in Sample	4030.5(1258.5)**	−759.0(301.9)**
Year	4248.1(619.4)**	−1496.7(159.5)**
Mid-term election	9284.8(3954.5)*	−1762.3(944.4)+
Balance of Power	−1099.8(188.2)**	615.5(46.2)**
In sample post-94	−17744.3(9979.7)+	8253.8(2624.9)**
Intercept	−9557628(1234818)**	2754804(317761.1)**
Se	149185.4(1309.3)	36683.0(340.7)
N	6694	7441
Prob. Chi2 > 0	0.000	0.000

**$p<.01$ *$p<.05$ +$p<.10$

All tests are two-tailed, and Standard Errors (SEs) are in parentheses. Dependent Variable is expenditures in each type of race. The model was estimated using tobit, and expenditures are in 2002 dollars.

TABLE 4.2   PAC INVESTMENTS IN SENATE RACES, 1984–2002

Variable	Safe Seats	Competitive
PAC Ideology	1930.9(683.6)°°	3403.6(729.3)°°
Distance from floor median	−4097.7(895.7)°°	4924.4(962.4)°°
Corporate PAC	9756.8(1392.2)°°	1603.7(1526.0)
Labor PAC	−3014.7(1809.2)+	4529.6(1945.7)°
Trade Association PAC	10805.6(1499.2)°°	1977.2(1638.6)
Non-Connected PAC	4757.8(1671.4)°°	6410.1(1799.8)°°
DC office	−293.9(851.7)	1367.5(917.5)
Total expenditures	17523.3(320.3)°°	10945.6(348.6)°°
Years in Sample	1453.1(233.3)°°	543.5(253.1)°
Year	14.8(75.3)	−653.7(82.9)°°
Mid-term election	5550.7(731.3)°°	3979.2(785.4)°°
Balance of Power	−1099.5(120.0)°°	2537.8(131.8)°°
In sample post-94	−3074.0(1937.0)	1998.4(2172.2)
Intercept	−240420.3(149961.6)	1159259 (164948.6)°°
se	28429.9(252.0)°°	29588 (292.3)°°
N	7441	7441
Prob. Chi2 >0	0.000	0.000

°°p<.01 °p<.05 +p<.10
All tests are two-tailed, and SEs are in parentheses. Dependent Variable is expenditures in each type of race. The model was estimated using tobit, and expenditures are in 2002 dollars.

both contribute higher amounts in safe seat contests (in both the House and Senate models), and corporate PACs contribute significantly less in competitive House races. This makes sense if these PACs care more about specific policies that relate to their industry and are therefore more concerned with currying favor (Grier and Munger 1991, 1993). Labor PACs invest significantly more resources in competitive House and Senate races. Labor has always been categorized as seeking to move Congress in a more liberal direction (Gaddie 1995), and this is suggested here with their aggressive mobilization in close races.

The political environment is also important. For PACs involved in an election after 1994, there appears to be some mobilization in favor of competitive elections and away from safe seat races (with the strongest effects for the House models). This makes sense if we assume that the elections of 1996 through 2002 are somehow different (at least more consequential or high profile) than the elections of 1984 through 1992. In addition, the balance of power measure shows the importance of chamber control in the distribution of resources. As the measure increases (moving from a negative number to a positive

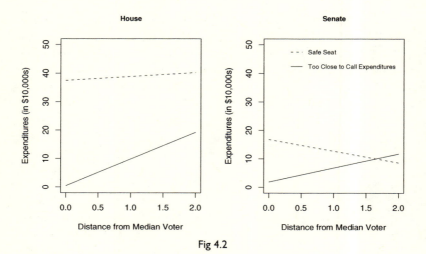

Fig 4.2

Predicted PAC Investments in House and Senate Races. Estimates are for a nonconnected PAC with a D.C. office, an ideology of 0.500, and an average level of expenditures. PAC—Political Action Committee.

number), PACs contribute less to safe seat candidates and more to competitive candidates.

To demonstrate the effect of ideological distance, I report predicted expenditures in Figure 4.2 for House and Senate safe seat and competitive races. I vary PAC distance from the median voter from 0 to 2 on the scale. This approach allows me to hold other variables constant and vary only the variable of interest. PAC ideological distance is, on average, about 0.440 for both the House and Senate, but some PAC distances range to a little over 3.

We can see in the graphs that the highest level of contributions are directed to safe seat House candidates (close to $400,000)—a consequence of there being so many such candidates. Nonetheless, for an average PAC that is farthest from the median voter, there is a steep increase in the aggregate amount spent on highly competitive House candidates (from nearly $0 when the PAC is located at the median voter to nearly $200,000). In the Senate models, the graphical results are striking. PACs with ideal points at the median voter spend virtually no money on competitive candidates; at the same time ideological outcasts spend significantly less on safe seat candidates.

Keep in mind, however, that contributing money to competitive candidates is valuable for PACs with ideal points near the median voter, if only to help maintain the status quo. And contributions to safe seat incumbents are valuable for ideological outcasts if only to maintain an open line of communication in an unfavorable policymaking environment. As such, the results demonstrate that PAC money is given by different groups for different reasons, but this does not mean that PACs forgo replacement or access completely. It only means that a PAC with limited resources will direct its contributions and expenditures to candidates in ways designed to optimize a favorable policymaking environment.

To investigate this issue further, I estimated four additional models (for safe seat and competitive contributions in House and Senate races) where the dependent variable was the average contribution (excluding independent expenditures and in-kind gifts) in each race type and chamber. These results are reported in Table 4.3. In these models, there are similar patterns for the distance measure in the House *and* Senate models. The farther a PAC is from the median voter in the House and Senate, the lower the average contribution to safe seat candidates and the higher the contribution to competitive candidates. Overall, these findings suggest that PACs direct their finite resources efficiently and in ways consistent with their ideological position.

All told, the results suggest that PACs contribute in ways that reach beyond candidate-specific relationships, but are influenced also by the policymaking and ideological environment as a whole. We might call this an ideoltropic response. Despite these strong findings, however, it is a lot to ask of PAC money to change the median voter to

TABLE 4.3   AVERAGE PAC CONTRIBUTION IN SAFE SEAT AND COMPETITIVE RACES, 1984–2002

	House	Senate
Safe Seats		
Distance from floor median	−87.14(22.40)°°	−273.06(49.14)°°
Competitive Elections		
Distance from floor median	221.29(34.98)°°	196.04(61.92)°°

°°$p<.01$

All tests are two-tailed, and SEs are in parentheses. Dependent Variable is the average competitive or safe seat contribution. The models were estimated using tobit, and expenditures are in 2002 dollars. Control variables are not shown.

a significant degree. Indeed, it may be rational for PACs to behave in these ways, but a PAC may realize more gains by helping a party regain or retain control of the House or Senate. By directing competitive money to a preferred party in elections in which the balance of power is tight, the PAC may gain huge policy benefits from an investment in partisan dynamics. I turn now to these questions.

Partisan Context

The early literature on political action committees hypothesized that PACs would compete with parties for resources and influence among candidates (Crotty and Jacobson 1980, Epstein 1980b). This research was motivated by the see-saw metaphor described in Chapter 3. Furthermore, consider again the 1989 reform proposal of President George H.W. Bush, mentioned at the beginning of this chapter. It contained a provision to let party committees spend more on coordinated expenditures with candidates. It also contained a plan to force all candidates to empty their war chests at the end of each campaign by either returning excess funds to contributors or donating the balance to party committees. As such, Bush's reform plan was not intended to reduce all money in elections, only PAC money.

Recent scholarship, however, has seen more room for collaboration between parties and PACs (Dwyre 1996, McCarty and Rothenberg 2000). For example, Sorauf and Wilson (1994, pp. 243, 247) note that, after PACs mobilized aggressively in the early 1980s, it became apparent how difficult it was for PAC leaders to play important roles across a set of elections (this is, in essence, exactly what James Madison would likely predict, were he alive at this time). As such, party leaders used their organization and coordination skills to act as brokers between PAC dollars and candidates. For PACs eager to gain access to incumbents or help elect favorable challengers, many learned to listen to the advice of party elites.

Not all PACs have a partisan preference, however, not to mention that how pro-party PACs invest in candidates might change under varying political conditions. In this section I test the partisan hypothesis, which predicts that PACs aligned ideologically with a party should increase their support for competitive candidates of their preferred party as parity between Democrats and Republicans increases in each chamber. Conversely, they should reduce such support for competitive candidate of the other party. This hypothesizes "party-picking."

In this section, I estimate models of PAC investments in Republican and Democratic safe seat and competitive races. The dependent variable in these models is the amount contributed to general-election Democrats in each race type minus the amount contributed for general-election Republicans. Thus, the variable is unbounded and can be negative. The dependent variable combines all expenditures by PACs in this realm, including contributions, independent expenditures, and in-kind gifts.

The virtue of this approach lies in combining partisan exclusivity with intensity. Large positive values of the dependent variable indicate a higher concentration of money spent on Democrats. Smaller numbers and zero values represent minimal PAC expenditures or no clear partisan preference. Large negative numbers indicate a higher concentration contributed to Republicans. For example, in 2000, the PAC for Shell Oil contributed $3,134 to competitive House Republicans and $0 for competitive Democrats.[11] The value of the dependent variable for Shell, then, is −3134. In contrast, the Airline Pilots Association contributed $25,078 to competitive House Democrats, but nothing to competitive Republicans; its value is 25078. Finally, the PAC for Morgan Stanley Dean Witter contributed $4,179 to competitive House Democrats and $14,629 to competitive House Republicans; the value of the variable for them is −10450.

I included many of the same independent variables as in the previous section, as well as the following. First, I included variables for whether the PAC was more liberal than the Democratic Party's median voter in either the House or Senate (depending on the model) or more conservative than the Republican Party median. This means that the PAC was more liberal or more conservative than the majority of members in their closest party. PACs with ideal points in between the party medians were the base category.

For example, in 2000, the median Democratic House member had an ideology of −0.393. Any PAC with an estimated ideology more liberal is coded as a pro-Democratic PAC. This includes the Association of Trial Lawyers (−2.51), the California League of Conservation Voters (−0.845), and the Michigan Credit Union League Legislative Action Fund (−0.493). In contrast, the Republican House median in 2000 was 0.468. Some pro-GOP PACs include the National Rifle Association Political Victory Fund (1.63), BP America PAC (1.01), and the National Association of Independent Insurers (0.568). In contrast, nonpartisan PACs include Land O' Lake Inc (–0.112) and Coca-Cola (0.247).[12]

In addition to the partisan PAC classification, I interacted the two variables with the party balance measure from the previous section. To do this, I simply multiply the two variables together, so as to assess how the combined condition is related to the dependent variable. In this case, the coefficient estimates for these interactions indicate how a PAC ideologically aligned with one or the other party reacts under varying electoral conditions. I expected the Democratic PAC interaction to be positive and significant for competitive races and negative and significant in the safe seat model. I expected the opposite for the Republican PAC interaction. This would indicate that Democratically aligned PACs increase their intense and exclusive support of competitive Democrats in years when majority control of the chamber is up for grabs, but they become more bipartisan in their support of safe seat candidates. Republican PACs should do the same, but with increased support for competitive Republicans in highly contested election cycles.[13]

Both results would indicate that partisan PACs close ranks in tight years in expenditures for competitive candidates, but hedge their bets on being with the out-party by spending higher amounts on safe seat candidates of the opposing party (that is, in races irrelevant to determining the balance of power). According to one interview respondent in 2003, PACs know very well the potential risks of electoral action in years when the balance of power teeters: "Would [our union] be better off with Pelosi as speaker—yes. But in between we have to work with what we have. Do we roll the dice and work against the GOP? What if we lose?"[14]

At the outset, consider this: why do partisan-oriented PACs ever support competitive candidates of the opposing party, regardless of the stakes of the election? This is a valid concern and one worth some consideration. While it is true that a very conservative PAC is less likely to support Democrats, this should not preclude that PAC from knowing at least a handful of competitive and conservative Democratic candidates. In addition, not all contributions are determined by the ideology of the candidate. It is possible that some Democrats serve in

TABLE 4.4   PARTISAN PAC INVESTMENTS IN HOUSE RACES, 1984–2002

Variable	Safe Seats	Competitive
Democratic PAC	55139.0(5338.8)°°	23495.5(1565.9)°°
Republican PAC	−13851.5(2555.7)°°	−9304.7(1332.5)°°
Dem PAC × Balance	619.7(275.3)°	541.5(80.4)°°
GOP PAC × Balance	281.0(107.4)°°	−178.9(58.7)°°
Corporate PAC	4948.1(3067.7)	5992.2(933.0)°°
Labor PAC	139786.5(10021.2)°°	26774.7(2715.5)°°
Trade Association PAC	−7623.1(3877.5)°	−470.4(1395.1)
Non-Connected PAC	−11874.8(3613.7)°°	1721.2(1311.1)
DC office	20110.3(3293.5)°°	5874.2(1024.6)°°
Total expenditures	10064.9(1313.8)°°	294.3(451.1)
Years in Sample	1147.3(478.9)°	323.0(190.7)+
Year	594.7(408.9)	199.9(136.1)
Mid-term election	2959.9(2651.3)	−655.2(887.6)
Balance of Power	−927.4(134.4)°°	10.5(40.3)
Democratic chamber	11027.3(4889.9)°	7356.6(1814.7)°°
In sample post-94	920.2(3528.4)	−1177.8(1206.9)
Intercept	−1337794.0(816863.3)	−415675.9(270438.3)
N	6694	7441
Prob. > F	0.000	0.000
R-squared	0.3231	0.1737

°°$p<.01$ °$p<.05$ +$p<.10$
All tests are two-tailed, and robust SEs are in parentheses. Dependent Variable is expenditures for Democrats in each type of race minus expenditures for Republicans. The model was estimated using OLS, and expenditures are in 2002 dollars.

influential committee positions that the conservative PAC cannot ignore.

I report the results of both models in Tables 4.4 and 4.5.[15] Because the dependent variable is continuous and unbounded in these models, we can interpret the coefficient estimates a bit more directly here. The relationship between the independent and dependent variables is still determined by the sign of the coefficient, but additionally, the size of the coefficient is instructive. A one-unit change in an independent variable is associated with a coefficient size change in the dependent variable. Again, however, the stars next to the coefficient determine whether the relationship is statistically significant.

The results show that, as expected, PACs ideologically aligned with either party spend resources to benefit candidates of that party. This is true for all four models. For example, Democratic PACs contribute, on average, a total of $55,139 more to Democratic safe seat House candidates than do nonpartisan PACs. They contribute over $23,000 more

TABLE 4.5   PARTISAN PAC INVESTMENTS IN SENATE RACES, 1984–2002

Variable	Safe Seats	Competitive
Democratic PAC	8058.4(1132.6)°°	11461.1(1268.1)°°
Republican PAC	–5785.9(631.5)°°	–5365.1(638.5)°°
Dem PAC × Balance	–317.8(137.9)°	2196.5(471.1)°°
GOP PAC × Balance	231.9(161.4)	–725.9(180.2)°°
Corporate PAC	–234.9(801.9)	931.6(927.2)
Labor PAC	11737.6(1175.0)°°	8616.9(2421.3)°°
Trade Association PAC	–1140.1(873.3)	–1801.9(1291.9)
Non-Connected PAC	–3862.3(2235.4)+	–2284.5(1551.5)
DC office	2380.6(835.1)°°	2572.4(822.1)°°
Total expenditures	–960.7(427.2)°	–678.6(337.2)°
Years in Sample	142.8(92.9)	–168.6(170.5)
Year	–174.6(77.6)°	–14.3(46.7)
Mid-term election	–2899.1(467.0)°°	–798.7(592.5)
Balance of Power	59.5(93.9)	–248.8(84.7)°°
Democratic chamber	6201.4(713.1)°°	1965.7(863.2)°
In sample post-94	600.9(1215.5)	638.9(951.8)
Intercept	353734.6(152546.6)°	33514.8(94111.7)
N	7441	7441
Prob. > F	0.000	0.000
R-squared	0.1008	0.0899

°°$p<.01$ °$p<.05$ +$p<.10$
All tests are two-tailed, and robust SEs are in parentheses. Dependent Variable is expenditures for Democrats in
each type of race minus expenditures for Republicans. The model was estimated using OLS, and expenditures are
in 2002 dollars.

than nonpartisan PACs to competitive House Democrats. Pro-Republican PACs invest more heavily than nonpartisan PACs in Republican safe seat and competitive candidates by about $14,000 and $9,000, respectively.

The effects for different PAC sponsors are also revealing. Labor PACs always favor Democratic candidates (the coefficient is positive and significant in all four models, with the strongest effect for House safe seats), and this is above and beyond the ideological location of these labor groups. Corporate PACs, however, show much less partisanship after controlling for ideology (only one of the four coefficient estimates—competitive House candidates—is statistically significant). The effects for trade association and nonconnected PACs show some tendency to favor Republicans, but these trends are only true for safe seat contributions. Indeed, despite the consistent effects for labor PACs, it seems much of the partisanship behind PAC donations can be attributed to the PAC's ideological location relative to the parties.

The key to the partisan hypothesis, however, is in the interactive effects, which investigate how partisan PACs alter their contribution strategies. In this regard, the results in both tables suggest strong support for the partisan hypothesis. Note that these effects are present in addition to the significant coefficient on chamber control. (In all four models, when the Democrats control the chamber, they benefit with slightly high contribution totals from all PACs.) Consider both competitive models first. The coefficient estimate on the interaction is positive and significant for Democratic PACs and negative and significant for Republican PACs. This indicates that as the balance of power moves from negative values (indicating an election where chamber control is unlikely to change) to positive values (where control is less certain), pro-Democratic PACs increase their investment in competitive Democrats. Republicans do the same in these years, lowering their support of competitive Democrats in favor of competitive Republicans.

The results in the safe seat models are less consistent, but still instructive. Pro-Democratic PACs do seem to support more Republican Senate safe seat candidates in years in which the balance of power is uncertain (note the negative and significant interactive coefficient for Democrats in the first column of Table 4.5). But they respond in the opposite fashion with contributions to House safe seat candidates. As expected, pro-Republican PACs appear to hedge their bets slightly in the House model (increasing their support of safe seat Democrats in years when chamber control is highly contested), but not in the Senate case. These trends will become clearer in the discussion below.

It should also be pointed out that the coefficient estimate for the balance of power variable can be interpreted as the change in contribution strategies for nonpartisan PACs. Because a variable for nonpartisan PACs is excluded (in order to appropriately estimate the statistical model), we can infer the behavior of nonpartisan PACs with the balance measure. As is demonstrated, nonpartisan PACs are only affected by the balance of power in two of the four instances: as the balance of power tightens, they favor Republicans in House safe seat candidates and Senate competitive candidates. In this latter case, the coefficient size indicates far less mobilization toward the GOP than the mobilization of pro-party PACs.

To demonstrate the importance of political conditions to partisan PACs, I show a series of predicted probabilities in Figure 4.3 and Figure 4.4. I estimate expenditures for a hypothetical pro-Democratic

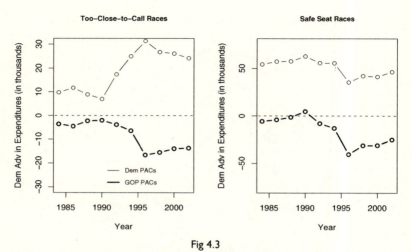

Fig 4.3

Predicted PAC Partisanship in House Races. Estimates are for a nonconnected PAC with a D.C. office. PAC—Political Action Committee.

and pro-Republican PAC in each year, letting the political conditions of each cycle vary. In other words, the only thing held constant in this simulation are the PAC characteristics. We can therefore see how pro-Democratic and pro-Republican PACs behaved in each cycle.

The results are quite striking. Note the significant polarization of partisan PACs in competitive House races after 1994. Democratic PACs are more partisan than ever in the elections of 1996–2002, giving far more to competitive Democratic candidates than in years past. Republican PACs follow a similar trend. Before the elections of 1994, pro-Republican PACs only moderately favored competitive GOP candidates. After 1994, these PACs mobilize heavily in favor of Republican candidates in competitive elections. Note that polarization is starkest in 1996, a year when there were 34 competitive races and only 13 seats necessary to change party control. In that year, pro-Democratic PACs favored competitive Democrats by more than $300,000, and pro-Republican groups favored competitive GOP candidates by nearly $200,000.

The trends in the safe seat panel of Figure 4.3 are also interesting. Republican PACs essentially split their safe seat money between Democrats and Republicans for most of the 1980s and early 1990s

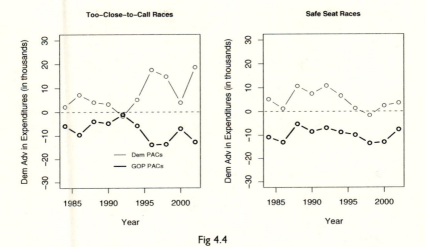

Fig 4.4

Predicted PAC Partisanship in Senate Races. Estimates are for a nonconnected PAC with a D.C. office. PAC—Political Action Committee.

(the predicted advantage in those years hovers around $0), but after the elections of 1994, they favored Republicans more strongly (by about $500,000 in 1996). Democrats also drop slightly in their support of Democrats after the 1994 elections (a change noted by many observers of PAC politics), but the drop reverses slightly in the elections of 1998–2002.

The Senate results are equally powerful. For competitive elections, both partisan PACs diverge after 1994, with the exception of 2000. But recall from Chapter 2 that the 2000 election cycle was the only one after 1994 in which Senate control seemed less likely to change. And there is divergence around the 1986 elections when the Democrats were successful in retaking control from the Republicans. In contrast, the safe seat panel shows the reverse trend for pro-Democratic PACs. Even as these PACs are more partisan after 1994 in how they gave to competitive Democrats, they are far more bipartisan in their contributions to safe seat candidates. Indeed, in the elections after 1994, Democratic PACs nearly split their safe seat contributions between Republicans and Democrats.

All told, the results are clear evidence for the partisan hypothesis. PACs with ideal points more extreme than the median of the closest party invest more exclusively and more intensely in their preferred party in years when competitive elections could determine control of the chamber. As such, cross-party support for competitive candidates comes in years when majority control is more secure.

Conclusion

PACs are shrewd electoral actors. As the results demonstrate, PACs respond to the political contextual factors that surround House and Senate elections. PACs that prefer the ideological status quo invest more resources in safe seat candidates, giving a smaller contribution to competitive candidates when they do give. PACs with extreme preference points direct resources to candidates most likely to win and give smaller average contributions to candidates who have virtually no chance of losing.

At the same time, pro-party PACs direct resources in ways to maximize members from that party, especially in years when the balance of power is tight. Most of the literature presumes that PACs focus on individual members for reasons ranging from ideology to the constituency the member represents, but this chapter shows not only that PACs consider or take account of the larger ideological and partisan contexts but they also direct their resources in ways that are most efficient. Indeed, we see evidence here that PACs are mobilized by consequential issues such as control of the chamber.

All told, this chapter is encouraging in that it provides important evidence that PACs respond to political contexts. PAC money, however, is not a new tactic. The puzzle that inspires this book relates to why interest groups in the mid-1990s began using tactics that appeared to circumvent the spirit of campaign finance law. I turn now to an examination of soft money contributions to the Democratic and Republican parties between 1991 and 2002. How much and how exclusively do corporations, labor unions, associations, and other groups give to the nonfederal accounts of the two parties? Are there trends in that data that reflect trends seen here?

5 Understanding Soft Money

On May 24, 2000 the Democratic Party held a fund-raiser at the MCI Center in Washington, D.C., dubbed by organizer Terry McAuliffe as a "down-home blue jeans and barbecue bash." DNC National Chairman Joe Andrew kicked off the event by declaring, "We don't care about the size of your wallet, just the size of your heart," and DNC General Chairman Ed Rendell proclaimed, "When we win this election in November, we are committed to getting rid of soft money. And four years from now, when we have a similar event—the top ticket is going to cost $100, and we're going to hold it in RFK Stadium." Ironically, the Democrats raised more than $26 million that night, with nearly 50 percent of those funds raised from a handful of individual, union, and corporate soft money donors.[1]

In the previous chapter, I examined the patterns of hard money donated by political action committees to candidates for federal office. In the mid-1990s, however, most campaign finance reform advocates lost interest in hard money and instead focused their ire on "soft money," those unregulated funds raised through the parties' nonfederal accounts (and at big fund-raisers like the Democrats' blue jeans bash). Congressman Marty Meehan (D-Mass.) and Senator John McCain (R-AZ) argued in 2001, for example, that "the current soft money system is a cancer on our democracy."[2] They asserted that parties were using soft money funds to aid electioneering efforts for federal candidates and that soft money was allowing interest groups to purchase influence with party leaders.

Proponents of soft money, however, warned that its elimination would spell doom for American politics. Senator Mitch McConnell (R-KY) declared a ban on soft money to be "mutual assured destruction of the political parties."[3] He believed the ban would damage the ability of both parties to form strong organizations and foster a party image. Legal scholars Joel Gora and Peter Wallison opined that soft money "helps [parties] maintain their organizations, motivate their followers and publicize their principles. Banning soft money denies parties the rights that we would not think of denying to other organizations."[4]

Despite being a major focus of campaign finance reform, however, little is known about, and little research has explored, the patterns of soft money giving. Indeed, what was the purpose of soft money, and what explains its dramatic rise? In this chapter I explore soft money contributions from all interest groups for the six election cycles between 1992 and 2002, which I term the soft money era. I investigate the **hard-to-soft hypothesis**, which predicts that donors will find ways of infusing money into the political process as a means of enhancing their resource capacity. I do this by testing whether large PACs (inhibited by upper limits on hard money contributions) were also large soft money donors. Second, I evaluate the **competitive hypothesis**, which predicts that many soft money donors were motivated to contribute because of their proximity to competitive federal races. Finally, I look for evidence of the **partisan hypothesis**, which expects some donors to give to both parties but many donors to invest exclusively in only one party.

Soft Money From PACs

There is nothing obvious linking interest group hard money with soft money. As explained in Chapter 3, well-funded hard money PACs might conceivably find no added value in making soft contributions to the parties' nonfederal committees. For example, if interest groups are hoping to gain access to specific influential policymakers, soft money to the parties seems a potentially inefficient route. After all, why would influential incumbents care whether an interest group donated to the party? The money never enters their coffers, and if they are a safe seat incumbent, it is unlikely the money would be used to benefit their electoral efforts. Further still, if a group is hoping to elect or defeat a candidate for office, helping the parties do this with soft money means trusting party leaders to spend the money in ways the group desires. At the outset, then, donating soft money seems to be a risky way to pursue access and replacement goals.

On the other hand, recall the actions recounted in Chapters 1 and 2 of the Walt Disney Corporation in the 2000 election. It contributed nearly $700,000 in soft money along with almost $300,000 in hard money. Indeed, much of the public concern over the explosion of soft money accorded with the conventional wisdom that donors were avoiding hard money limits by augmenting contributions with soft dollars. For example, in an affidavit for one campaign finance case (*Mariani v. United States*), former General Counsel for the DNC, Joseph Sandler, submitted testimony and documentation of how the DNC abided to regulations in the raising of soft money. Consider the following excerpt from a memo between Sadler and the DNC finance staff on how to write hard and soft money checks:

> Checks for federal contributions must be made payable to "DNC/Federal Account." Checks for nonfederal contributions must be made payable to "DNC/Nonfederal Account." Checks for the building fund must be made payable to "DNC Building Fund." If an individual contributor who has not already given the maximum amount to the DNC federal account ($20,000 per year per person, $40,000 per year per married couple), *you should do everything possible to encourage the donor to write two separate checks*, one check to the "DNC/Federal Account" for the maximum that contributor can still give to the federal account, and the other check for the remainder of what the donor wants to give, made payable to the "DNC/Nonfederal Account" (italics in original).[5]

Given this attention to detail, I hypothesize that interest groups with PACs and PACs that spent a lot of hard money were also to be the most prevalent interest group soft money contributors. In Chapter 3,

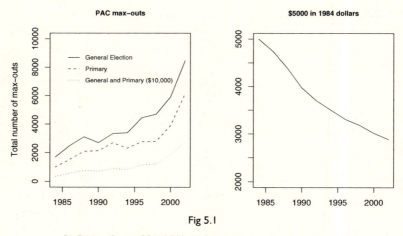

Fig 5.1

PAC Max-Outs, 1984–2002. PAC—Political Action Committee.

I argued that this dynamic might be a response to changes in the resource context. As inflation devalued hard dollars, interest groups
should seek to expand tactical capacity by finding new avenues by
which to act on their goals.

Figure 5.1 illustrates the number of "max-out" ($5,000) PAC con-
tributions over time. As the graph demonstrates, the number of primary and general election $5,000 contributions steadily increased over
the last 20 years (from just under 2,000 general election and 1,000 primary contributions in 1984 to more than 8,000 and 6,000, respectively,
in 2002). The bottom line in the left-hand graph shows the number of
$10,000 contributions—that is, when PACs donated both a primary
and general election maximum to the same candidate. That number
rose from almost none in 1984 to more than 2,000 in 2002. The right-
hand graph shows the declining value of a maximum contribution;
$5,000 dollars in 1984 was worth less than $3,000 in 2002. If soft
money was motivated by the effects of inflation on hard money, both
graphs in Figure 5.1 are necessary but not sufficient evidence.

We can directly test for whether PACs that contributed a lot of
hard money were also those groups that gave soft money to the Democrats and Republicans. First, we have the universe of PAC hard money
contributions, which is stored at the FEC and is easily downloadable.

These are the same data used in Chapter 4. Second, data on soft money contributions are also available from the FEC, although they are stored in a rather obscure setting. This method of storage deserves some explanation.

The FEC splits its contributor files by contributor type—one for hard money contributions to candidates and parties from PACs and one for hard money contributions to candidates and parties from individuals. Put simply, if one is interested in tracking contributions from the Walt Disney Corporation's PAC, one looks in one file, but if one is interested in tracking contributions from Michael Eisner (the former CEO of Walt Disney), one examines a different file. Oddly, the individual contributor files for the six election cycles between 1992 and 2002 also contain soft money contributions from individuals and interest groups.

The Federal Election Commission maintains these records of soft money contributions because of a court challenge by Common Cause in the late 1980s (*Common Cause v. FEC*). Common Cause complained that existing FEC regulations did not mandate federal parties to disclose the source of nonfederal funds (like they did for hard funds), thus limiting the extent to which party money was disclosed. The U.S. District Court in Washington, D.C., ruled in 1988 that the FEC had to make the source of party soft money public, which the Commission did starting with the 1992 election cycle. It seems apparent, however, that the Commission did not consider the contributions significant enough to put them in a separate file, choosing instead to lump them with hard money data on contributions from individuals.

I selected and saved all interest group soft money contributions of this type from these files.[6] This allowed me to create databases of interest group soft money contributions for each of the six election cycles between 1992 and 2002. As explained in Chapter 2, there were only about 11,000 soft money contributions in 1991–1992, but nearly 50,000 by 2001–2002. The files are an incredibly valuable source of information on which groups donated soft money and the level of that investment. For example, the data show that the average interest group soft money donation in 2002 was only $9,000. It was just under $10,000 in 2000. This finding challenges the conventional wisdom that most soft money donations were in the hundreds of thousands or even millions.

With both data sources in hand, an ideal cross-reference would compare all active PACs with the soft money contributor files for each election cycle. However, in each cycle there are more than 3,000 active PACs and, as noted, thousands of soft money contributors. To compensate, I sampled from the list of PACs, choosing about 10 percent in each election cycle (300 PACs in each cycle). This produced a stratified random sample of 1,800 PACs. From this list, I checked whether the PAC or the PAC's sponsoring organization made a soft money contribution in that cycle.

There is one immediate complication, however. The FEC assigns each PAC a unique identifier code. General Motors, for example, has a PAC named the Civic Involvement Program/General Motors, and its FEC code is C00076810. The unique identifiers make it easy to aggregate contributions by the PAC and track its activity over election cycles. Soft money contributors, however, are not given unique identifier codes and are only identifiable by the name of the contributor. Furthermore, if a group makes multiple contributions in an election cycle, it might make each contribution under slightly different name iterations. In 2000, for example, General Motors made three soft money contributions. Two were made in the name of General Motors, but one was made in the PAC name, Civic Involvement Program. To cross-check the PAC and soft money files, then, means matching on the listed contributor name. This can prove to be quite difficult and undoubtedly introduces measurement error into this investigation.[7]

Table 5.1 shows the results of two slightly different models estimating the amount of soft money contributed by each PAC. All told, 30 percent of the 1,800 PACs were soft money contributors. The models include variables that might conceivably be associated with making a soft money contribution. For example, I control for the organizational type of PAC; there were 140 labor unions in the sample, 822 corporations, 165 nonconnected PACs, and 361 trade associations. I also include a variable for whether the PAC had a D.C. office listed in the PAC committee file (290 PACs did), and a trend variable for the election cycle.

Of course, the principal set of variables concern the hard money activity of the PAC. I account for this activity in several ways. For example, I include three measures from Chapter 4 for whether the PAC had an estimated ideology. Recall, PACs with ideology scores were very active hard money donors. I controlled for whether the estimated

TABLE 5.1   SOFT MONEY FROM PACS

Variable	Model 1	Model 2
Hard money contributed	.503(.048)**	
Number $5,000 contributions		.524(.063)**
Year	4.311(.741)**	4.255(.756)**
Democratic PAC	24.417(6.66)**	38.420(6.40)**
Republican PAC	17.670(5.72)**	28.291(5.65)**
Non-Partisan PAC	22.589(3.19)**	29.328(3.15)**
DC Office	16.164(3.37)**	19.492(3.41)**
Corporate PAC	27.632(3.88)**	29.192(3.99)**
Labor PAC	7.776(6.11)	9.848(6.20)
Non-Connected PAC	−26.382(7.69)**	−28.469(7.86)**
Trade Association PAC	−5.140(4.59)	−.709(4.64)
All hard money for competitive candidates	−3.813(6.80)	−5.338(6.94)
All hard money for safe seats	−8.461(4.37)+	−10.569(4.45)*
Percent hard money for competitive	1.425(5.61)	.726(5.71)
Intercept	−70.075(5.44)**	−71.032(5.57)**
N	1800	1800
Prob. chi2>0	0.0000	0.0000
log-likelihood	−3038.792	−3057.4037

**$p<.01$ *$p<.05$ +$p<.10$
All tests are two-tailed, and SEs are in parentheses. Dependent Variable is the amount of party soft money (in $10,000s) contributed from each PAC. The model was estimated using tobit, and all amounts are in constant 2002 dollars.

score was more liberal than the Democratic congressional median (I used the more liberal floor median of the two chambers, which accounted for 81 PACs), more conservative than the Republican median (I used the more conservative median of the two chambers, and there were 66 such PACs), or an ideology in between these medians (of which there were 281). The base category, then, was any PAC that did not have an estimated ideology score, meaning the PAC was not in the top 500 in that election cycle.

I also include a more direct measure in Model 1 of the amount of hard money contributed by the PAC. If the hard-to-soft hypothesis holds, this variable should be positive and significant, indicating that more hard money funds predict a higher level of soft money. In Model 2, I include a variable for the number of maximum contributions made by the PAC (combining general election and primary contributions); that is, the number of $5,000 contributions in that election cycle. These hard money variables are similar but represent alternative operationalizations of hard money activity. A group might contribute a lot of hard money but make almost no maximum contributions (this was true of the NRA Political Victory Fund in 2002); or a group might contribute lots of $5,000 contributions, but still contribute only a modest amount of hard money (as was true of the Communication Workers of America PAC in 2002).

Finally, I include three measures that disaggregated hard money spending. I include a variable that measured the percentage of all hard money given to candidates in competitive races (defined here as "leaning" or "too-close-to-call" House and Senate races according to *Congressional Quarterly's* pre-election estimates); I expected this measure to be positive and significant. I also include two variables identifying whether the PAC made only House or Senate competitive or safe seat expenditures. I expected a PAC only making competitive contributions to be more likely to give soft money, and groups only participating in safe seat races to be less likely to make nonfederal contributions.

There are three important sets of results from Models 1 and 2. The first concerns the variables tapping the type of PAC. Corporate PACs contribute a lot of soft money; nonconnected PACs contribute significantly less; and the coefficients on labor and trade association PACs are insignificant in both models. Thus, in the universe of active PACs, corporations were the predominant soft money givers. For example, of all corporate PACs that contributed some soft money, the average contribution was $114,000. For comparable nonconnected PACs, the average was $51,000. Some examples of corporate soft money donations include Pfizer ($1,500,000 in 2000 and more than $800,000 in 1998), Atlantic Richfield Corp. ($1,120,000 in 1998), Bristol-Myers Squibb (only $1,300 in 1992, but more than $550,000 in 1996), and Metlife Insurance ($390,000 in 1996 and more than $200,000 in 2002). Also significant are PACs with D.C. addresses, which contribute significantly more than those outside the beltway. The average contribution for a D.C. PAC was $230,000, significantly more than the $96,000 average contribution for a non-D.C. PAC.

Second, there is persuasive evidence that connects hard money to soft money. To that end, PACs with estimated ideologies—from Chapter 4—contribute higher levels of soft money than PACs with no ideology score. Furthermore, in Model 1, the "hard money" variable is positive and significant, as expected; this finding indicates that PACs spending a lot of hard money also contributed higher levels of soft money. And in Model 2, the variable for the number of hard money maximum contributions is also positive and significant. To illustrate these effects, I estimate predicted soft money contributions for a non-partisan corporate PAC in the 2002 election. If this PAC contributes $100,000 in hard money, it is expected to contribute $270,000 in soft money. If it contributes $700,000 in hard money, the model predicts $580,000 in soft money. And if it gives out $1.6 million in hard money, it should contribute just over $1 million in soft money.

Finally, there are some interesting results for the competitiveness and safe seat variables. The percentage of all hard money that goes to competitive candidates has no effect on soft money giving, nor does the signifier for PACs making only competitive contributions (I predicted a positive and significant result on both). On the other hand, if a PAC only makes safe seat contributions, it contributes significantly less soft money than other PACs. This indicates that PACs only interested in helping safe seat incumbents were not likely to seek access indirectly through soft money.

All told, the results of the PAC analysis provide evidence in favor of the hard-to-soft hypothesis. Nonetheless, it is important to note the issue of causation. These results do not necessarily mean that hard money predicts soft money—only that the factors compelling PACs to spend heavily with hard money also compelled them to spend soft money. In other words, whatever factors push interest groups to be active participants in the electoral process applied both to hard and soft money. In this sense, soft money was not a qualitatively different form of election money—simply an extension of hard money (with obvious implications for those opposing BCRA under the assumption that soft money should be considered a unique party resource).

Taken alone—that is, with only the hard-to-soft test—we still lack the convincing causal mechanism driving the rise in soft money. Beyond the inflation argument, what makes a group want to extend its presence in elections with soft money? I turn now to a series of tests for whether (and how) soft money is related to competitive and partisan elections.

Soft Money From States

When during the election cycle do interest group donors contribute the bulk of soft money? If access politics dominates soft money giving, we might expect minimal increases in soft money donations closer to Election Day, and we might see higher levels of soft money at key policy votes or even in off-years. In contrast, if electoral politics principally motivates soft money, we might predict large increases as the campaign draws to a close.

In Figure 5.2 I show the amount of money in each month of the six cycles, adjusting the totals to 2002 dollars. As the graph demonstrates, there is more soft money contributed in later cycles. In particular, note the difference between 1992 and the two other presidential elections. The parties also raised millions more for the 2002 mid-term elections than for the 1998 and 1994 cycles.

More importantly, the graphs appear consistent with contributions for both access and replacement goals. For example, there are periodic spikes in contribution totals throughout the two-year election cycle. These spikes are particularly extreme in 2000 and 2002, for which there are surges in contributions every few months. This pattern could

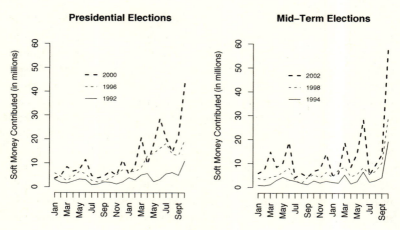

Soft Money Contributed by Month During Two-Year Election Cycle, 1992–2002. All values are in constant 2002 dollars.

be indicative of contribution strategies designed to curry favor with key party leaders (i.e., donating at party fund-raisers well in advance of the upcoming elections). For example, consider again the Democratic fund-raiser noted at the beginning of the chapter. The party raised $26 million in May, six months before the November elections. As for the Republicans, the *Atlanta Journal-Constitution* reported in June 2001, for example, that President Bush was hoping to raise millions in soft money at a party fund-raiser that month—16 months before the 2002 mid-term elections.[8]

At the same time, however, the month with the greatest contribution activity is always October of the election year; in particular, note October 2002, when the parties raised nearly $60 million from interest groups. In addition, the trend lines tend to track upward over the election cycle (especially the spikes, which get higher and higher as the election cycle progresses). In the debate over issue advocacy—the focus of the next chapter—proponents of reform pointed to the dramatic rise in nonmagic word issue advertisements toward the end of the campaign. Indeed, the Supreme Court used this empirical pattern as partial justification in upholding BCRA's restrictions on advertising. In these graphs, the same pattern holds for soft money contributions, and one might take this as limited but persuasive evidence of an electoral dynamic to soft money.

Does this rate of increase vary, however, across competitive states? In this analysis I examine the amount of soft money contributed from each state in each month of the six election cycles in the soft money era. If the competitiveness hypothesis holds, I expect states that were classified as competitive to have had a higher rate of increase in the amount contributed than noncompetitive states. For example, consider Michigan in 2000. Voters there were exposed to an intense Senate contest between incumbent Senator Spencer Abraham and challenger Debbie Stabenow. Al Gore and George Bush were also locked in a tough battle for the state's electoral votes. Might donors in Ann Arbor or Detroit or Grand Rapids be particularly susceptible to party appeals for soft money donations? After all, their soft money contribution might tip the balance in that state and help give control of the Senate and the White House to their preferred party. Compare this to donors in Connecticut, who were likely ignored by party leaders. Joe Lieberman was Gore's running mate that year, but he was also a shoo-in for re-election as Senator, and Gore was assured of winning the state's electoral votes. Perhaps donors in Hartford or Bridgeport or Fairfield were not solicited as aggressively.

To test for this dynamic, I estimated two separate statistical models—one for presidential election years and one for mid-term election years—predicting the total amount of Democratic and Republican soft money contributed from each of the 50 states between January 1991 and October 2002; this totals more than 6,700 state-month observations. For example, all interest group donors in Massachusetts contributed a combined total of $702,875 in soft money in October 2002; this was up from $280,850 in September and $33,550 in August.[9]

I control for several variables that might predict contribution totals from each state-month. For example, I account for the 22-month election cycle with a trend variable. I expect the results to show that months closer to Election Day generate larger amounts of soft money. I also include a lagged measure of contributor totals from that state in the previous month; this is done to control for the fact that contributions in any state-month are likely correlated to surrounding months (i.e., donors from Maine in September of an election year might be motivated by the same factors as donors from Maine in October).[10] In addition, I include variables for year-specific effects to account for the fact that there is more soft money in 2000 than in 1996, and more in 1998 than in 1994.

I also include several variables tapping the competitiveness of the state, as well as a variable for the absence of a Senate election in that state. These variables are key to testing the competitive hypothesis. In the mid-term model I define Senate competitiveness using *Congressional Quarterly's* pre-election estimates (where 1=safe seat, 2=favored race, 3=leaning campaign, and 4=too-close-to-call). This is the same competitive ranking used for Chapter 4. I also interacted states identified as "leaning" and "too-close-to-call" with the month variable for each of the three mid-term elections. This allows me to assess the rate of change in competitive elections for each of the mid-term races. In 1994 and 2002 there were 13 such competitive Senate races, and in 1998 there were 12.

In the presidential election year model, I control for Senate competitiveness and presidential competitiveness, which I define as any state in which the election was decided by less than 5 percent of the votes.[11] I interacted the month variable with any state competitive in *both* the Senate and presidential race, which I term a "super" competitive state. In 2000, these "super" states were Michigan, Minnesota, Florida, Nevada, and Washington. In 1996, they were South Dakota, Georgia, North Carolina, Kentucky, and Montana, and in 1992 they were New Hampshire, Ohio, Wisconsin, North Carolina, Arizona, and Colorado. These three interactions (one for each presidential election year), as with the mid-term model, allow me to assess the rate of change in highly competitive states in each of the three presidential elections.[12]

The results in Table 5.2 show evidence for the competitiveness hypothesis. The coefficients to focus on are the ones listed under the Competitive°Month row. They show the rate of change in competitive states over the course of the campaign. Positive numbers indicate that, as the campaign progressed, money donated from competitive states outpaced contribution totals from noncompetitive states. In the mid-term model (the right column), the rate of change in competitive Senate races is significant in 1998 and 2002. In the presidential model (left column), the rate of change in competitive "super" states is significant in 2000. All told, these results indicate that in the elections of 1998, 2000, and 2002, as Election Day grew closer competitive states generated much higher contributions than noncompetitive states.

As for the other variables, the month variable is positive and strongly significant, as is the lagged contributor variable. The variables for election cycle also show an increasing amount of soft money with each new election. In the mid-term model the number of electoral votes in each state is in the expected direction, but fails to reach significance, as is the "no Senate race" variable (which I expected to be negative; such a result would indicate that with no Senate race to motivate contributions, donors are less aggressive givers. This prediction is not borne out.).

I demonstrate the competitiveness effects more clearly in Figure 5.3, where I compare predicted contribution totals in competitive and noncompetitive states in the 1998, 2000, and 2002 elections. Both graphs show that, at the start of the campaign, noncompetitive states contributed slightly more soft money than the eventual competitive states. For example, in January 1999 a state that is not competitive by

TABLE 5.2   SOFT MONEY FROM STATES

Variable	Presidential	Mid-Terms
Amount contributed previous month	.521(.019)**	.203(.024)**
Month	.625(.056)**	.510(.070)**
1996(1998)	3.70(.860)**	2.79(1.06)**
2000(2002)	5.81(.862)**	8.27(1.09)**
Electoral votes in state		.919(.570)
Competitive presidential state	−1.74(1.00)+	
Competitive Senate state	−.609(.516)	−2.03(.737)**
No Senate race in state	−1.77(1.31)	−.654(1.40)
Competitive × Month		
1992(1994)	−.045(.155)	.147(.157)
1996(1998)	.035(.168)	.547(.173)**
2000(2002)	.623(.173)**	.598(.160)**
Intercept	−2.56(1.55)+	−9.31(6.48)
N	3150	3150

**$p<.01$; +$p<.10$

All tests are two-tailed, and SEs are in parentheses. Dependent Variable is the amount of soft money (in $10,000s) from each state in each month. The model was estimated using cross-sectional times series with fixed effects for states. Washington, D.C is excluded, and all amounts are in constant 2002 dollars.

fall 2000 contributed about $100,000, compared to about $80,000 from a competitive state. By the end of the campaign, however, donors in competitive states contribute an average total of about $320,000, compared to states with no competitive election (which donate an estimated total of $220,000).

All told, the graphs show that although parties raised more soft money from everyone as the campaign progressed (evidence enough to demonstrate the importance of soft money to the parties' efforts in elections), they did so at even higher rates in competitive states. This is consistent with the competitiveness hypothesis. For donors in these states, being in the midst of a competitive federal election likely means being exposed to aggressive solicitation efforts by party leaders. It also gives donors interested in replacement goals an additional motivation to contribute; their contributions might help the parties battling for control of Congress and the White House do so on the donors' home turf.

Of course, there is no evidence that the nature of the race was important in the elections of 1992, 1994, and 1996. However, there is nothing disconcerting about this finding. As we know, soft money developed over the course of the 1990s into an important party resource,

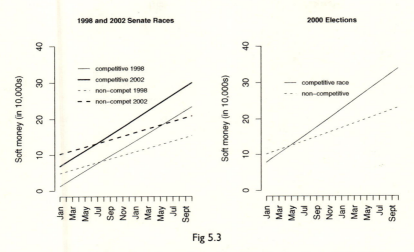

Fig 5.3

Predicted Soft Money From States During Two-Year Election Cycle, 1998–2002.

but that development likely took time as party leaders become more sophisticated in their soft money fund-raising. It makes sense that party leaders in the first half of the soft money era were less efficient in their solicitation and that the patterns observed here become evident only after parties had learned the value of soft money dollars.

Soft Money From Large Donors

Soft money, by definition of course, is partisan. Up until now, though, we have seen only that active hard money PACs were also participants in the soft money system and that contributors in competitive states tended to give more than interest groups in noncompetitive settings. These are very important findings that confirm two of the hypotheses laid out in Chapter 3, but it is crucial that any investigation of interest group soft money concern itself with its relationship to partisan politics.

In that regard, two initial observations must be made. First, soft money contributors can give to both parties, and to the extent that a contributor gives to Democrats and Republicans, the partisanship of soft money declines (Apollonio and La Raja 2002). For example, the

Atlanta Journal-Constitution reported in 2001 that the insurance company AFLAC had contributed substantial sums of soft money to both Democrats and Republicans. According to Kathleen Spencer, AFLAC's director of corporate communications, "That's something that typically we do because we do have an active role on both sides of the aisle in terms of support."[13] Such an approach was not pursued by all contributors, however. The article also reported that, as of June 2001, Philip Morris had contributed $350,000 in soft money, all of it to the Republicans, and accounting firm Buttenwieser and Associates had contributed all of its $300,000 in soft money to the Democrats.

In this section I focus on all large soft money donors—that is, any group giving at least $25,000 in any of the six election cycles. All told, there were 3,360 unique interest groups giving more than $25,000 between 1991 and 2002, a sampling frame representing only about 10 percent of all interest group donors but about 75 percent of all interest group soft money contributions.[14] In Figure 5.4 I show two histogram plots for the percentage of large donors giving to Democrats. In the left graph, the bar for 0 indicates that the donor gave all soft money funds to the Republican Party, and the bar at 1 indicates exclusive Democratic giving. The figure shows what we might expect—the majority of donors were exclusive partisans. It also shows that there were more exclusive Republican donors than exclusive Democratic donors (nearly 1,000 more).

In addition, there is a right skew to the distribution between 0 and 1. This is seen more clearly in the right panel, where I show the histogram of donors giving between 0 and 100 percent of soft money to Democrats (that is, leaving out exclusive partisan donors). The figure indicates that when donors gave most of their money to Democrats (those groups to the right of .50 on the x-axis), they were more likely to be exclusive donors. More specifically, 68 percent of pro-Democratic givers were exclusive donors to the Democrats. This contrasts to donors giving most of their money to Republicans (those groups to the left of .50 on the x-axis). For these groups, only 57 percent gave solely to the GOP.

Of course, we should be able to predict which groups are more inclined to invest in only one party. Further still, as made clear in Chapter 3, the partisan hypothesis expects such exclusive investment to go up over the life of soft money (in the same way that PACs became

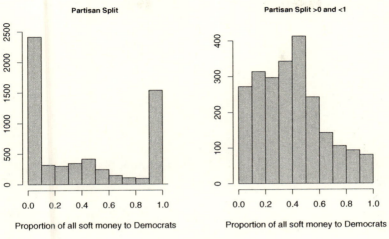

Fig 5.4

Partisanship in Soft Money Donations, 1992–2002.

more partisan in their use of hard money). Finding such a pattern will allow us to connect the dramatic rise in soft money to changes in the partisan environment.

To investigate these expectations, I report the results of a statistical model in Table 5.3, where the unit of analysis is a group in an election cycle and the dependent variable is the amount contributed in Democratic soft money minus the amount contributed to the Republican Party. This is the same approach used in Chapter 4 to investigate the partisan advantage in hard money. Because my sample of large donors in this chapter is left censored at $25,000, values on the dependent variable that approach $0 indicate interest groups that have split their contributions between both parties. High positive values indicate more money for the Democrats, whereas negative numbers indicate a stronger Republican preference. Also, because the 3,360 unique contributors often participated in several cycles, unique donors could appear in this sample a number of times.

I collected a range of information on these large donors to help control for factors that might predict a partisan preference in soft money contributions, including whether the group was a labor union,

TABLE 5.3   DEMOCRATIC ADVANTAGE FROM LARGE DONORS

Variable	Estimates
Labor group	−44.46(13.79)**
Labor group × Year	19.27(4.44)**
Fortune 500	−4.28(2.01)*
Fortune rank	.029(.005)**
Fortune 500 × Year	−2.16(.501)**
Democratic issue area	.181(1.67)
Democratic issue × Year	.921(.466)*
Republican issue area	−.830(1.28)
Republican issue × Year	−.698(.357)+
Percent from D.C.	3.73(2.24)+
Percent from D.C × Year	−1.06(.738)
Corporation	−.762(1.16)
Trade Association	−2.18(1.72)
Hard money	.051(.038)
Democratic PAC	25.31(5.52)**
Republican PAC	−10.09(1.48)**
Year	−.127(.102)
Unknown	.020(.950)
Intercept	252.32(204.28)
N	5774
Prob. >F	0.0000
R-squared	.2355

**p<.01 *p<.05 +p<.10
All tests are two-tailed, and robust SEs are in parentheses. Dependent Variable is the Democratic soft money minus GOP soft money (in $10,000s) for every contributor giving more than $25,000 in one cycle. The model was estimated using OLS, and all amounts are in constant 2002 dollars.

corporation, bank, law firm, party committee, candidate committee, Native American tribe, ideological group, trade association, membership group, sports team, Internet company, or university. I cross-checked corporations with a list of Fortune 500 companies (Hansen, Mitchell and Drope, 2005) and cross-checked all large donors with PAC files to establish which donors also maintained a hard money committee. Corporations accounted for 73 percent of all large donors; 20 percent of these donors (and 15 percent of all donors) were Fortune 500 companies. Labor unions made up only 3 percent, trade associations accounted for nearly 9 percent, and law firms represented only 4 percent of the sample. Finally, 41 percent of large donors had a PAC with some hard money activity.

In addition, I categorize each contributor's issue area, searching for a wide range of potential issues, from ideological concerns such as abortion and the environment (of which there were few soft money donors) to business-related issues such as personal and home products as well as financial services or information technology support.[15] The issue areas with the greatest representation were finance (11 percent of the sample), energy (8 percent), real estate (8 percent), food (6 percent), health care (5 percent), and insurance (5 percent).

I reduced many of these codes into pro-Democratic or pro-Republican issue areas. First, I defined any Indian tribe or law firm, as well as any group coded as media, health professionals, health services, education, the environment, homosexuality, and women as a Democratic issue group; this was true for 870 contributors. Some examples of Democratic groups include Blockbuster Videos, Black Entertainment Television, Blue Cross and Blue Shield, California Elementary Education Association, and Martha Stewart Living. Second, I defined any bank, as well as groups coded as finance, energy, insurance, drugs/pharmaceuticals, defense, or guns as a Republican issue group; this was true of 1,634 groups. Some examples of Republican groups include Freddie Mac, AG Edwards and Sons, Foxmeyer Drug Company, Southern California Edison Company, and Cantor Fitzgerald Securities.

These are obviously arbitrary issue assignments, but there is only limited guidance in the political science literature in determining which specific issue areas are best considered Democratic or Republican issues. For example, Petrocik (1996) uses survey data (and a plurality of respondents preferring one party's position on the issue) to classify issues as owned by the major parties. For example, he codes civil liberties and civil rights, social welfare spending, women, labor, social class, and agriculture as issues owned by the Democrats. According to Petrocik, Republicans own civil and social order, defense spending, and the concept of big government. I used this research as guidance in sorting large soft money donors into these partisan categories.

In estimating the model, I include the above contributor variables, plus a number of others. For example, if the group had a hard money PAC, I include how much total hard money it expended in that election cycle (2,414 groups made some hard money expenditures); whether the group sponsored a pro-Democratic or pro-Republican PAC is defined the same way as in the PAC analysis from earlier in the chapter. There were 179 pro-Democratic and 321 pro-Republican PACs in the sample. Finally, because there may be some incentives— for some groups—to keep their donor names hard to track, I include a variable for whether I could not find any information on the contributor. All told, 251 of the 3,360 large soft money contributors were classified as "unknown."

To test for evidence of the dynamic partisan hypothesis, I interacted the variables for labor group, Fortune 500 corporation, and Democratic and Republican issue groups with the trend variable. This indicates how the contribution strategies of these groups changed between the 1992 and 2002 elections. This approach is slightly different from the dynamic test in Chapter 4, where I correlated Democratic and Republican PACs with the balance of power in the House and Senate. I take an alternative approach here because I am using a smaller number of election cycles and because the linear time trend is a rough approximation of how tight the balance of power was in this time frame. In 1992, the out-party needed 52 House seats and 7 Senate seats; in 1994, it was 42 and 7; in 1996 it was 13 and 3; in 1998 it was 10 and 5; in 2000 it was 6 and 5, and in 2002 it was 6 and 1.

The results in Table 5.3 suggest strong support for the partisan hypothesis.[16] As expected, donors with partisan PACs preferred their party by significant margins. For example, all else being equal, pro-Democratic PACs favored the Democratic Party by more than $250,000. In contrast, groups with a very conservative PAC favored the GOP by more than $100,000.

More importantly, the interactions show an increasing partisanship over the course of the soft money period. Labor groups drastically increased their Democratic soft money in the late 1990s. For every election cycle after 1992, they increased their preference for the Democrats by nearly $200,000. Figure 5.5 demonstrates this more clearly, showing that an average labor union contributed very few soft money dollars (with little Democratic advantage) in 1992, but gave more than $1,000,000 in favor of the Democrats by 2002. Indeed, in the entire sample of large donors there were only a few examples of any labor union soft money contributions to the Republicans, so the increasing Democratic advantage was not the consequence of less Republican support, but more investment overall by labor unions.

In contrast, Fortune 500 companies favored Republicans, and this

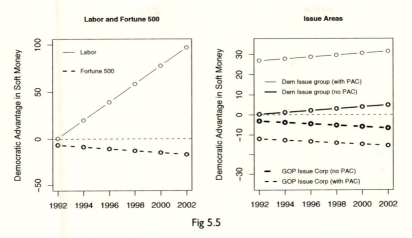

Fig 5.5

Predicted Democratic Advantage From Large Donors. Values on all y-axes are in $10,000s.

advantage grew by more than $21,000 with every election. For example, Figure 5.5 shows that a Fortune 500 company slightly favored the GOP in soft money contributions in 1992, but that advantage grew to more than $120,000 by 2002. Note also (from the results in Table 5.3) that as a Fortune 500 company's rank grows (higher rank denotes a smaller corporation) Republican preference decreased. In other words, for every increase in rank (from 120 to 121, for example) the Republican advantage declines by $290.

The left panel in the graph, then, shows that the Democrats got their greatest support over time from labor unions (overall unions demonstrated the most aggressive mobilization toward a political party of all groups in the sample), whereas the strongest Republican allies were from large Fortune 500 companies. By 2002, both major interests had diverged toward their preferred party. It should be noted, though, that because labor unions account for a small percentage of the large donor sample (recall, they make up only 3 percent, compared to 15 percent for Fortune 500 firms), *the total amount* of soft money from unions does not approach the pro-Republican financial advantage from Fortune 500 corporations. (Francia 2006, pp. 80–83, makes a similar point). For example, in 2002, labor unions contributed about

$34 million (nearly all of it to the Democrats), but Fortune 500 companies contributed almost $75 million (with nearly three-quarters of that going to the Republican Party).

As for partisan issue groups, there is additional evidence of divergence toward their preferred party between 1992 and 2002 (although to a less dramatic extent than shown by unions and large corporations). As the figure shows, Democratic issue groups increased their pro-Democratic contributions by nearly $10,000 with every election cycle, and pro-Republican issue groups favored the GOP by nearly $7,000 more in successive elections.

We learn from this analysis that soft money—already a partisan beast—became more partisan as soft money became more prevalent. Cross-partisan support from labor groups was nearly nonexistent throughout the life of soft money, but labor unions increased their support of Democrats significantly. Cross-partisan support declined heavily for Republican corporate allies, so that by 2002 a pragmatic bipartisan contribution strategy became the province of those organized interests less disposed to heavily favor one party. Indeed, if you rerun the statistical model above and look for a change in soft money contribution patterns among groups with no obvious partisan disposition, you can find no evidence of it. All told, then, we see in these results some evidence of groups pursuing an access strategy with soft money (witnessed with significant contributions to both sides of the aisle), but also, and more importantly, an increasing level of exclusive partisan giving (evidence of a growing replacement strategy).

Conclusion

The party soft money era ended when BCRA became law after the 2002 elections, but its impact on American elections in the 1990s and early 21st century is without question. Soft money was such a prominent part of federal elections during this time that many feared the consequences of its elimination. Senator Mitch McConnell, for example, warned that a soft money ban would transform interest groups into the Home Depot of American politics, and parties into the local ACE hardware (McConnell 2004). In other words, McConnell not only predicted that interest groups would become the new beneficiaries of an altered campaign finance regime but also that parties would lose power in the end.

Ansolabehere and Snyder (2000, p. 619) also contemplated the end of soft money in their *Columbia Law Review* article in 2000. They made a striking claim: "Eliminating all current soft money expenditures, we estimate, would lead to a 2 percent decline in voter turnout—without soft money, approximately 2 million fewer Americans would have gone to the polls in 1996." They added that at least one additional benefit of soft money (and expanding party finances more generally) was to reduce the influence of interest groups in elections; that is, "by lessening the unique campaign finance advantages of incumbents, which derive substantially from interest group contributions" (pp. 599–600).

Both arguments worry about the consequences of the soft money ban. Consider, though, the claims of Ansolabehere and Snyder. There is little evidence in this chapter that the soft money era was characterized by a weaker sphere of influence for interest groups. Indeed, with parties able to raise millions in unregulated funds, there was opportunity for intense mobilization by interest groups in conjunction with party electioneering efforts. Interest group soft money donors were very often also active hard money contributors. And interest groups with pro-party affiliations increased their soft money participation and invested more heavily in their preferred party when partisan control of Congress was up for grabs. Labor unions mobilized aggressively to that effect. Indeed, it is safe to conclude that the soft money system enhanced the power of interest groups, albeit through the mechanism of party financing.

In the next chapter, I turn to how interest groups spend independently in elections, through 527s and issue advocacy advertisements. It is in this realm that we might better test the assertions of those worried about a party soft money ban. That is, what are interest groups doing on their own on behalf of candidates? Did that advocacy become more hard-hitting after the passage of BCRA?

6 Following 527s and Watching Issue Advocacy

I n Chapter 4, I demonstrated that partisan PACs altered their hard money contribution strategies in the late 1990s, becoming more partisan in years when the control of Congress hung in the balance. In Chapter 5, I broadened the analysis to soft money contributions. Both empirical analyses focused on how interest groups contribute funds to other political actors. In this chapter, I switch the analysis to examine how interest groups raise and spend money independently of the candidates or parties they are trying to help.

I focus the chapter on interest group advertisements in the 2000, 2002, and 2004 federal elections and on the activity of 527s in the 2004 elections. Both political advertisements and 527s have been the topic of considerable debate in recent years. Bernadette A. Budde of the Business-Industry Political Action Committee had this to say about issue advocacy in 1998: "[It] could have caught people off-guard in '96. In '98 it may look new. By 2000 it's not going to be a new technique anymore. The campaign world will have adapted."[1] Budde was exactly right, and the presence of nonmagic word ads in 1996–2000 compelled reformers in 2002 to establish restrictions on which groups could fund political ads.

These changes spawned the "explosion" of 527s in the 2004 elections. As noted in Chapter 2, 527s spent more than $150 million in

October 2004, including $82 million in television and radio ads that featured federal candidates. According to Stephen Moore, co-founder of the Club for Growth, "Here's the whole irony of McCain-Feingold. [Congress] didn't even understand their own law made 527s more powerful, not less powerful."[2]

Indeed, political advertising and 527s have altered the landscape of interest group electioneering. But what explains the dramatic rise in interest group political ads, and why are 527s so important a tactic in the aftermath of BCRA? How can we tie the findings from previous chapters to the investigations in this one? In this chapter, I examine Wisconsin Advertising Project data on political advertisements, testing both the **competitive** and **partisan hypotheses**, which predict that interest group ads will be predominantly focused on competitive races and that groups will only advocate for candidates of one party. After this analysis, I transition to a study of 527s, and using IRS data that track receipts and expenditures by 527s between 2002 and 2004, I investigate whether the largest donors to 527s were also large party soft money donors; this would be evidence of "water finding the cracks" in the **soft-to-soft hypothesis**.

Political Television Advertisements

For any interest group hoping to move votes and persuade the electorate, hitting the airwaves is arguably the most crucial tactic of all and has been for more than a generation. Even in the 1980s, groups like the National Conservative Political Action Committee spent millions of dollars on ads against Senate candidates and on behalf of President Reagan. And the most famous political advertisement in the last generation—the Willie Horton "Weekend Passes" ad—was funded by a PAC, the National Security Political Action Committee. That group spent $8,552,666 on advertising in 1988, all of it paid for with hard dollars. In 1996, however, interest groups and the Democratic and Republican parties began spending millions in unregulated money to fund nonmagic word ads that, until BCRA, went largely unregulated. By 2000, some groups were spending close to $6 million dollars in issue advocacy ads in the final eight weeks of the campaign (recall Table 2.1 from Chapter 2).

In this section, I rely on data from the Wisconsin Advertising

Project, which has coded advertisements in the largest media markets since 2000. Coders classify unique ads on several dimensions, including the tone of the ad, the favored or opposing candidate, issues mentioned, and ad sponsorship. This information is then appended to frequency data in which each entry represents the airing of one ad. When merged, the data show every ad that aired in the top 75 media markets, with information on the time of day when it aired, the show in which it aired, and the content codes from the coders' assessments.[3]

My initial focus was on the number of groups that invested in House, Senate, and presidential contests, and the extent to which groups aired ads for only one political party. Under the partisan hypothesis, I expect interest group ad expenditures to be the most partisan of all forms of interest group electioneering. More specifically, when interest groups choose to spend money on public communications that mention or picture federal candidates, groups should only do so for candidates of their preferred party (unlike in other chapters where we saw nontrivial contributions to both sides). As noted in Chapter 3, however, such intense partisanship is not obvious if interest groups care more about issues than party labels.

In Figure 6.1, I show a scatterplot of interest groups airing ads for House candidates, where the y-axis is the number of pro-Democratic ads minus the number of pro-Republican ads (including general and primary election ads), and the x-axis is the number of participating campaigns. Figure 6.2 repeats the scatterplot for Senate contests, and Figure 6.3 shows the presidential case (with the x-axis in that figure being the number of media markets). In all three graphs, I do not distinguish group type (527s vs. PACs vs. labor unions), and I add a histogram showing the number of groups that aired ads exclusively for Democrats and the number of groups with exclusively pro-Republican ads.

I draw several important conclusions from these figures. First, it is apparent that far fewer groups aired advertisements than contributed hard and soft money. In the House, only about 50 interest groups advertised between 2000 and 2004. In the Senate races, that number was about 60, and in the presidential case, about 100 (with the bulk of those in 2004). Compare this to the nearly 3,000 active PACs in any election cycle and the 50,000 or more interest group soft money contributions in the 2000 and 2002 elections.

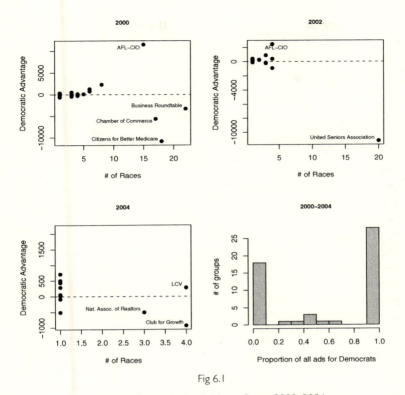

Fig 6.1

Interest Groups Active in House Races, 2000–2004.

On the other hand, a number of groups were highly invested in multiple House and Senate races and in dozens of presidential markets. In 2000, for example, the AFL-CIO sponsored more than 10,000 advertisements in 15 House races, and the Citizens for Better Medicare funded more than 10,000 ads for Republican candidates in 18 House races. In 2002, the United Seniors Association aired more than 10,000 ads for House Republicans in 20 campaigns, dwarfing the AFL-CIO's still impressive 2,000-ad campaign in 5 races. The largest mobilization came in the 2004 presidential contest, in which MoveOn .org and the Media Fund combined to air more than 80,000 ads in about 50 markets. Note also that a number of groups were involved in only a handful of campaigns, but mobilized significant resources to that effect.

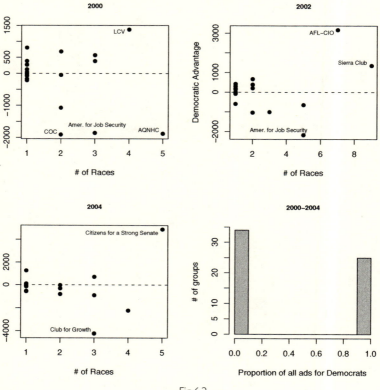

Fig 6.2

Interest Groups Active in Senate Races, 2000–2004.

This was particularly noticeable in the 2004 House case, in which a small number of groups mobilized in only one campaign but aired upward of 500 ads for their preferred candidate.

Finally, the figures demonstrate that advertising is highly partisan. In no Senate or presidential case did an interest group air ads for candidates of both parties. Of course, we should expect this in the presidential case. Why would an interest group advocate for both Kerry and Bush in 2004, for example? On the other hand, these advertising totals include ads aired in primary elections, where it is at least conceivable that groups might air ads on both sides (supporting Bill Bradley over Al Gore in 2000, for example, *and* John McCain over George Bush). The

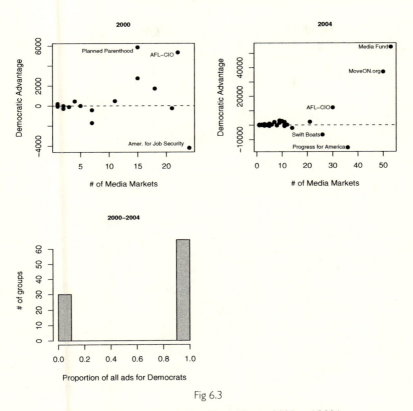

Fig 6.3

Interest Groups Active in Presidential Races, 2000 and 2004.

absence of such activity in Senate races, however, is less obvious and true testimony to the partisan nature of Senate races in all three years.

However, a handful of groups did air ads on both sides for House candidates. In 2000, for example, Americans for Term Limits made limited partisan distinctions, aiming their efforts at a handful of Democrats and one Republican, George Nethercutt of Washington. In 2002, the United Seniors Association, despite airing more than 10,000 pro-Republican ads, funded 879 pro-Democratic ads for three House Democrats: Steve Israel, Ralph Hall, and Collin Peterson. In 2002 and 2004, the League of Conservation Voters elevated stance on the environment over partisanship; they aired 408 pro-Democratic ads and 568 pro-Republicans ads in 2002, and 497 pro-Democratic and 223 pro-Republican ads in 2004. Finally, the National Association of Realtors aired 138 pro-Democratic ads despite supporting Republicans in other contests.

I take the results in all three figures as persuasive evidence of a partisan dynamic to television advertisements. But I also expect groups to focus their advertising efforts in competitive House districts and Senate states; that is, those electoral environments where moving votes matters most.[4] Throughout the book, I have shown the draw of competitiveness for interest groups. For example, there are important distinctions between which PACs contribute to competitive vs. safe seat candidates, and there is evidence that interest group donors in competitive states contributed more soft money and closer to Election Day than groups in states with no statewide competitive federal race. As such, we should see evidence that interest groups direct their candidate-mention ads to races where moving votes has the potential to affect the outcome.

It is important to keep in mind, however, that competitiveness in this analysis is important because of the partisan dynamic surrounding federal elections in recent years. As the balance of power has tightened in the House and Senate—and as interest groups see the policy-making potential of party over candidate alliances—moving votes in competitive races becomes intimately tied with political party goals.

In Tables 6.1 and 6.2, I show evidence of the competitiveness hypothesis. These tables show statistical models predicting, first, the to-

TABLE 6.1   HOUSE ADS BY DISTRICT

Variable	All Ads	Interest Group Ads
Open Seat	232.14(248.22)	104.06(60.39)+
Number of Markets	796.43(256.63)**	−189.57(53.75)**
2000	−525.82(283.90)+	−282.75(89.53)**
2004	−60.19(318.75)	34.69(43.78)
Electoral Votes	−16.65(7.12)*	−.367(1.13)
Competitive × 2000	1355.95(191.54)**	310.56(69.96)**
Competitive × 2002	1168.33(164.13)**	92.173(36.80)**
Competitive × 2004	1166.47(212.04)**	27.65(15.15)+
Intercept	−1145.35(329.74)**	−116.48(88.51)
R-squared	0.4393	0.2127
N	464	464

**$p<.01$ *$p<.05$ +$p<.10$

All tests are two-tailed, and SEs (clustered by state) are in parentheses. Dependent Variable is the number of ads in each House race where there was at least one ad aired. The model was estimated using OLS.

TABLE 6.2   SENATE ADS BY STATE

Variable	All Ads	Interest Group Ads
Open Seat	3188.81(2083.14)	−526.88(261.86)+
Number of Markets	2904.90(903.62)°°	36.22(70.36)
2000	−1755.42(2484.85)	292.05(230.33)
2004	−1027.64(2253.87)	−109.53(260.49)
Electoral Votes	−67.54(126.05)	−2.84(11.82)
Competitive × 2000	4719.81(1428.42)°°	443.10(169.11)°°
Competitive × 2002	3398.18(632.34)°°	540.82(128.32)°°
Competitive × 2004	4356.59(1450.20)°°	708.46(189.84)°°
Intercept	−5878.98(1482.84)°°	−707.95(183.70)°°
R-squared	0.7129	0.4392
N	82	82

°°$p<.01$ °$p<.05$ +$p<.10$
All tests are two-tailed, and SEs (clustered by state) are in parentheses. Dependent Variable is the number of ads in each Senate race where there was at least one ad aired. The model was estimated using OLS.

tal number of ads in House and Senate races (combining ads sponsored by candidates, parties, and interest groups) and, second, the number of interest group ads in these races. I only examine races where at least one ad aired.[5] It should be noted that the statistical estimation for this analysis is a standard regression framework, so we can interpret the coefficients as direct effect sizes—a one-unit increase in an independent variable corresponds to a coefficient size change in the dependent variable.

I include any independent variables that might be related to a campaign's advertising volume. For example, I account for whether the seat was an open seat and for the year of the election cycle. I also include a variable for the number of media markets covered by the district (for House races) or state (for the Senate). On this latter variable, media markets often cross district and state boundaries. Consider Michigan. Parts of the state are covered by the Detroit, Flint, and Grand Rapids media markets. This means that candidates, parties, and interest groups have several ABC, NBC, CBS, and Fox affiliates to choose from, potentially increasing the number of television ads aired. Finally, I include measures of the competitiveness (again using *CQ*'s four-scale measure) of the House and Senate seats. I do this by interacting the year and competitiveness measures so as to assess the impact of competitiveness for each of the three election cycles.

There are important differences across both models in the House and between the House interest group and Senate interest group models. First, in both the House and Senate case, in models predicting the total number of ads (left column in both tables), competitiveness was the driving force in 2000, 2002, and 2004. For example, as House races move up the competitiveness scale (from safe, to favored, to leaning, to too-close-to-call), there are over 1,300 more ads at each stage for House races in 2000 and almost 1,200 more ads for each race type in 2002 and 2004. In the Senate case, the ad totals are even larger. A Senate race in 2000 that is too-close-to-call is expected to have over 14,000 more ads than a safe seat race that year. The numbers are comparable for 2002 and 2004. Note also that the number of media markets that cover a House or Senate race is also an important predictor of ad volume. Every additional media market means almost 800 more ads in House races and nearly 3,000 more ads in Senate races.

In the House case, however, note the declining importance of competitiveness in predicting interest group advertisements (right column in Table 6.1). In 2000, for example, we can expect to see more than 1,200 interest group ads in a highly competitive House race, compared to a predicted 100 ads in such races in 2004. By contrast, interest group ads in Senate races are always most abundant in competitive elections; predicted ad totals in highly competitive races are 1,720, 2,160, and 2,832 in the elections of 2000, 2002, and 2004, respectively.

What prompted interest groups to become far less active in House races in 2004? Part of the answer relates to the balance of power in the House. In 2000, the Democrats needed 6 seats to regain majority status, with 16 competitive elections. In 2002, the Democrats needed 6 seats with 13 competitive contests. In 2004, though, the Democrats needed 13 seats, but with only 6 competitive campaigns. This is significant. Indeed, in 2004 the larger stakes of U.S. House elections changed—with control a less salient force than in 2000 and 2002. Given a 13-seat differential and only 6 seats considered toss-ups, it makes sense to avoid lending significant resources to House candidates. This stands in contrast to the Senate partisan context, in which the elections of 2000–2004 were very competitive—especially 2002 and 2004 when the minority party needed only one and two seats respectively, and six seats were considered highly competitive in both years.

Of course, the public face of the Democrats suggested that the House was in play in 2004. According to House Democrat Nancy Pelosi in July 2004, "If the election were held today, there would be no question but the Democrats would take back the House. We have to be on guard for the venom that the Republicans will pour into the races and, of course, the money that will accompany that. But we're ready to fight." On the other hand, Larry Sabato of the University of Virginia contradicted Pelosi: "Is there some small chance the Democrats in the House could pull off an upset? Yeah. But is it probable? No."[6] All told then, it appears interest groups made the efficient decision to spend resources in the far more competitive Senate and presidential contexts. This is a trend that—according to some reports—was reflected in the level of interest group participation in the House ground war (i.e., door-to-door activities, mailings, and phone calls; Greene and Heberlig 2005, Kolodny and Gollob 2005).

It is important to consider the source of the changing partisan context in the 2004 House elections. Many attribute the stronger GOP hold on House power to the actions of Tom Delay and his redistricting plan in Texas. I first recounted this in Chapter 1. According to a *New York Times* editorial in the aftermath of the 2004 elections, "victorious Republicans are already shaping a fresh agenda in Congress. In the House, the Democrats' impotence can only deepen as their bare-knuckled nemesis, Tom DeLay, the majority leader, returns more powerful than ever after his gerrymander of Texas delivered [an] increase in the G.O.P. majority."[7] Another report noted, "After a rare election in which the incumbent [president] was re-elected while his party gained power in both houses of Congress, DeLay now appears to have the votes and momentum to roll back significant portions of the New Deal legislation on the books for more than 70 years. 'The Republican Party is a permanent majority for the future of this country,' an elated DeLay declared."[8] Of course, the elections of 2006 proved Delay wrong, but in the context of 2004, and with the Texas redistricting controversy, it certainly seems plausible that interest groups interpreted the political context in much the same way Delay did.

All told, the results in this analysis demonstrate that interest group advertising was highly partisan and focused in highly competitive elections. The competitive results are a necessary condition of interest group response to the political context; the partisan results are the sufficient condition. In the one major case in which the balance of power seemed out of reach—House elections in 2004—we see exactly what we might expect: little interest group participation. These results are encouraging evidence that interest group advertising is motivated, in part, by issues relating to the balance of power in Congress.

Contributions to Partisan 527s

In this section I switch the focus to 527s. Were corporations, trade associations, labor groups, and ideological groups who donated large sums to nonprofit 527s in 2004 the same groups that contributed to Democratic and Republican soft money party accounts before BCRA's passage? Can we find evidence of "water finding the cracks" with the end of party soft money, where interest groups eager to avoid hard money restrictions funnel large sums to unregulated 527s?

The IRS mandates that 527s that expect to raise or spend at least $25,000 in any taxable year record all contributions from persons or groups making donations that aggregate $200 or more per calendar year. It also mandates that 527s record all expenditures that aggregate $500 or more a year per person or group. These data contain information on the date of the expenditure, the stated purpose of the expenditure, and information on the location and occupation of the recipient (for example, money disbursed to a marketing firm to produce GOTV leaflets).

I downloaded all available electronic 527 data through January 2005.[9] These data contain information filed on two forms: Form 8871, which is filed by each 527 within 24 hours of its establishment (and contains information about the 527's location and purpose), and Form 8872, which records the 527's receipts (labeled type A) and expenditures (type B).

One of the weaknesses of the IRS set-up is that prior to 2003 527s could file their 8872s by paper. These data are not included in the electronic downloads.[10] For example, Tom Delay's Texans for a Republican Majority filed all its forms by paper with the IRS. This makes it hard to track systematically activity by some 527s. Nonetheless, in October

2002 Congress mandated that any 527 raising or spending $50,000 must file forms electronically.

In this section I examine the list of donors who contributed at least $25,000 to 527s in 2003–2004. I cross-reference this list with my datasets on soft money donors in 2000 and 2002. There were 1,081 large contributors to 527s. Of that, 543 groups (50.2%) were also former soft money donors in either 2000 or 2002. I split donors into three categories: corporations, labor unions, and all other groups. Table 6.3 shows the cross-tabulation of donors to 527s with whether they were soft money donors in either 2000 or 2002.

As the table shows, the majority of corporate donors were also party soft money donors: 426 of 730 corporations, nearly 60 percent. For example, Anheuser-Busch contributed $669,000 to 527s in 2003–2004, $968,000 in party soft money in 2000, and $1,773,376 in party soft money in 2002. Altria Corporate Services, which is affiliated with Kraft Foods and Philip Morris USA, contributed more than $1 million to 527s, but nothing in soft money in either 2000 or 2002.

In contrast to corporations, only 25 percent of 170 labor unions were former soft money contributors, which include the United Auto Workers, Service Employees International Union, and the Teamsters. Most labor unions that contributed to 527s but not to party soft money accounts were local union affiliates. For example, Laborer's Union Local 169 contributed $45,000 to 527s but nothing to party soft money accounts.

Finally, 41 percent of 181 other groups contributed nonfederal party funds in either 2000 or 2002. For example, the National Rifle Association contributed more than $860,000 to 527s in 2003–2004, compared to almost $1.5 million in soft money in 2000 and $533,000 in

TABLE 6.3   COMPARING LARGE DONORS TO 527S BY FORMER PARTY SOFT MONEY ACTIVITY

	Soft Money Contributor	Non-Soft Money Contributor
All Contributors	543 (50.2%)	538 (49.8%)
Corporations	426 (58.3%)	304 (41.7%)
Labor	42 (24.7%)	128 (75.3%)
Other	75 (41.4%)	106 (58.6%)

°Percentages are row.

2002. The American Trucking Association contributed $360,000 to
527s, and nearly $1 million in soft money between 2000 and 2002. In
contrast, the American Heart Association contributed no party soft
money (in 2000 or 2002) but more than $59,000 to 527s, and the
Young Democrats of America contributed $0 in soft money but
$30,000 to 527s.

As a first cut, then, it seems that many contributors to soft money
were not averse to becoming contributors to 527s. Furthermore, of
these large contributors, former soft money donors also gave in larger
amounts to 527s than those with no prior soft money activity. For example, among labor unions, the median contribution to a 527 was
more than $300,000 for former party soft money contributors, but
$73,000 for unions with no soft money history. For corporations, for-
mer soft money contributors gave a median contribution of $82,000 to
527s, compared to $50,000 for all other corporations. And of the
"other" groups, soft money donors gave a median contribution of
$86,000 to 527s, whereas those groups with no soft money history gave
a median contribution of $60,000.

Of particular interest, of course, is how these donors allocated their
contributions to 527s. Did former soft money donors give to 527s that
appeared tied to a particular party? To assess this, I aggregated these
donors' contributions to certain "partisan" 527s. I coded 59 committees
as leaning Democratic and 34 as leaning Republican. To assign codes,
I relied on the purpose codes in each committee's Form 8871 (on
which groups might state explicitly their desire to help state, local, or
federal candidates of a certain party), in addition to coder assessments
from Weissman and Hassan (2005), who also used interviews and press
reports to identify partisan 527s. I excluded labor unions from the list
of partisan groups so as not to conflate labor union transfers with partisan contributions.

For example, I coded the following as pro-Democratic 527s: Democratic Governor's Association, Democratic Victory 2004, Democrats for
America's Future, and Democratic Attorneys General Association. I also
coded America Coming Together, the Media Fund, Texans for Truth,
Planned Parenthood Votes, and Progressive Majority as pro-Democratic groups. The list of pro-Republican 527s includes College Republican National Committee, Greater Republican New Orleans

Fund, National Federation of Republican Women, Republican Governor's Association, Republican National Lawyers, Progress for American Voter Fund, and the National Association of Realtors.

It is important to note that identifying "partisan" 527s requires important decisions on operationalization. In two recent examinations of 527s in the 2004 election, Dominguez and Pearson (2005) and Weissman and Hassan (2005) restricted their study to 527s concerned *only* with federal elections—for example, the Media Fund, America Coming Together, and Progress for America Voter Fund. It should come as no surprise that Dominguez and Pearson (2005) found no relationship between interest group soft money donors and donors to these 527s, as these groups likely fall under the MCFL exemption (see again the discussion in Chapter 2; in brief, MCFL groups rarely if ever accept interest group donations). Instead, as we might expect they did find a stronger relationship between individuals who contributed soft money and individuals who contributed to federal-only partisan 527s.

I broaden my analysis, however, to include 527s that might be concerned only with state and local elections—for example, Republican Governors Association, Republican Legislative Majority of North Carolina, and Democratic Attorneys General Association. These groups might not have spent money directly in 2004 on electioneering communications that mentioned or pictured federal candidates, but their electioneering efforts through grassroots activity or voter mobilization might have helped federal candidates indirectly, especially in states with both a presidential and gubernatorial race. In addition, donors wishing to signal their support of a partisan platform might have conveyed such support with soft money donations to these groups. According to a May 2004 Associated Press story, for example, posted on the Republican Governors' Association (RGA) Web site, "Presidential politics and economic turmoil will have a major impact on the 11 gubernatorial races this fall, with the interplay between national and state politics most critical in four states where the 2000 race was dramatically close—Missouri, New Hampshire, Washington and West Virginia."[11]

The basic question in comparing partisan 527 donors to former soft money donors is simple: in the wake of a post-BCRA environment where parties are without soft money, "[Can or] do 527's add up to a Party?"(Skinner 2005).[12] Table 6.4 shows the correlations between

TABLE 6.4   CORRELATION OF PARTY SOFT MONEY WITH PARTISAN 527
CONTRIBUTIONS

	Democratic Advantage	Pro-Democratic	Pro-Republican
2000			
All groups	0.6046(453)*	0.6544(453)*	0.2381(453)*
Corporations	0.2853(351)*	0.2262(351)*	0.4623(351)*
Labor unions	0.6159(38)*	0.6281(38)*	0.3626(38)*
All other groups	0.2805(64)	0.7615(64)*	0.1637(64)
2002			
All groups	0.5733(488)*	0.6462(488)*	0.2189(488)*
Corporations	0.3778(382)*	0.4489(382)*	0.4299(382)*
Labor unions	0.5727(39)*	0.5832(39)*	0.3425(39)*
All other groups	0.1678(67)	0.7727(67)*	0.1066(67)

*$p<.05$
Numbers in parentheses are the number of groups in each category. The Pro-Democratic column correlates Democratic Party soft money in 2000 or 2002 with pro-Democratic 527 contributions in 2004. The Pro-Republican column does this for Republican contributions.
*Bars for federal, state/local, and issue 527s are those not also classified as labor unions.

partisan 527 donations in 2004 and party soft money contributions in 2000 and 2002. These correlations test whether patterns in party soft money giving are reflected in patterns of partisan 527 contributions. The first column shows the relationship between the 527 and soft money Democratic advantage in contributions (contributions to Democrats minus contributions to Republicans), the second column only correlates the amount given to Democrats, and the final column shows the correlation for Republican funds. I also indicate where the correlation between the two measures is statistically significant, indicating that the co-variance between the two measures is not attributable to chance.

For all groups, the advantage measure correlates at .6046 and .5733 in 2000 and 2002, respectively, with the highest correlation for labor groups (.6159 and .5727 in 2000 and 2002). Democratic contributions correlate at .6544 for all soft money givers in 2000 and at .6462 in 2002. In general, the correlations between Democratic soft money and Democratic 527 contributions are higher than correlations for Republican contributions. The highest correlation for Republican contributions is for corporations (.4623 for 2000 soft money donors and .4299 for 2002 contributors).

There is really only one instance where the correlations are not statistically significant—for pro-Republican contributions among "other" groups in both years. Although these groups have very high correlations for pro-Democratic 527 activity (.7615 in 2000 and .7727 in 2002), these groups did not translate that relationship to pro-Republican 527s. For example, the National Education Association gave just over $1 million in soft money to the Democrats in 2002 and nearly the same to pro-Democratic 527s in 2004. In contrast, the Grocery Manufacturers of America gave more than $330,000 in soft money to the Republicans in 2002, but only $28,000 to pro-Republican 527s in 2004. In general, then, it seems that pro-Democratic interest groups made the smoother transition from party soft money to 527s. Pro-Republican interest groups with a significant party soft money history were not averse in 2004 to donating to pro-Republican 527s (and these 527s are certainly active in a post-BCRA environment, as we will see), but that mobilization is far less aggressive than on the Democratic side. In evaluating the soft-to-soft hypothesis, then, it seems apparent that pro-Democratic interest groups offer the strongest evidence.

As one final analysis of partisan 527 donations, Figure 6.4 repeats two graphs from Chapter 5, but for 527s (see Figure 5.4). As the left panel shows, the vast majority of groups contributed all their partisan 527 money to one party: more than 300 groups for Republicans and about 250 for Democrats. The right panel shows the histogram for all groups giving at least some money to 527 committees on both sides. As with soft money from Chapter 5, the histogram indicates that donors that give most money to Democrats are more likely to be exclusive donors, whereas of the donors giving most of their money to Republicans, there is a good chance the donor will also give to the Democrats. In other words, of all pro-Republican groups (those to the left of the .50 on the x-axis), 60 percent gave exclusively to pro-GOP 527s; in contrast, of all pro-Democratic contributors (those to the right of .50), 74 percent gave exclusively to the Democrats. That this pattern is reflected in both party soft money and partisan 527 contributions is rather striking.

The results of this analysis represent strong evidence of the soft-to-soft hypothesis. Nearly 50 percent of large donors to 527s in 2004 were also former soft money donors. Further still, these former soft money donors acted in very similar ways with respect to partisan preference; indeed it seems that if a group contributed large sums to the Democratic (and to a lesser extent, Republican) parties' nonfederal accounts pre-BCRA, it did so at similar levels post-BCRA to pro-party 527 allies.

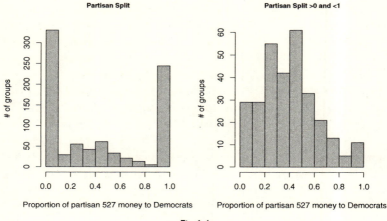

Fig 6.4

Partisanship in 527 Donations.

Expenditures by 527s

What do 527s do with all of their contributions, however? Of course, we know that some spend money on radio and television advertisements, but which are the most active 527 spenders? The unit of analysis in this section is each 527 that received contributions and made expenditures in the 2004 election cycle.

To begin assessing group-level differences, I first classified each 527 for whether it was sponsored by a labor union. Second, I examined each stated purpose code from the group's Form 8871 and coded each group into one of four categories: issue advocacy, state and local, federal, and unclear. Issue advocacy groups, in my coding scheme, are those groups whose stated purpose is to educate voters or to get-out-the-vote. State and local groups are those whose stated purpose is to contribute to or aid candidates for nonfederal office. Federal 527s are groups whose stated purpose includes either a specific reference to helping federal candidates or a generic reference to aiding candidates. Finally, unclear groups are 527s whose stated purpose is too vague to be classified. Below, I list an example of each type.

- Texans for Justice. Code: issue advocacy. Purpose: To educate voters on the records and views of candidates for public office and to promote interest in political issues and participation in elections
- New Century Leadership Fund. Code: state and local. Purpose: To receive contributions and make expenditures in connection with nonfederal elections in the Commonwealth of Virginia
- HILLPAC-NY. Code: federal. Purpose: To support Democratic candidates and committees
- Americans United to Preserve Marriage. Code: unclear. Purpose: To engage in exempt function/activity

In Figure 6.5 I show the amount of contributions received by labor, issue, federal, and state/local 527s between January 2002 and October 2004. Labor 527s received the largest set of contributions from other labor groups. State and local 527s received the most funds from corporations, and federal and issue advocacy 527s received the bulk of contributions from individuals.

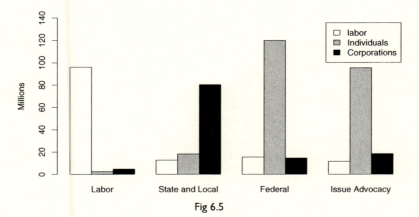

Fig 6.5

Contributions to 527s by Source, 2002–2004. Bars for federal, state/local, and issue 527s are those not also classified as labor unions.

I then assigned a code to each unique expenditure purpose; the codes are listed in Table 6.5. I classified the codes into four major types—campaign-related, contributions, fund-raising, and operating expenses. Campaign-related expenditures were funds spent on media and advertisements, direct mailings, voter registration, GOTV efforts, phone banks, and generic campaign assistance. I do not mean to imply here that these expenditures are *always* spent on advocating for candidates. Indeed, issue-related 527s might protest that their direct mail expenditures, for example, were completely unrelated to elections. On the other hand, the veracity of my coding scheme will be put to the test in the analysis below. If I am incorrect in making the assumption that these expenditures are related to campaigns, we should find some evidence of that.

Operating expenses included funds for salary, food, supplies, accounting, taxes, computers, insurance, security, fees, gifts, entertainment, and equipment rental. Contributions were direct donations or fund transfers to a candidate for office (mostly state and local candidates), to other interest groups, or to state political parties. Fund-raising expenses were any reported funds spent on tickets to fund-raisers or checks written at a fund-raiser.[13]

TABLE 6.5 PURPOSE CODES FOR EXPENDITURES BY 527S

Campaign-related	Operating Expenses	Other
Media/advertisements	Salary	Travel/parking
Direct mail	Rent	Reimbursement
Voter registration/GOTV	Food	Hospitality
Phone banks	Supplies	Refund/void
Campaign assistance	Accounting	Signs/bumper stickers
	Taxes	Polls/focus groups
Contribution/donation	Computers/IT	Data/research/lists
	Insurance	Consulting
Fund-raising/receptions	Security	Lobbying
	Equipment rental	Website
	Entertainment	Public relations
	Gift/awards	Mail/postage
	Fees	Telephone/email/DSL
		Printing/copying
		Legal
		Fund transfer
		Convention/conference
		Training/recruitment

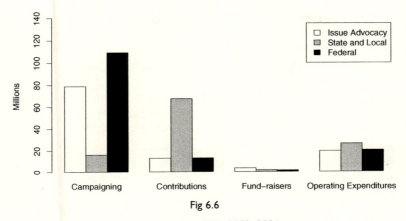

Fig 6.6

Expenditures by 527s, 2002–2004.

In Figure 6.6 I show how much federal, state, and local and issue advocacy 527s spent on campaigning, contributions, fund-raising, and operating expenses between January 2002 and October 2004. The graphs demonstrate important differences across groups in different forms of spending. For example, state and local 527s contributed more than $60 million to candidates, parties, and other interest groups, far in excess of the contribution behavior of other 527s. For example, the Carpenters PAC of Philadelphia and Vicinity—a state and local 527—reported making more than $1.1 million in contributions between 2003 and 2004. One of their contributions included a $27,000 donation to John Perzel, former Speaker of the Pennsylvania legislature. Another state and local 527, the Democratic Attorneys General Association, reported more than $600,000 in contributions, including $27,500 to the Louisiana Democratic Party and $240,000 to the Washington State Democratic Party. (These last two examples serve to illustrate the myriad ways unregulated money can enter the system. Imagine an interest group that donates to a state and local pro-party 527; that money is then channeled to a state party committee, which in turn spends the money on GOTV efforts and mobilization. These expenditures would serve to increase the store of partisans voting on Election Day, thereby helping federal candidates by proxy.)

In addition, all three 527 types spent comparable amounts on operating expenditures. Club for Growth, for example, reported $2,765,510 in 2004 for expenses such as salary ($1,126,740) and credit card fees ($309,319). Democrats 2000 reported more than $240,000 in expenses for, among other things, payroll (nearly $160,000) and membership dues ($40,000).

In terms of campaign activity, though, state and local groups expended very few funds in comparison to federal and issue advocacy committees. For example, one issue advocacy 527, And for the Sake of the Kids, spent more than $3 million in campaign costs in 2003–2004. This amount included $270,000 to WV Media on September 27, 2004, for "advertising spots."[14] Another example is Issues Matter, coded as a federal-oriented 527; it spent almost $300,000 in campaigning in 2004, including a $67,000 expenditure on October 22 to Joe Slade White and Company, a well-known Democratic consulting firm. All told, issue-oriented 527s reported nearly $80 million in campaign-related activities, and federal 527s reported more than $100 million.

In Figure 6.7 I show these 527s' reported expenditures over a one-year period, from October 2003 through October 2004. The results show that federal 527s made campaign-related expenditures throughout most of 2004, including $15 million in February and $20 million in July. They spent next to nothing in this area in October 2004. In contrast, issue advocacy 527s made almost no such expenditures until August, September, and October of 2004, spending, for example, nearly $35 million on campaign-related activities in the month before the November elections. The differences are likely rooted in MCFL classifications. Because issue advocacy groups claim to be advancing only a policy agenda, they have more freedom in funding campaign ads close to Election Day. Federal-oriented 527s are tied more explicitly to electioneering, and because of BCRA's restrictions on electioneering communications, they likely avoided campaign activities closer to November.

From this evidence, then, we can see important variation in the way different 527s raised and spent funds in 2004. To get at these differences more specifically, and to control for a number of factors simultaneously, I ran two multivariate models predicting the level of campaign expenditures and contributions for active 527s in 2003–2004. There are more than 400 groups in this analysis. The dependent variables are the amount spent on each type of expenditure.

In addition to variables for 527 type (in these models there were

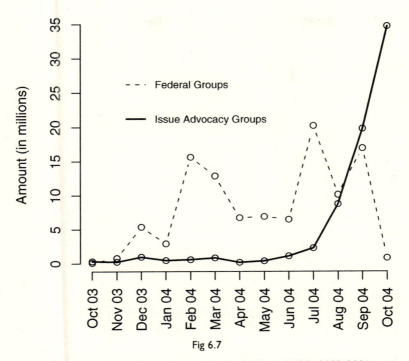

Fig 6.7

By-Month Campaign Expenditures for Issue and Federal 527s, 2003–2004.

120 federal 527s, 165 issue advocacy groups, 109 state and local committees, and 67 unclear groups), I include several other variables that
might predict increased levels of expenditures. For example, I include
a variable for whether the 527 lists Washington, D.C., as its mailing address; this is to control for the likelihood that these beltway 527s are
more active than state-based groups. I also include four variables that
measure the percentage of 527s' contributions coming (1) from individuals, (2) in the last 60 days before the general election, (3) from
too-close-to-call Senate states (as classified by *Congressional Quarterly*), and (4) from competitive presidential states (where the election
was decided by less than 5%).

I also account for whether the group has an FEC-registered federal PAC (there were 107 such groups) and whether the group filed
an electioneering communication report with the Federal Election

Commission. After BCRA, any qualified nonprofit group that spends soft money on an electioneering communication mentioning or picturing federal candidates (but avoiding magic words) within 60 days of the election must notify the FEC of the communication. The Commission assigns the group a committee code in its files. For example, the Swift Boat Veterans for Truth does not have an active FEC PAC that makes contributions, but because it spent money on television ads close to the election, the FEC tracks the expenditures. I also interacted this variable with the percentage of contributions from competitive presidential and Senate states. Finally, I include variables for whether the 527 was one of the partisan committees from the previous analysis.

Most importantly, I expected electioneering communication groups to be the most active campaigners. These are groups that raised and spent money on electioneering designed to help federal candidates (most specifically, presidential candidates). Their expenditures should dwarf the amount raised by state and local groups. As such, I also expected the issue advocacy and federal variables to be positive and significant, as compared to state and local groups and unclear groups (the base category). Third, I expected groups with federal PACs to be more active than those without them, and I expected groups that raised more funds from competitive states to spend more (another implication of the competitiveness hypothesis).

In a sense, there is an apples-and-oranges question here. In PAC models, each committee is directly comparable, as all FEC-registered PACs are concerned directly with federal elections (by definition). In this analysis, however, I am comparing 527s of very different stripes—at least potentially. State and local 527s might raise less than issue groups or 527s with federal committees, perhaps because the concerns of issue and federal groups extend beyond one state. This is not immediately obvious, however. One of the criticisms of BCRA is that 527s can spend money in ways that help or hurt federal candidates, but remain unregulated. That is, imagine a local 527 in a competitive presidential state. It might be motivated to raise and spend more money on grassroots activity that remains unregulated but relates—even indirectly (i.e., voter registration and GOTV)—to federal races. (I speculated on this above.)

Indeed, it appears that in the wake of the 527 explosion, many in Congress agreed that state and local-oriented 527s might be active spenders. In the congressional debate in 2005 over legislation to regulate 527s, Congress considered two specific changes that would force some state and local 527s to partially fund nonfederal activity with hard dollars. For example, under the proposed changes, any 527 that spends on state and local candidates but that mentions a party in those communications (i.e., Vote for Governor Doyle, Democrat) would have to pay for that advocacy with 50 percent hard money. And should a federal candidate appear in the ad to endorse a local or state candidate, the group would be mandated to use 50 percent hard money. The proposed legislation did not become law in 2005, but many in Congress continue to advocate for such changes.

The results are reported in Table 6.6. In the campaign activity model, electioneering PACs dwarf all others, while the variables for DC groups and Republican groups are also positive and significant. Thus, electioneering 527s spent more than groups not supporting federal candidates in the weeks before the election; Republican groups spent more on campaign activity than their Democratic foes; and groups close to power in Washington, D.C., spent more than state-based committees. Interestingly, 527s with PAC committees spent no more or less than those without them, which is counter to what I expected.

It should be noted that some electioneering PACs were also partisan groups (6 of 26 Republican 527s and 12 of 59 Democratic groups). This means that the insignificant coefficient for Democratic 527s does not indicate that Democratic groups avoided campaigning. The results merely imply that pro-GOP 527s spent even more than Democratic groups, all else being equal. This is important because even though John Kerry and other Democrats were aided by the millions of dollars spent on television ads from groups like America Coming Together and MoveOn.org, some pro-Democratic 527s were also more likely to shift money between each other before spending it on campaigning. For example, the Joint Victory Campaign spent more than $72 million in 2004, but none of it on campaigning. This is because they were essentially the fundraising arm of America Coming Together and the Media Fund, and the group's expenditures were mostly fund transfers to these 527s.

As for contributions, we see important distinctions from the campaigning model. First of all, electioneering 527s spent no more or less than other groups. Labor groups contributed more than issue groups,

TABLE 6.6   PREDICTING EXPENDITURES BY 527S IN 2004 ELECTION

Variable	Campaign Activity	Contributions
Federal	.331(.742)	−.472(.394)
State and Local	.743(.779)	.248(.412)
Issue	.496(.706)	−.909(.388)°°
Labor	.788(.710)	1.09(.364)°°
Paper filer	−1.03(.581)+	.631(.292)°
PAC	−.313(.554)	.206(.295)
Electioneering PAC	8.05(1.36)°°	−.409(1.16)
Democratic group	−.338(.706)	.698(.424)+
Republican group	3.64(.800)°°	.527(.498)
% from individuals	.005(.626)	−.248(.328)
% from competitive Senate state	.050(.721)	.238(.397)
% from competitive Pres state	−.359(.663)	.131(.358)
% in 60-days	−.106(.660)	−1.41(.397)°°
DC address	1.77(.547)°°	1.53(.322)°°
% competitive pres × elec PAC	−3.06(3.22)	−1.94(4.25)
% competitive Senate × elec PAC	−7.15(3.18)°	−2.08(3.50)
Intercept	−2.40(.822)°°	−.436(.433)
Log likelihood	−778.13502	−694.45633
N	439	439

°°$p<.01$ °$p<.05$ +$p<.10$
All tests are two-tailed, and SEs are in parentheses. Dependent Variable is the total amount spent on each type of activity. Both models were estimated using tobit, and all amounts are in millions.

which contributed less than the base category ("unknown" 527s). D.C. groups contributed more (making them more active campaigners and contributors than state-based 527s). In addition, both Democratic and Republican 527s had positive coefficients on contributions, but the Democratic coefficient was weakly significant. This is partly because of the point made above about fund transfers between some pro-Democratic groups. Finally, the higher percentage of funds raised in the final two months of the campaign results in smaller contribution totals at the 527 level (no surprise), but no more or less electioneering (which is somewhat of a surprise). These last two findings suggests a cycle of fund-raising *and* spending for electioneering activity, and fund-raising *then* spending for contribution activity.

Conclusion

In this chapter, I shift the analysis from an investigation of contributions by groups to candidates and parties to an analysis of expenditures by groups on behalf of candidates and parties. I examined the distribution of political advertisements in the last three House and Senate contests, finding a strong relationship between ad volume and competitiveness. Indeed, the weakest case of that relationship occurred in the 2004 House elections—when the Republicans held the firmest grip on power since becoming the majority in 1995. I followed with an analysis of 527s, and I found strong evidence of a soft-to-soft dynamic, in which interest groups responded to a constrained resource context (with the end of party soft money) by investing in high amounts and in similar patterns with partisan 527 money. Finally, I examined the expenditures of 527s, comparing across group type, finding evidence that the most active 527s were those hoping to affect federal elections and that Republican- and Democratic-allied 527s spent their money in slightly different ways.

This analysis of 527s is one of the first to examine how these groups raised and spent money in the 2004 elections. Their presence that year caused many citizens and political activists considerable angst. Columnist O. Ricardo Pimental had this to say in September 2004 about 527s' political ads that year: "There is a sad truth we can glean from this election year. Dirt works. Mud and lies work. Appealing to fears and baser instincts works best of all. It's quite likely that the winner will not be the most persuasive person but merely the person with the last, best dirt. Or, with the advent of the so-called 527 groups, the person for whom surrogate campaigners dish the best dirt. To the spoilers belong the electoral spoils on Nov. 2."[15] I have said nothing about whether political ads or expenditures by 527s have any impact on citizens, but the analysis in this chapter is important in helping us understand why so many interest groups invest in elections so aggressively.

All told, in Chapters 4–6 I have focused on the political determinants that drive interest group electioneering. I have argued that the balance of power in Congress is the principal driving force in the rise of soft money and issue advocacy. I have also shown evidence that PACs—long the focus of interest group scholarship—shifted strategies to become more partisan in recent elections. Politics, however, does not complete the story. After all, there are political, legal, civil, and even criminal costs to using tactics with a degree of legal uncertainty to them. As that uncertainty decreases, such tactics should be

144 = Chapter 6

employed more often. In the next chapter, I switch gears by focusing on the regulatory and legal environments that surround campaign financing, and I argue that changes in the legal context worked in tandem with changes in the political environment to produce this most recent "explosion" in interest group politics.

7   Tracking the Regulatory Context

I n this chapter, I shift from a focus on how the ideological and partisan context structures interest group electoral goals (which in turn drive tactical choices) to a discussion of how the regulatory context structures the capacity to act in campaigns—which (also) affects tactical choices. At the outset, it makes sense to assume that political actors are concerned about whether innovative or untested tactics have criminal, civil, or political penalties to their employment. After all, "Federal campaign law is a freakish mess."[1]

Indeed, between 1977 and 2003, more than 1,200 candidates, parties, and interest groups sought official legal counsel from the FEC, giving us insight into common questions and interpretations about the scope of campaign finance law. For example, in 1979, Rexnord, Inc., of Milwaukee, Wisconsin, asked the FEC if it could use corporate funds to pay for a newspaper advertisement that said simply, "Please Register to Vote" (AO 1979-48). The company considered such activity a generic public service. The FEC responded that the proposal as conceived could be funded only with regulated PAC funds. We learn a lot from the example. First, questions about regulated and unregulated political communications to the public date back further than we might assume (a point made in Chapter 2); second, the FEC was tough in its interpretation of the boundaries of regulated election activity.

The main question in this chapter, then, is how and when political actors seek out such knowledge and to what effect. I leverage a diverse and unique set of data tracking changes in the regulatory environment in testing two main hypotheses about how interest groups incorporate the regulatory context into the decision calculus on how to engage electoral politics.[2] First, it is often said that political actors must learn about election law before knowing how to exploit loopholes or implement innovative tactics. If such a process takes place, we should see evidence of the **political learning hypothesis**. Second, the FEC is often blamed for being too partisan or too lax. If this is true, however, there should be systematic evidence of the **lenient FEC hypothesis**. Taken together, both hypotheses identify how changes in the regulatory context affect tactical selection. As interest groups learn about the law and as the FEC alters its application, interest groups are freer to adopt new tactics. This has direct importance to the rise of soft money, issue advocacy, and 527s.

Advisory Opinions: Signposts for Tactical Capacity

The discussion in Chapter 2 identified the sources of changes in election law—from Congress, the FEC, and the courts. In this chapter I rely principally on advisory opinions from the FEC, and I begin with an in-depth discussion of these data and their utility. Advisory opinions are an important means for political practitioners to better understand the dimensions of federal election law; they become particularly relevant when the boundaries of permissible activity are not clearly understood.

For example, in 2004 a controversy emerged over advertising for Michael Moore's controversial documentary, *Fahrenheit 9/11*. Did advertising for the film, which mentioned and pictured President Bush, constitute an electioneering communication that fell under BCRA? Or did such advertisements come under a media exemption that permits news organizations and news broadcasts to editorialize for or against a candidate? The question was relevant (although ultimately the FEC never addressed Moore's advertisements) because of two advisory opinions issued by the FEC in the summer and fall of 2004 (AO 2004-15 and

2004-30). In both AOs, the FEC ruled that advertisements for two proposed political documentaries about the 2004 presidential election (one by the Bill of Rights Educational Foundation and the other by Citizens United) were regulated electioneering communications that could not be funded with corporate money. Both groups conceded that advertisements publicizing the films would feature the candidates running for the White House. The decision created a stir among opponents of BCRA's new provisions because it hinted at the possibility that numerous forms of film or book advertising might be deemed illegal if they occurred too close to an election.

Below, I review five examples of advisory opinions to give a better sense of the range and diversity of questions posed to the FEC through the AO process.

1. In November 1985, the National Conservative Political Action Committee (NCPAC) asked the FEC if it could use PAC funds to purchase a life insurance policy on its chairman, John Dolan. The group asked for clarification on whether the proceeds of the insurance policy, on Mr. Dolan's death, would be considered a contribution from the insurance company to NCPAC; it hoped not. Second, the PAC hoped to use the proceeds—in excess of $100,000—to make contributions to candidates and to pay for the overhead costs of running NCPAC. The FEC responded that so long as the insurance policy was purchased at the normal rate, it could implement such a plan (AO 1985-34).

2. In September 1995, the Coastal Employee Action Fund, the separate segregated fund of the Coastal Corporation in Houston, Texas, asked the FEC if it could send a PAC newsletter via email to members of its restricted class. Recall, election law restricts connected PACs (or separate segregated funds) to collecting contributions from a specified class of employees. The Coastal Corporation was worried that, since some executives in the company did not have or use computers, the executives' secretaries—who were not in the PAC's restricted class—would print the newsletter for their employer to read and would therefore be exposed

to PAC solicitations. Would this constitute a prohibited solicitation outside the restricted class? The FEC responded that "the secretary's receipt of the newsletter would be pursuant to the usual and normal function of routing such communications on to the supervisor"—and was permissible (AO 1995-33).

3. In November 1984, the Amerifirst Good Government Committee, the separate segregated fund of the Amerifirst Federal Savings and Loan Association, asked the FEC if two law firms that represented Amerifirst could be included in the PAC's restricted class for purposes of solicitation. The PAC hoped to increases its resource base by expanding its restricted class. The FEC concluded that, because the lawyers in both firms were compensated by their parent firms and not by Amerifirst, they were not included in the restricted class. Further still, the FEC argued that since only one employee of Amerifirst was actually compensated, that individual, W.H. Walker, Jr. (Chairman of the Board), was the only individual in the restricted class. As a consequence of the ruling, it was determined that only Walker could contribute money to the Amerifirst Good Government Committee (AO 1984-55).

4. In April 1982, the Sprik and Andersen law firm in Grand Rapids, Michigan, asked the FEC about radio and print advertisements it sponsored. Dale Sprik, one of the partners in the firm, had run for Congress in 1978 and 1980, and was considering a run for Congress in 1982. The firm wanted to know if advertisements airing on radio and television, which stated the firm's legal services and mentioned Sprik but did not mention his candidacy, constituted in-kind contributions to Sprik's campaign or independent expenditures on his behalf. The FEC responded, "It appears to the Commission that these advertisements will be aired, televised and written irrespective of any possible candidacy for Congress in 1982 by Mr. Sprik. Therefore, the Commission concludes that since the ads will not identify Mr. Sprik as a candidate for Congress, or any other public office and since the frequency of such ads will not be accelerated immedi-

ately preceding any 1982 primary or general election, no purpose to influence an election would arise in those circumstances." Note that in this example, the classification of political advertisement extends beyond a magic word test to include the timing and frequency of the ads[3] (AO 1982-15).

5. Finally, in July 1988, the non-PAC Section 527 group, San Joaquin Valley Republican Associates—self-described as organized "for the express purpose of promoting political ideas . . . with 'no ties' to any political party"—asked the FEC if it could engage in some issue advocacy that might be construed as expenditures adversely helping or hurting candidates for federal office. This activity included disseminating newsletters highlighting political issues (mostly putting Republican candidates in a positive light), holding luncheons with contributors to the group, and maintaining a campaign library that would contain, among other things, contributor lists accessible to any member of the group. The group believed that it should not be classified as a PAC because the activity highlighted would not constitute a majority of its political activity; the group referenced *FEC v. Massachusetts Citizens for Life, Inc.* (MCFL), where— recall from Chapter 2—the Court argued that some groups are exempt from having to register with the Federal Election Commission. The FEC disagreed with San Joaquin Valley Republican Associates, arguing that the MCFL case referred to groups only occasionally expending in ways to help candidates (AO 1988-22).

These examples demonstrate that petitioners ask the FEC for legal advice on questions that range from permissible solicitation behavior to how a group is classified (and what its responsibilities are in reporting to the Commission). In Table 7.1, I show the purpose codes I used to categorize each advisory opinion. I coded each AO on up to five of the codes listed. I split the codes into three general categories—one for electioneering, meaning opinions related to campaign activity of some sort; one for questions relating to fund-raising; and one catch-all category for purpose codes that do not fit naturally into the previous two. Indeed, many of these catch-all codes are highly correlated with

TABLE 7.1   PURPOSE CODES FOR ADVISORY OPINIONS

ELECTIONEERING	"OTHER"	
Use of funds	Committee designation	Candidate death
Independent expenditures	Committee affiliation	Personal funds
Coordinated expenditures	Committee organization	Redistricting
Other expenditures	Administrative expenses	Public financing
Issue or express advocacy/GOTV	Reporting requirements	501c or 527
Fund transfers	Membership	
Campaign activity	Restricted class	
Endorsements	Loans	
Excess funds	Campaign debts	
Candidate appearance	Internet	
Soft money	Lobbying	
Advertisements	Refunds	
Bundling/conduit	"Testing the waters"	
Media exemption	"Winding down"/termination	
Contributions to someone	Federal contractors	
	Donations	
FUND-RAISING	Foreign nationals	
Fund-raising	Use of FEC database	
Solicitation	Banks	
Honoraria	Partnerships	
Legal expenses	Interns	
Tax check-off/state funds	Election recount	
What is an election?	Disclaimer on ads	
Contributions from someone	Conventions	

electioneering or fund-raising requests. For example, "restricted class" is most often associated with solicitation. However, because it is possible that the restricted class purpose code might also go with an electioneering request, I separate purpose codes that clearly fall into electioneering and fund-raising classifications.

This coding scheme allows me to track the kinds of questions that are asked over time. I also coded each AO on how the FEC responded; that is, whether the petitioner's question is denied, affirmed, or a mixture of both. From this, I can track both when questions are asked and why, and how the FEC responds.

In Table 7.2 I report results from two statistical models predicting who is more likely to request electioneering (left column) or fund-raising AOs (right column) for all decided opinions between 1983 and 2003.[4] I include variables for whether the petitioner is a political party, a candidate in a competitive race, an incumbent candidate, or a challenger. I also control for several interest group identifiers. For exam-

TABLE 7. 2   UNDERSTANDING THE RELATIONSHIP BETWEEN PETITIONER AND AO-TYPES

Variable	Electioneering	Fund-raising
Party	.872(.287)**	−1.293(.348)**
Competitive candidate	.212(.245)	−.2441(.250)
Incumbent	.700(.304)*	−.0912(.313)
Challenger	.197(.282)	.128(.292)
PAC Ideology	.148(.191)	.077(.182)
PAC Expenditures (10,000s)	.0013(.001)	−.0013(.0014)
Non-registered Group	.704(.255)**	−1.100(.290)**
Corporate PAC	−.818(.323)**	.522(.307)+
Labor PAC	−.220(.701)	.340(.689)
Non-Connected PAC	.213(.465)	−.793(.541)
Trade Association PAC	−1.01(.376)**	1.09(.355)**
Year	−.037(.026)	−.008(.027)
Intercept	−.246(.266)	−.340(.279)
N	802	802
Prob. chi2>0	0.0000	0.0000
log-likelihood	−519.292	−477.783

**$p<.01$ *$p<.05$ +$p<.10$
All tests are two-tailed, and SEs are in parentheses. Dependent Variable is whether AO was an electioneering or fund-raising request. The model was estimated using probit.

ple, I measure whether the group had a registered PAC or not and, if so, who sponsored the PAC (i.e., corporation or labor union). I also control for the PAC's ideology (0 if no ideology was estimated; 1 if the PAC had an ideology score in between the party medians; and 2 if the PAC ideology was more extreme than one of the party medians) and for the total expenditures of the PAC in the most current election cycle. If there were multiple interest groups jointly making the AO request, variables are coded if at least one petitioner fits the category. Finally, I control for the year the AO was requested.

Initial expectations are that competitive candidates should be more likely to make both types of requests; these candidates are more likely to spend higher amounts and in diverse ways in their campaigns. I expected groups not registered with the FEC to be more concerned with electioneering than fund-raising. This is because these interest groups would have to be classified first as electioneering interest groups for their fund-raising to comply with election law. Finally, I expected corporate and trade association PACs to be more concerned with fund-raising than electioneering; recall that in Chapter 4 we confirmed that these PACs are more concerned with access politics than replacement politics.

The results indicate that, when the FEC considers electioneering and fund-raising requests, they are more likely to come from predictable petitioners. Although my expectation about competitive candidates was not borne out (competitive candidates were no more or less likely than any other petitioner to ask electioneering or fund-raising requests), political parties were more likely to ask electioneering questions than fund-raising questions. Finally, I found evidence for my expectations about different interest groups. Groups not registered with the FEC are significantly more likely to make electioneering-related requests, while trade and corporate PACs are significantly more interested in fund-raising questions.

This analysis is but a preliminary investigation into the types of petitioners that seek out FEC clarification. Of course the model is conditional on the FEC considering this request. What we see in this analysis, however, is that AO requests are not random or idiosyncratic. Petitioners with particular stakes are the ones most likely to seek out relevant FEC input.

A Brief Defense of Advisory Opinions

Advisory opinions are a very public forum in which political actors can take account of the regulatory environment, and political actors pay close attention to FEC deliberations. Consider the following comments from two Commissioners on the importance of the AO process.

- Commissioner Scott Thomas: "Congress intended advisory opinions to serve a valuable interpretive function. Recently, this was underscored by a request from the Committee on House Administration for prompt action to make such opinions more accessible on the Internet. Rather than downplay their significance, commissioners should cite them when appropriate and use them to educate the regulated community and encourage compliance with the law passed by Congress" (AO 1999-11A).
- Commissioner Thomas: "The Commission's advisory opinion process can and should be an educational vehicle" (AO 2001-17A).

- Commissioner Frank Reiche: "I believe the Commission has a responsibility in issuing advisory opinions to provide guidance for others in similar circumstances" (AO 1981-25A).

The point is larger, however. AOs are but one way to incorporate legal considerations into tactical choices. There are other methods of seeking out even minimal legal advice, ways that are far more common but almost impossible to track systematically. For example, political actors can use lawyers to answer questions about permissible tactics. Most candidates, parties, and interest groups likely have easy access to legal counsel, especially when considering innovative electioneering strategies.

Political actors can also rely on other methods of considering how election law affects their capacity to act. For example, the FEC has an anonymous 800 help-line that anyone can use to ask for nonbinding legal clarification. The Commission reports the total number of calls to this hotline each year in its annual report (first issued in 1996); for example, the FEC reported more than 34,000 calls in 1996, 61,000 in 1998, 54,000 in 2000, and 20,000 in 2002.

Moreover, political actors can also participate in FEC-sponsored conferences and roundtables that deal explicitly with election law compliance. These conferences have workshops for questions ranging from fund-raising and solicitation to electioneering and political advertising. The FEC sponsors close to six conferences a year at various locations across the country (although because of budget constraints they have scaled back in recent years). I attended one of these conferences in September 2003. Some interest group participants included American Electric Power, AFL-CIO, Chicago Mercantile Exchange, Illinois Bankers Association, National Association of Realtors, Aristotle International, MetLife Insurance, Whirlpool Corporation, the Northern Trust Company, National Society of Professional Engineers, Devon Energy Corporation, and the Illinois Corn Growers Association.

These points demonstrate that while an analysis of AOs is not one I can generalize to the entire universe of political actors, we should not expect AOs to be random; they are the most public forum by which political actors consider and respond to the regulatory environment. As such, I am making a modest claim in this chapter. By tracking advisory opinions over time, we gain insight into one avenue by which political actors consider the scope of election law in their decision calculus.

Political Learning

I define political learning as the process by which political actors come to understand and evaluate different campaign tactics. Learning can take many forms. For example, candidates, parties, and interest groups may abandon tactics that prove unsuccessful. Alternatively, they may be introduced to new or innovative tactics through interpersonal networks. I focus here on political learning with respect to the regulatory environment.

To investigate this dynamic, I report statistical models in Tables 7.3 and 7.4 predicting the number of advisory opinion requests made to the FEC in every month between 1977 and 2003.[5] This set-up is analogous to the state-month soft money analysis in Chapter 5 in that the statistical technique must account for the correlation of requests across months and years (i.e., the number of issue advocacy requests in January of 1978 might be related to the number of requests of this type in February of 1978).

The two models in the Table 7.3 test for frequency effects in the broad categories encompassing electioneering and fund-raising requests, using the purpose codes from Table 7.1. I combined requests from candidates, parties, interest groups, and individuals. The two models in Table 7.4 are for more focused requests—issue advocacy requests from interest groups and matching fund requests from presidential candidates. I chose these two categories because there have been a number of relevant regulatory changes in these areas. By contrast, for the vast majority of categories reported in Table 7.1, the law has remained fairly static.

I estimate these models with a number of important independent variables that tap (changes in) the regulatory environment. First, I account for whether BCRA was law (any month between November 2002 and the end of the 2003). Second, I include a variable for whether an FEC regulatory change became effective or an amendment to FECA passed in that month or the month before. These use the data reported in Figure 2.7 and Table 2.2. I expected both types of

TABLE 7.3   POLITICAL LEARNING FOR ELECTIONEERING AND
FUND-RAISING AOS

Variable	Electioneering	Fund-raising
Other requests in month	.090(.025)**	.049(.019)*
Regulation or Amendment (2 Months)	.302(.135)*	−.047(.119)
Reg or Amend (3–4 Months)	.311(.150)*	.078(.150)
Reg or Amend (5–6 Months)	−.189(.192)	.035(.156)
BCRA is law	.486(.310)	.721(.280)**
Election Year	.298(.091)**	.036(.102)
Democratic House	−.245(.194)	−.683(.205)**
Democratic Senate	−.107(.093)	.131(.088)
Year	−.053(.012)**	−.096(.011)**
Month	−.032(.012)**	.010(.012)
Intercept	105.96(24.13)**	190.98(21.37)**
N	320	320
Prob. Chi2 > 0	0.0000	0.0000
log-likelihood	−509.853	−462.815

**$p<.01$ *$p<.05$
All tests are two-tailed and robust SEs are in parentheses. Dependent Variable is the number of requests of each
type made to the FEC in each month. The models were estimated using Poisson.

variables to be significantly positive. This would indicate that in a
month with some recent legal change, the number of AOs in that area
increased. I interpret such a relationship to be evidence of political
learning.[6]

In addition, I control for a number of other factors that might predict the frequency of AOs. I include two variables for whether the
House and Senate were controlled by the Democratic Party. I include a year variable that controls for the downward trend in AOs, as
reported in Figure 2.8. I also control for whether the month is in an
election year (either mid-term or presidential) and a trend variable for
the month.[7] Finally, I control for the number of other requests (outside of the category under investigation) in that month, to capture the
effect of a higher number of opinions for reasons not specifically controlled for here.

I draw three conclusions from the results in both tables. First, the
political environment often motivates the volume of requests. For example, electioneering requests were higher in election years, and
matching fund requests were higher in presidential election years, as
we should expect. Fund-raising requests were not more frequent in
election years, which makes sense given that fund-raising is also an

TABLE 7.4 POLITICAL LEARNING FOR ISSUE ADVOCACY AND MATCHING FUND AOS

Variable	Issue Advocacy	Matching Fund
Other requests in month	.132(.042)°°	.035(.043)
Regulation or Amendment (2 Months)	1.054(.561)+	.612(.283)°
Reg or Amend (3–4 Months)	.501(.687)	.200(.381)
Reg or Amend (5–6 Months)	−.409(.993)	.148(.362)
BCRA is law	.669(.681)	−.065(.568)
Election Year	.089(.266)	
Mid-term		−.629(.425)
Presidential		.624(.245)°°
Democratic House	.092(.606)	−1.094(.497)°
Democratic Senate	−.046(.278)	−.242(.343)
Year	−.018(.036)	−.046(.033)
Month	−.036(.039)	−.009(.033)
Intercept	33.661(71.048)	91.27(65.95)
N	320	320
Prob. Chi2 > 0	0.0000	0.0000
log-likelihood	−141.581	−75.060

°°$p<.01$ °$p<.05$ +$p<.10$
All tests are two-tailed and robust SEs are in parentheses. Dependent Variable is the number of requests of each type made to the FEC in each month. The matching fund model was estimated using logit. The issue model was estimated using Poisson.

off-year concern. For example, in a nonelection year, the probability of at least two electioneering requests in a given month is about .38. That probability rises to almost .50 in an election year. The probability of a matching fund request in an off-year or mid-term election year is about .10, but rises to .25 in a presidential election year.

Second, and most important in testing the hypothesis of political learning, changes in election law matter. After the large-scale changes in BCRA redefined campaign finance law, the number of electioneering and fund-raising requests increased (note that the BCRA variable in the electioneering model is insignificant, but has a p-value of .117). Indeed, the number of fund-raising requests is much higher post-BCRA, but this makes sense considering that the scope of the law did change in this area, especially in terms of how party leaders and candidates could raise and solicit soft money for outside groups and state parties.

In addition, smaller scale regulatory changes made between FECA and BCRA also increased the number of electioneering requests, matching fund, and interest group issue advocacy requests. Regulation

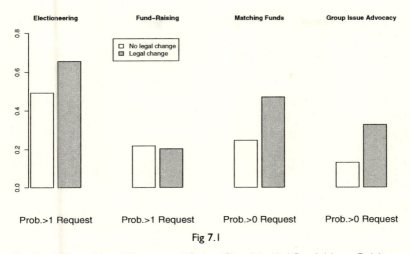

Fig 7.1

Predicted Effect of Legal Changes on AOs in a Given Month. AO—Advisory Opinion.

changes did not affect fund-raising AOs, mostly because these regulatory changes (based on my reading) concerned some fairly idiosyncratic areas of the law.[8] In Figure 7.1, I report predicted probabilities for all four models for months where there has been a recent regulatory change and for months where there has not.[9] In the electioneering case, the probability of at least two requests in a given month rises from about .50 to more than .60 in the aftermath of a regulatory or statutory change. That probability changes from a little over .20 to over .40 in the matching fund model, and from .10 to .30 in the issue advocacy model.

As a final observation, it is apparent that learning is quick. The more time has passed since a regulation becomes effective, the less likely that change will result in higher AO requests. I track this relationship with three variables for regulation changes: one or two months prior, three or four months prior; and five or six months prior. I do this as a further test for political learning. We have no reason to expect political learning to occur rapidly, but if the effect of a recent regulatory change decreases the further in time we get from that change, we can be confident that the significant coefficient results are more persuasively related to the regulation change.

All told, I take this as evidence of some limited political learning. Indeed, finding evidence in this realm is encouraging, as it is likely the hardest case in which to find learning effects. More specifically, political actors likely learn directly from advisory opinions, as the earlier quotes from the FEC commissioners stated, but we may never see that explicitly (for example, it might occur behind closed doors in meetings between group leaders and their legal counsel). To find it in the very public forum of AO requests is persuasive evidence that it occurs more frequently in areas we cannot see.

Nonetheless, the learning hypothesis is less satisfying given that parties and interest groups have been asking questions about the distinction between regulated and unregulated money for more than two decades. Are we to assume that, in the realm of soft money and issue advocacy, learning took more than 20 years? But this begs the question—was the regulatory environment so porous? Or have the FEC and the courts taken more aggressive stands on the expansion of electioneering tactics? I turn now to investigations of the lenient FEC hypothesis.

Lenient FEC

When the FEC approves an AO, the capacity for the political actor making the request is likely enhanced. When the AO is not approved, capacity is either restrained or maintained. I assume at the outset that petitioners who win on their AO are more likely to use or employ that tactic than petitioners who lose. The relevant test of the lenient FEC hypothesis, then, is whether interest groups, parties, and candidates have fared differently in the approval of requested AOs. Such an examination should tell us something insightful about why issue advocacy and soft money tactics took so long to emerge on the political scene.

The FEC is often criticized for being lax enforcers of election law, as was discussed in Chapter 3. For example, Jim Drinkard of *USA Today* once wrote, "A close look . . . at the FEC's 27-year history reveals an agency that puts protecting the interests of the Democratic and Republican parties ahead of policing election laws or guarding public confidence in the integrity of campaigns and elections."[10] Recent reform proposals in the wake of BCRA often include suggestions on revamping or eliminating the FEC. For example, in both 2003 and 2006, Senators John McCain (R-AZ) and Russ Feingold (D-WI), and Representatives Chris Shays (R-CT) and Marty Meehan (D-MA) proposed the Federal Election Administration Act, which sought to replace the FEC with a new Election Administration composed of an independent three-member commission and administrative law judges. John McCain testified in front of the Senate Rules Committee in 2003 that "the Federal Election Commission has continually acted as a bureaucratic barrier to reform of the system. Time and time again, these unelected officials of the FEC have thwarted the enforcement of the nation's campaign finance laws in deference to the partisan wishes of those who have appointed them."

The lenient FEC hypothesis seems vulnerable to critique, however. Recall the Rexnord advertisement described in the beginning of the chapter, about which the FEC argued in 1979 that an exhortation to vote was within the purview of regulated electioneering. And consider a 1992 AO where the FEC went beyond the magic word distinction in concluding that the National Rifle Association could not pay for proposed political advertisements from its general treasury (AO 1992-23). Their argument is worth citing at length:

> To limit the concept of express advocacy to certain key phrases would preserve First Amendment rights "only at the expense of eviscerating" [FECA] and would permit independent campaign spenders to "remain just beyond the reach of the Act by avoiding certain key words while conveying a message that is unmistakably directed to the election or defeat of a named candidate." Instead, to be express advocacy under the Act, speech "must, when read as a whole, and with limited reference to external events, be susceptible of no other reasonable interpretation but as an exhortation to vote for or against a specific candidate."
>
> The Commission concludes that each of the ads are such an exhortation and not simply issue discussion. . . . The content and timing of these advertisements lead us to determine that they expressly advocate the election or defeat of a Federal candidate. All of the sample advertisements were run in close proximity to [the candidate]'s election. The written advertisements

provided to the Commission make specific reference to the date of the election (which is referred to as "doomsday"), and the requester states that the radio advertisements would be "similar" to the [candidate's] radio commercials. These ads encourage no action in connection with the issues mentioned (such as urging the Congressman to vote for or against specific bills).

Indeed, it seems more likely, given the previous section, that political learning does occur, but that the FEC (as enforcer of the law) has played an active role in defining those boundaries. Indeed, we might expect the pattern of responses from the FEC to vary across time and petitioner. In that sense, I complicate the political learning hypothesis by asserting that it takes place in an environment that varies in the intensity of its constraints. And I expand the lenient FEC hypothesis by asserting that weakness or partisanship might not be uniform or consistent. Perhaps Drinkard and McCain are right in that the FEC historically favors parties, but this might not preclude them from disfavoring organized interests, and for those evaluations to change over time.

Before proceeding, it is important to consider what costs truly exist. Recall that the FEC has enforcement powers in relation to action proposed (with advisory opinions) and action taken (with administrative fines and court cases). There is evidence that the FEC is particularly weak in the latter case (Lochner and Cain 1999), which has direct effects on the weight that interest groups give to the FEC's advice on activity proposed. Nonetheless, any potential litigation, audits, or investigations are significant costs to election law violators. Another component in the criticism of the FEC is that it pursues too many violations, even frivolous ones (and at the expense of more serious violations). The FEC's effectiveness at enforcement is not the focus of this analysis, and I assume that political actors (in asking for advice through an AO) have given the FEC some legitimacy on the issue.

To assess the lenient FEC charge, we can examine systematically how the FEC has evaluated AOs between 1977 and 2003. In the statistical models reported below, I focus the analysis on the FEC's decision in each AO—whether the petitioner wins, loses, or gets a mixed response. Winning AOs are when the FEC considers a petitioner's request and green lights the action. Losing AOs are either when the FEC decides that the action proposed does not conform to existing regulations (such as in the NRA example above) or when the FEC deadlocks on a decision and cannot provide guidance. Mixed response AOs are those in which the FEC approves only part of the request but denies the rest. I order the three-category variable from a losing AO to a winning AO, with mixed decisions in the middle. The distribution of wins and losses is skewed heavily toward a win: 65 percent of all decided AOs (801) are wins, 15 percent (182) are mixed, and 20 percent (243) are losses.

I estimate two slightly different models using the following independent variables. First, I include variables that distinguish the type of petitioner. I ignore AOs asked by individuals (of which there were only a handful) and focus on requests from interest group, parties, and candidates (the latter being the excluded category in these models). I interact interest groups and parties with pre-1995 and post-1994 measures to assess any temporal change in the rate at which these petitioners win. I use 1994 as the cut point because, as we know, this was around the time that issue advocacy and soft money exploded onto the political scene. Second, I include a number of variables that categorize the AO. Was the AO about fund-raising, electioneering, both, issue advocacy, or soft money? In addition, I interacted petitioner type with the code for whether the AO is an electioneering request.

Finally, I include a variable tapping the make-up of the FEC— that is, the number of FEC commissioners appointed by a Republican president. The law requires the Commission to be balanced 3-3 between Democrats and Republicans, but this does not prevent presidents from appointing (or re-appointing) commissioners who match their party's philosophy. At the same time, there exists an unofficial norm that presidents allow the opposing party to select half the president's nominees, as in the case of Clinton's most controversial nominee, conservative Republican Brad Smith. As such, it might be very difficult to sort out statistically whether the political make-up of the six commissioners is related to AO outcomes.

The results are shown in Table 7.5. Because the three-category dependent variable is ordered from a win to a loss, positive coefficients mean that, as the independent variable increases, the FEC is more likely to approve the AO; negative coefficients indicate that the FEC is

TABLE 7.5 PREDICTING APPROVAL OF ADVISORY OPINIONS

Variable	Model 1	Model 2
Interest Group		−.039(.103)
IG × Pre-1995	−.142(.109)	
IG × Post-1994	.464(.200)*	
IG × Electioneering AO	−.368(.159)*	−.379(.158)*
Party		.040(.192)
Party × Pre-1995	−.035(.218)	
Party × Post-1994	.224(.258)	
Party × Electioneering AO	−.398(.284)	−.445(.278)
Year		.018(.005)**
Pre-1995	−.108(.150)	
Fund-raising AO	.173(.104)+	.189(.104)+
Electioneering AO	.524(.137)**	.511(.137)**
Fund-Raising and Electioneering	−.391(.170)*	−.365(.169)*
Issue Advocacy AO	−.344(.149)*	−.320(.148)*
Soft Money AO	.039(.235)	.083(.231)
Numb GOP-Appointed Commiss.	.000(.032)	−.009(.031)
threshold 1	−.784(.204)**	−.553(.172)**
threshold 2	−.313(.203)	−.088(.172)
N	1206	1206
Prob. chi2>0	0.0000	0.0000
log-likelihood	−1035.39	−1044.40

**$p<.01$ *$p<.05$ +$p<.10$
All tests are two-tailed, and SEs are in parentheses. Dependent Variable is whether AO was denied (y=−1), mixed (y=0), or affirmed (y=1). The model was estimated using ordered probit.

more likely to disapprove the request. The most important result from this analysis is a change in how the FEC evaluates interest group requests over time. In Model 1, the coefficient on outcome is negative (and insignificant) for interest groups pre-1995, but the coefficient is positive and significant for interest groups post-1994. This means that in the late 1990s, the FEC became more likely to approve interest group requests, all else being equal.

The results also show that interest group electioneering requests are more likely to lose (Model 2), as are issue advocacy requests (negative coefficients in both models). Because I did not look for a temporal shift with these variables, this means that, across all of the years in the analysis, the FEC has been more likely to look unfavorably on these types of requests. Compare this to the results for party electioneering requests and soft money requests, which are not evaluated in any consistent way by the FEC.

Interestingly, all electioneering and fund-raising requests are

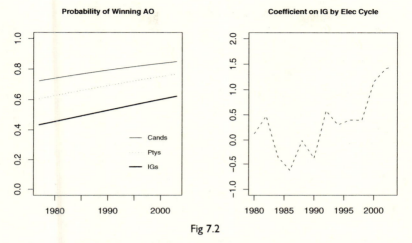

Fig 7.2

Predicted Success Rate of Electioneering AOs. AO—Advisory Opinion.

more likely to be approved (controlling for petitioner), but when the requests become complicated enough to involve both types of questions (which I treat as a rough proxy for innovative and aggressive requests), the AO is more likely to be denied. In addition, the variable tapping the make-up of the FEC has no effect,

To demonstrate the temporal shift in AO evaluation, I show in Figure 7.2 (in the left panel) the probability over time that candidates, parties, and interest groups obtain approval of important AOs, using estimates from Model 2. The result in Model 2 shows that, regardless of sponsor, the FEC is more likely to approve AOs as time progresses (the positive and significant coefficient on the "Year" variable). The figure shows the probability of an interest group winning an issue advocacy request, along with the probability of a party winning a soft money request and a candidate winning an electioneering request. As the figure demonstrates, the probability of a group winning an issue advocacy request is about .40 in the early 1980s, but rises to .60 in the late 1990s. The same patterns hold for parties and candidates, but they always have a higher probability of winning than interest groups.

I also plot the coefficient estimates (shown in the right panel of the figure) from a third model that allows the coefficient for interest groups to change for each election cycle. More specifically, I correlate the interest group measure with a variable for each election cycle between 1978 and 2002. The interactive effect shows the likelihood that the group wins the AO request in each election. Again, negative coefficients indicate a likelihood of losing, but positive coefficients suggest a higher chance of winning. The graph shows the coefficient for interest groups increasing over time, from a low of −.5 in 1986 to more than 1 by 2000. These results indicate that the FEC was more likely to say "no" to interest groups in the late 1970s and throughout the 1980s, but it was far more likely to say "yes" in the 1990s and early 2000s.

One explanation for this shift is a *weakening* of the FEC's historic aggressiveness concerning interest group electioneering. In 1995, the FEC issued a rule change that expanded the express advocacy distinction beyond magic words—a bold move. The Commission argued, "The definition of express advocacy included in [the new regulations] includes elements from [a variety of definitions], as well as the language in [previous court] opinions emphasizing the necessity for communications to be susceptible to no other reasonable interpretation but as encouraging actions to elect or defeat a specific candidate. Please note that exhortations to contribute time or money to a candidate would also fall within the revised definition of express advocacy" (issued on July 6, 1995; note also it contains some of the same language from the above-cited NRA advisory opinion).

The FEC was relying in part on a decision from 1987 by the Ninth Circuit Court in *FEC v. Furgatch* that extended the definition of express advocacy beyond magic words; the court in this case established that the context of the communication might be used to help distinguish express from issue advocacy. The FEC regulation, however, was ruled unconstitutional in 1996 by the First Circuit Court in *Maine Right to Life Committee, Inc. v. FEC*. The decision was upheld in federal appeals court, and the Supreme Court in 1997 refused to hear the case. Although the Commission kept the expanded regulation on the books in the aftermath of the ruling, the rebuke from the courts essentially prevented the FEC from applying the broader test.

Maine Right to Life Committee was not the only development, however. There appeared to be a conscious shift by FEC commissioners to accept the magic word standard. For example, by 2000, the FEC had concluded that some public communications containing magic words were outside the scope of election law. In an advisory opinion for Third Millennium (a nonprofit group not registered with the Commission), the FEC concluded that the organization could engage in an Internet project investigating voter apathy among young people (AO 2000-16). The research design for the project included an Internet survey of 40,000 young adults, who would be exposed to a variety of Internet presidential advertisements, some of which would be provided by the presidential campaigns. The question asked was whether this activity was regulated electioneering or academic issue advocacy.

The FEC ruled that it was the latter, and in concurring with the opinion, three commissioners argued:

> In determining whether or not corporate communications are prohibited by the Act, we are required to engage in a two-step analysis. The first step is to determine whether or not the communications contain "explicit words of advocacy of the election or defeat of a clearly identified candidate." Only after determining that express advocacy is involved is it necessary to examine whether or not the communications are for the purpose of "influencing an election" (AO 2000-16).

As such, the FEC concluded that the project was not intended to influence the outcome of the election; in so doing, it created the potential for even magic word communications to be unregulated, so long as the intention is considered academic or issue-based. What is more, whereas the earlier regulation change expanding the magic word distinction compelled regulators to take account of other factors in the timing and scope of the communication, the commissioners here allowed that second standard to be applied only *after* magic words have been used.

In an April 15, 2004, hearing on creating new regulations for 527s and 501cs, Commissioner Scott Thomas made note of the San Joaquin Valley Republican Associates advisory opinion from 1988 (noted earlier). Thomas defended the decision (applied to that group) to extend the express advocacy test beyond mere magic words and to force the group to register as a political committee. According to Thomas, "As I see it, it is still good law. It has never been overturned." This was in response to an earlier comment from Larry Noble, former General Counsel at the FEC, who noted that it was the Commissioners' change in standards in the late 1990s that created a perception on the ground that the inclusion of magic words was the acceptable bright-line test. Noble argued:

> Up until the late 1990s, the Federal Election Commission was using a broad standard, an electioneering message standard [the NRA example], when it was dealing with political organizations. Starting, again, as best as I can tell, with the Clinton and Dole audits [surrounding the controversy in the 1996 elections of party soft money used for issue advocacy], there were four commissioners finally who said, No, we're not going to do that anymore; we're going to use express advocacy. If you look a the history of this, this is about the time that these stealth PACs, what have been called stealth PACs, the 527s, really took off because I think some very bright lawyers . . . realized that there's now a way, if you're going to use the express advocacy standard, to do a lot of what would normally be considered campaign work through these PACs.[11]

This discussion and the results in Table 7.5 point to a dramatic shift in the mid-1990s in the regulatory context, toward more permissiveness in the arena of express advocacy. As such, we can surely tie the expansion of interest group electioneering to this change. But it also helps explain the puzzle of why there was a 20-year delay between the magic word standard created in *Buckley* and its widespread adoption by the interest group community. The analysis of AOs points to an FEC that was for a long time unwilling to permit interest groups too much latitude to influence the electoral process, but one that eventually became a willing ally in issue advocacy's explosion.

In total, then, the evidence points in part to a lenient FEC, but a leniency that is relatively recent. Another implication of the hypothesis, however, is that the FEC favors parties and incumbents. *Washington Post* columnist David Broder has described the FEC as an agency "whose six members are famously responsive to the members of Congress who put them in their jobs."[12] We have already seen that the FEC has historically viewed party-based electioneering requests more favorably than interest group ones, as shown in Figure 7.2, and that the FEC also favors candidate requests at rates even higher than parties. These are key findings.

As an additional test, I add some contextual information to the models reported in Table 7.5. I include variables for whether candidate petitioners are in competitive races and for whether they are incumbents or challengers. I do not provide the full results in a table, but they demonstrate that incumbents are significantly favored over challengers. The coefficient on incumbent petitioners is 0.632 and is statistically significant ($p<.05$), but the coefficient for challengers is 0.047 and is indistinguishable from 0.

It is possible, of course that a reason for the FEC's evaluative change relative to interest groups lies also in a change in the nature of the request. In 2002, for example, the FEC permitted the distribution of political advertisements through wireless telecommunications networks, and it did not require disclaimers on such communications (AO 2002-9). The FEC argued that the request was innovative, and in a concurring opinion two commissioners argued, "We believe it to be sound policy to allow political advertisers to explore the benefits of this evolving and exciting communications technology without being hamstrung by a rigid and sterile application of the Commission's disclaimer rules, which were promulgated years before this technology was ever developed." Indeed, between 1995 and 2003, 26 AOs involved fund-raising and electioneering activity using the Internet.

The most compelling piece of the story thus far, however, revolves around the relationship between the FEC and the courts. The decision in *Maine Right to Life Committee* and the subsequent overturning of the broader regulation on express advocacy seem to be important pieces of the puzzle. In the final section of the chapter, I explore the possibility that the FEC's relationship with the courts might also explain the observed interpretative shift.

The FEC v the Courts

In April 1996, in the aftermath of the overturned express advocacy regulation, election lawyer Jan Baran had this to say about the FEC's relationship with the courts on the question of issue advocacy: "The FEC has spent 20 years trying to stamp this out. They're like a dog that refuses to be house-trained and gets beaten over the nose with a rolled-up newspaper by the courts."[13]

The FEC suffered a particularly humiliating defeat in 1996 when the Fourth Circuit Court of Appeals ruled in *FEC v. Christian Action Network* that the Action Network did not expressly advocate the defeat of presidential candidate Bill Clinton in a 1992 television ad and two newspaper ads. The FEC argued that, despite the absence of magic words, the ads could only be interpreted as advocating against the election of Clinton, especially because of the ominous music and coloring in the television ad and the question posed to viewers about Clinton's stance on rights for homosexuals: "Is this your vision of a better America?" Judge Luttig of the Fourth Circuit, however, argued that the FEC standard for judging express advocacy was too broad and recommended that the Commission pay heed to "its string of losses in cases between the FEC and issue advocacy groups." The court went further and ordered the Commission to pay Christian Action Network's court costs.[14]

Smith and Hoersting (2002, p. 166)—Smith being a former Commissioner on the FEC—conclude in this regard: "Far from being a timid enforcement agency in the field of express advocacy, it is clear that the FEC has devoted substantial resources over a lengthy period of time to promoting an aggressive interpretation of the law that has been uniformly rejected by the courts, even if one includes the decision in Furgatch."

To investigate this relationship more systematically, I read and coded court case abstracts from 327 court cases. This list of cases comes from the Federal Election Commission, but it is by no means a complete universe of election law litigation. As compared to the universe of Advisory Opinions, the universe of court cases related to election law (even in a minor way) is almost impossible to track. The court cases included here deal almost exclusively with federal election law issues and with litigation involving the FEC. Recall from Chapter 2 that I listed some descriptive information about these cases in Figure 2.9.

This court case database is insightful. I coded each case on the identity of the defendants and plaintiffs, whether the case was heard in a district or appeals court and by the Supreme Court, what the focus of the case was (using the codes from Table 7.1), the final decision date (as well as the initial date the case was heard by the lowest court, although that information is missing in the majority of cases), and the outcome (plaintiff or defendant win, settlement, dismissal, or still pending). As noted before, the AO data relate to proposed activity by candidates, parties, and interest groups and whether such activity should be permitted; the court case data relate to reactions to past behavior and contentions surrounding whether such activity should be punished. In that sense, although I have said very little about the FEC's strength in responding to action taken, this analysis will provide some perspective on the ability of the FEC to defend its role as effective election law enforcer.

There have been a number of interesting court cases in the last 30 years, and by example, I quickly highlight two strange but significant ones. First, in 1990 the FEC filed suit in D.C. District Court against the National Right to Work Committee (NRWC) for allegedly hiring private detectives (spending $100,000) to infiltrate the AFL-CIO, the National Education Association (NEA), and the Mondale for President Committee to gather evidence that the AFL-CIO and the NEA were using general treasury money to support Mondale's candidacy. NRWC used the information from the detectives as evidence in an administrative complaint filed with the FEC. The NEA countered with its own complaint, claiming the $100,000 spent by NRWC should be considered illegal corporate contributions. The FEC agreed and filed suit against NRWC, but the D.C. District Court dismissed the suit because the statutory of limitations had run out. Second, in April 1997, the U.S. District Court for the Eastern District of Michigan granted an FEC request to dismiss a case filed by Detroit resident Alfonzo Jones. Jones claimed the FEC had acted improperly by not certifying him for public financing for the 1996 presidential campaign. As a result, Jones sought $249 *trillion* in damages.

Strange examples aside, I show in Table 7.6 the results of a statistical model predicting the probability of the FEC winning its case (that is, as plaintiff or defendant). I looked only at cases where the FEC was a party in the suit, and I excluded *Buckley* and *McConnell*. I included a variable for whether the FEC was the plaintiff and whether the case concerned issue advocacy, soft money, contributions, or the larger categories (used earlier) of fund-raising or electioneering. Because I coded each case on up to three purpose codes, these are not mutually exclusive categories. I also included two measures for whether the court was heard in appeals court or the Supreme Court. Finally, I include a post-1994 variable for any court cases decided in the last 10 years.

TABLE 7.6   PREDICTING AN FEC VICTORY IN COURT

Variable	
FEC is Plaintiff	−.543(.237)*
Issue Advocacy Case	−1.575(.414)**
Soft Money Case	−.733(.559)
Contributions Case	.359(.313)
Electioneering Case	−.138(.302)
Fund-Raising Case	−.068(.433)
Reached Appeals Court	−.191(.232)
Reached Supreme Court	−.604(.434)
Final Decision After 1994	−.294(.234)
N	223
Prob. chi2>0	0.000
log-likelihood	−85.424

**p<.01 *p<.05
All tests are two-tailed, and SEs are in parentheses. Dependent Variable is whether FEC won or lost the case. The model was estimated using probit.

As the results demonstrate, the FEC has a much higher probability of losing issue advocacy cases than other cases (just as Jan Baran noted), including ones relating to party soft money. The FEC also has a greater chance of losing as the plaintiff (implying that their record as the defendant is better), which is evidence that challenges to their enforcement decisions are often thrown out by the courts. All told, the results of this analysis are evidence that issue advocacy and interest group electioneering have historically faced a tough and unreceptive Federal Election Commission, but the courts have been a tough and unreceptive judge on that stance.

I argue that this dynamic was a major factor in delaying the expansion of these tactics across the political spectrum. Indeed, the evidence is in favor of the claim that issue advocacy tactics and related electioneering strategies emerge partly from changes in the regulatory environment.

Conclusion

In this chapter, I argued that the regulatory environment is a factor that determines in part the capacity of an interest group to act in electoral politics. Based on previous research, we know that external constraints on organizational behavior can vary in their intensity and that organizations can and do learn about how to navigate such constraints. I presented evidence that interest groups are not only embedded in a regulatory environment that has become more permissive over time, but that political actors (including interest groups) actively learn about election law as it changes.

There is one outstanding question. How is it that the regulatory environment became most permissive of soft money and issue advocacy tactics in the densest of regulatory environments? After all, these innovations occurred after years of regulatory decisions and court challenges. To allow these new tactics meant navigating all of this complex precedence. The answer lies in the powerful force of politics. Namely, politics compelled interest groups not only to expand their goals beyond mere candidate-picking but also to force open the regulatory environment through consistent pressures on its watchdogs.

All told, understanding the regulatory context completes the story begun with an investigation of the political context. Both the presence of political incentives and the reduction in tactical costs to using soft money, issue advocacy, and 527s worked in tandem to produce the "perfect storm" witnessed in the last 10 years. I complete the analysis in the next chapter by summarizing the results and by discussing the larger implications of the findings.

8 Conclusion

During a third season episode of NBC's *The West Wing* ("Gone Quiet," which originally aired on November 14, 2001), staffers of fictional president Josiah Bartlett convened to plan strategy for Bartlett's upcoming re-election campaign. When the conversation turned to campaign advertising, Toby (the president's communications director), Sam (Bartlett's speech writer), Bruno (the campaign manager), and Connie (Bruno's assistant) had the following exchange[1]:

> TOBY: Look, we can't spend soft money on a primary ad anyway, so . . .
>
> SAM: No, he's passing the magic words test.
>
> TOBY: What magic words test?
>
> SAM: The US Supreme Court, *Buckley v. Valeo*. The court created a loophole by ruling [that hard money] only applies to communications that in express terms advocate the election or defeat of a clearly-identified candidate for federal office.
>
> BRUNO: You don't put "vote Bartlett" in the ad, you can pay for it with unmarked bills from a bank heist if you want to.
>
> CONNIE: And we should know. There's also endnote 52, where the Court said campaign-finance laws only apply to com-

munications with the terms "vote for," "elect," "support," "cast your ballot for," "Smith for Congress," "vote against," "defeat," "reject," and that's it. [Pause] I'm savant-like.

TOBY: If it doesn't use those specific words . . .

BRUNO: It is an issue ad.

CONNIE: You know what they say about money and politics.

SAM: No.

CONNIE: It's like water on pavement.

SAM: Why is it like water on pavement?

CONNIE: That's a good . . .

BRUNO: It finds every crack and crevice.

SAM: The standard ought to be, does the ad try to influence the outcome of the election? If so, you can't use soft money, period.

BRUNO: Well, zippity-do-dah, Sam.

SAM: Excuse me?

BRUNO: That isn't what the standard is. And I think we should run in the same election as everybody else.

In Chapter 1, I posed a puzzle. Given that magic words and soft money were concepts created in the late 1970s, why did most interest groups and political parties wait until 1995 and 1996 to use issue advocacy campaigns in such high numbers, eventually warranting the passage of the most significant campaign finance reform in a generation? One might even see the puzzle in the fictional exchange above. Why do staffers for a sitting president—already veterans of one presidential campaign—need a tutorial in election law? Indeed, separating fact from fiction in this case is difficult; Dick Morris's account of Clinton's re-election efforts tells a tale not unlike the exchange above (Morris 1997).

In the last seven chapters, I have offered evidence that helps answer the puzzle. In this conclusion, I first review the major findings and follow with some speculation on the larger implications of this research. I conclude by offering some predictions about campaign finance in the coming years.

What Do We Know Now?

In Chapter 3, I asserted the following model:

$$T = f\ (G,C,e)$$

Interest group tactical choices (T) are a function of a group's goal (G) weighted by its capacity to act (C). I argued that understanding tactical changes implies understanding goal changes or capacity changes or both. As such, I focused on two factors that might change interest group goals—the ideological and political contexts that surround elections—and two factors that might change tactical capacity—the regulatory and resource contexts.

Let me briefly summarize the empirical results. In Chapter 4, I demonstrated that PACs respond to the political contexts that surround House and Senate elections. PACs that prefer the ideological status quo invest more resources in safe seat candidates, giving a smaller contribution to competitive candidates when they do give. PACs with extreme preference points direct resources to candidates most likely to win and give smaller average contributions to candidates who have virtually no chance of losing. At the same time, PACs aligned with a political party direct resources in ways to maximize members from that party, especially in years when the balance of power is tight. Indeed, the results are convincing that some PACs are mobilized by big-deal issues such as control of the chamber.

In Chapter 5, we learned that soft money—already a partisan beast—became more partisan as soft money became more prevalent. Cross-partisan support from labor groups was nearly nonexistent throughout the life of soft money, but labor unions increased their support of Democrats dramatically. Cross-partisan support declined heavily for Republican corporate allies, so that by 2002 a pragmatic bipartisan contribution strategy became the province of organized interests less disposed to heavily favor one party. I also connected soft money giving to competitive federal campaigns, showing that states with competitive presidential or Senate races contributed more and contributed closer to Election Day than states with no statewide competitive federal race. In addition, we saw evidence of "water finding the cracks," in that active hard money PACs were also active soft money donors.

In Chapter 6, I switched to an analysis of political advertisements and expenditures by 527s. We saw first that groups airing political ads almost never do so for candidates of both parties, making this form of electioneering the most partisan of the tactics tracked in this analysis. Second, interest groups direct almost all of their advertising dollars to candidates in competitive races, except for House races in 2004 (when the Republicans held a firm control on the chamber). In addition, we saw that large donors to partisan 527s were also former party soft money donors, further evidence that interest groups continue to seek new ways of influencing electoral politics when old ways are closed off.

Finally, in Chapter 7, I offered evidence that the regulatory environment is a factor that determines in part the capacity of an interest group to act in electoral politics. Based on previous research, we know that external constraints on organizational behavior can vary in their intensity, and organizations can and do learn about how to navigate such constraints. I presented evidence that interest groups are not only embedded in a regulatory environment that has become more permissive over time, but that political actors (including interest groups) actively learn about election law as it changes.

These results, taken together, point more generally to the importance of the political and regulatory context in mobilizing interest group electioneering. Responses and reactions to the ideological and partisan contexts that surround elections compel interest groups to adopt replacement or access tactics. This influence is, of course, mediated by the group's capacity to support different tactics, which is itself a function of existing interpretations of election law.

Madisonian Majoritarianism?

These results also allow us to draw larger conclusions about the state of American elections. For example, consider the consequences of aggressive interest group electioneering on representation in American politics. There is a large literature in political science that investigates whether campaigns can persuade voters to vote for particular candidates, and while there is empirical evidence that persuasion can happen, it is not a foregone conclusion (see Holbrook 1996, for example). Most might presume that Democratic and Republican efforts balance out, especially in competitive races. Thus, interest group participation

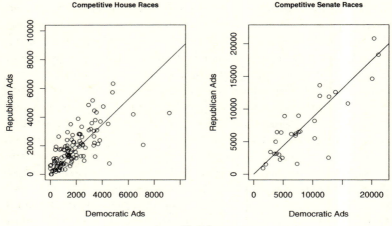

Fig 8.1

Political Ads in Competitive House and Senate Races, 2000–2004. Line is 45-degree line. Both axes include the total number of Democratic or Republican ads in the race (candidates, parties, and interest group allies). Competitiveness is defined as any race CQ listed as "too-close-to-call" or "leaning." (*Source:* Courtesy of Wisconsin Advertising Project.)

in campaigns becomes a costly effort to keep up with the other side, but with no real consequences for election outcomes.

But impacts on outcomes become more likely when Democratic and Republican efforts do not cancel out, and when one side has an advantage in the flow of information (Zaller 1996). Figure 8.1 is relevant to this point. I show a scatterplot of the number of pro-Republican or pro-Democratic advertisements in "leaning" and "too-close-to-call" House and Senate races between 2000 and 2004. As we can see, there are a number of races above and below the 45-degree line. In these races, the Republican or the Democrat has the advertising advantage; this is a highly valuable asset in races where every vote counts. Thus, electioneering does not always balance or cancel out, and to the extent that voters are influenced by campaign messages, in these races advertising advantages might have determined the outcome.

If so, it is at least possible that the outcome diverged from the "true" desires of the constituency. Put differently, it might be the case that the political advertising advantage (or another form of electioneering) convinced a handful of citizens to vote in ways they might not have normally. Kahn and Kenney (2004), for example, present evidence that 75 to 80 percent of advertisements are judged to contain some factual inaccuracies. If enough viewers see enough television or radio ads, or receive enough telephone calls or pro-candidate mail, it is possible that they might be temporarily disposed to vote for a candidate; and that persuasion might be achieved on the basis of a twisted form of facts. This is not to say that the content of all campaigns is untruthful—just that it is possible in the rough and tumble world of a competitive campaign to play loose with the facts for electoral advantage. Interest groups, in mobilizing aggressively in elections, can help their preferred candidate try to carve out such a campaign advantage.

This is really only consequential, however, in a political context highly polarized and balanced, such as the political environment of the late 1990s and early 2000s. A few tipped races in this context can have large consequences for what policies are made and what constituencies get represented. Imagine a case where the National Rifle Association or the Sierra Club mobilizes in only a handful of competitive races and pumps enough money into those races (either through contributions or independent spending) to give their preferred candidates an edge. Should those candidates win, and give their party a majority in the House or Senate, the NRA or Sierra Club would be partly responsible. And should the resulting Congress implement important gun or environmental legislation, the NRA or Sierra Club would and could rightly take some credit.

What are we to say then about a political environment in which the NRA's or Sierra Club's participation in a few races (and whose messages are seen by only a fraction of the 100 million voting citizens in America) can help determine the future of gun legislation or environmental policy? Of course, isolating the effects of any one group's participation might be empirically impossible, but the likelihood of their being such an effect is greater today than it was 20 years ago.

Indeed, this points to a possibility where the cacophony of interest group voices—a reflection of the pluralism James Madison supported—works in tandem with organized and strong party organizations, both with the goal of winning majorities. Madison and the Framers, in their defense of the Constitution, argued that more voices would dilute influence, that the large nation would deflect groups from amassing significant power. Might not interest group participation in only a handful of races, but for majoritarian ends, puzzle the Framers? Are interest groups playing minoritarian politics (hoping to tip only a few races with small advertising and expenditure advantages) for majoritarian gain (hoping to elect a party over a candidate)?

In 2006, two influential liberal bloggers proposed an electoral agenda for progressives that seemed to reflect this majoritarian aim. Armstrong and Zuniga (2006, p. 66) argued that "combining [electoral] efforts works better than working in each group's silo. Working to make sure Democrats win control is more important than sabotaging the chances of any candidate that doesn't check off every box on the liberal laundry list."

Their proposal was in response to a controversy in early 2006 over the failure of two pro-choice groups (NARAL Pro-Choice America and the National Organization for Women) to endorse Senate Democrat candidate Jim Langevin in Rhode Island because he was pro-life. Instead, NARAL endorsed incumbent Republican Lincoln Chafee because his record on abortion issues seemed more palatable to the group. Progressives were furious over the endorsement because the Rhode Island Senate seat was crucial to the Democrats' chances at regaining the majority in the Senate. Armstrong and Zuniga (2006, p. 42) made this appeal: "Who is in a better position to protect [abortion rights]—a lone pro-choice Republican or two within a governing party hell-bent on destroying those rights, or a lone antiabortion Democrat or two in a governing party determined to protect those rights?" Both bloggers made an impassioned appeal to liberal progressives to support the Democratic agenda in 2006 (and all competitive Democratic candidates) in the attempt to win control of Congress.

These implications run counter to Clemens' (1997) investigation of interest groups in the early 20th century. She argued that interest groups came to recognize that the organizing power of the political party acted as a constraint to changes in the political system. That is, groups such as farmers and laborers became convinced that so long as two-party politics endured, independent group concerns would never be adequately addressed. To compensate, these groups altered their tactics and chose to challenge the party process and to work to dismantle the two-party system. In my analysis, I argue that interest groups altered their tactics and chose to *reinforce* the party process and the two-party system. In both the historical and contemporary case, however, interest groups pursued (and pursue) the tactics that they perceive as having the highest pay-off. That doing so can mean working to undermining the party system in one time period while working to bolster it in another is a testimony to interest groups' ability to adapt.

There are also important normative issues to consider. First, there may be a trade-off for those reformers who want to remove money from electoral politics. As I have shown, it is political parity between the Democrats and Republicans that motivated the expansion of interest group electioneering. Any attempt to constrain the resource context for interest groups may stem the flow of money in elections for a time, but as interest groups react to a polarized political context, they will mobilize to expand their resource base. Indeed, the speedy explosion of 527s in the 2004 elections stands in contrast to the slow emergence of issue advocacy. If the latter development is curious because it took so long, the former is intriguing because it happened so fast. But both changes are explained by the same mechanism: water will find the cracks when there is a political motivation to find them.

Thus, on the one hand, many have serious concerns about the flow of money into the political process, especially when election outcomes significantly determine the foundation of power in Washington. Here's the trade-off, though. Party theorists are thrilled to see a competitive political process where parties are polarized and differences matter. Although the continued decline in the number of competitive House elections seems to counter the argument that elections are consequential, real differences between Republican and Democratic agendas are important when each party has the chance of winning control.

What do we value more, however? A competitive partisan context where interest groups continue to spend vast sums on elections (to the dismay of reform advocates), or an electoral process where groups play a more limited role but where the outcome is pretty much known (to the dismay of many democratic theorists)? Indeed, I am not sure we can escape such a trade-off.

Consider this question also: is interest group money spent on electioneering better for democracy than money spent on lobbying? Which should we prefer, independent and uncoordinated interest group electioneering that directly touches the voter, or less visible interest group lobbying on K Street obtained in part through hard and soft money contributions? In a 2004 letter to the FEC (accessed from www.fec .gov), the National Voting Rights Institute and the Fannie Lou Hamer Project argued,

> Donors who previously made $100,000 contributions to the RNC or DNC in order to purchase access to and influence with elected officials will make the same donations to a 527 organization established to elect or defeat particular candidates. Candidates will understand the source of the largesse and will be grateful for the assistance. Persons able to make such large donations will have far more influence and access than ordinary citizens who cannot afford to participate through their checkbooks. The goal of a truly participatory democracy will be further subverted.

I have shown evidence to reinforce their first point (about party money directed into 527 accounts), but their normative argument remains open to debate. The bulk of empirical evidence suggests that PAC money almost never buys votes on the House and Senate floor, but it does buy access to policymakers at key moments of policymaking (Ansolabehere, de Figueiredo and Snyder 2003, Smith 1995). And we can be pretty sure that party soft money bought even more access than $5,000 hard money contributions. But if indirect partisan support through 527s also buys policymaking access, might this be more dangerous? For example, what happens when corporations or other groups give millions to a 527 active in competitive Senate races? If the preferred candidates win, how would we feel about the victorious candidates granting access to those groups that helped fund negative attack ads through 527s?

Democracy works best with transparency and when it is easy for voters to see the process in action. With 527s acting as "shadow parties," often looking for and exploiting loopholes in election law, the political process loses some transparency. It becomes harder to see who the players are and to track the source of the money. Indeed, if reform was intended to minimize influence from checkbooks, BCRA may have failed. With indirect access through 527s, it may have even exacerbated the problem.

On the other hand, I may be overstating the case. Much of the debate now about 527s and issue advocacy revolves around the regulation of television ads, not access during congressional sessions. In that regard, the struggle over which groups can fund soft money issue ads up until Election Day might not be so worrisome. After all, this struggle concerns who is funding the ads voters are seeing on television or hearing on the radio. But when interest groups try to convince voters to vote for certain candidates, voters keep the power. If concerned citizens are worried about soft money ads and who funds them, voters will discount the messages. American voters are not stupid, and if they do not like certain political products (like obvious electioneering disguised as issue advocacy), we might expect them to vote with their remote controls and turn the channel. And if voters care not about issue ads and soft money (which seems to be the case, since respondents in public opinion polls almost never list campaign finance as a major problem in American politics), then all of the hand-wringing over finance reform may be misplaced energy.

Not everyone is convinced, however. Consider an additional exchange from the same West Wing episode:

BRUNO: Instead of "Jeb Bartlett's fighting to rebuild crumbling schools," we'll make it "We're fighting to rebuild crumbling schools."

CONNIE: And we've got a picture of the President on the screen.

SAM: Yeah.

BRUNO: And we change "Vote Bartlet for America" to, uh, "Paid for by Democrats for America."

SAM: You've changed five words.

CONNIE: Magic words.

SAM: They're not magic.

CONNIE: It's an illusion.

SAM: It's a scam.

CONNIE: Yeah. [Enter TOBY]

TOBY: Where are we?

SAM: Bruno and Connie have managed to fight their way out of the straitjacket of our campaign finance laws.

Sam's frustration—conceivably, he would have been fine with keeping the five magic words and funding the ad with hard money—exemplifies that felt by many reform advocates. To them, issue advocacy and soft money are loopholes that undermine the spirit of the law, and this alone is enough to warrant additional constraints on campaign finance. At the end of the day, reformers are worried about the impact of money in ways we cannot see and in ways that are impossible to track. They would like a political system where candidates do not need large sums to fund campaigns, where competition between candidates is great, and where interest groups have only a limited impact on political outcomes. Such a goal may be impossible to obtain, however, even if it is a worthy pursuit.

Lessons From the 2006 Elections

What's next? How will interest groups respond in the coming years? The answer lies in the nature of the partisan and regulatory environments. The partisan political context leading up to the 2006 mid-term elections suggested that control of Congress was very much in play; the Democrats needed 15 seats in the House and 6 in the Senate. Indeed, the Democrats took joint control of the House and Senate for the first time since 1994.

In March 2006, seven months before the election, an editorial at *The Washington Post* had this to say about the political environment[2]:

If you're a Democrat, life is good right now. The Republicans are mired in Iraq and domestic political difficulties. The White House is rearranging the deck chairs. For now, Democrats can sit back and watch the GOP self-destruct: "They're on fire," says one party strategist. "Don't say anything. Let them destroy themselves." The experience of being out of power and being the targets of Karl Rove's relentless attacks has made the Democrats a tougher and more cynical party. They think more about winning than about governing. Some strategists even see a virtue in the party's lack of a clear agenda or leader—since it denies the Republicans easy targets. This strategy may not serve the country in the long run, but for angry Democrats this year, there is only the short run—taking back control of Congress in the midterms and the White House in 2008.

That sentiment persisted into the fall campaign. In its October assessment of House and Senate races, *Congressional Quarterly* ranked 18 House seats as too-close-to-call and predicted that 4 Senate Republican incumbents were likely to lose, with 3 other races as toss-ups. The Democrats ended up with the necessary 6 seats in the Senate and won 30 seats in the House.

In this sense, the partisan environment seemed to be ripe for aggressive interest group electioneering. A review of interest group behavior in the campaign seems to bear out this prediction. In late October, for example, the *New York Times* reported that Democrats were getting donations from corporate PACs in higher amounts than previous cycles[3]:

> The shift in political giving, for the first 18 days of October, has not been this pronounced in the final stages of a campaign since 1994, when Republicans swept control of the House for the first time in four decades. Though Democratic control of either chamber of Congress is far from certain, the prospect of a power shift is leading interest groups to begin rethinking well-established relationships, with business lobbyists going as far as finding potential Democratic allies in the freshman class—even if they are still trying to defeat them on the campaign trail—and preparing to extend an olive branch the morning after the election.

This pattern is consistent with the findings from Chapter 4, in which PACs acted strategically with hard money contributions by being sensitive to the partisan context. With control of Congress hanging in the balance, many PACs chose to hedge their bets by shifting at least some support to the opposing party.

The 527s were also very active in 2006. Even without a presidential campaign to motivate spending, the Center for Responsive Politics reports that 527s spent more than $405 million in the 2006 elections. If you discount some partisan 527s—such as the Republican Governors

Association—the total is still more than $200 million. And according to a breakdown of those expenditures, at least $33 million went to advertising and nearly $30 million was spent on contributions to other interest groups or to candidates. Furthermore, based on FEC reports, more than two dozen 527s reported electioneering communications in the final 60 days of the general election or in the final 30 days of a primary. Expenditures for these ads totaled almost $21 million, including $6 million from the group, Economic Freedom Fund, and nearly $4 million from Americans for Honesty on Issues. Pete Maysmith at the reform group Common Cause noted that this activity in 2006 makes clear that 527s have "become the new way to do business in politics."[4]

At the same time, we should not discount the regulatory context surrounding the 2006 elections. No doubt the aggressive spending by 527s in 2006 was partly the consequence of the partisan context, but by the fall of 2006, the FEC appeared to endorse exemptions for many 527s, leaving their activity relatively unregulated. For example, as discussed in Chapter 2, the ability of 527s to fund electioneering communications with unregulated funds was defended by these groups under the MCFL exemption, for which a nonprofit group can qualify if the primary purpose of the organization is issue advocacy and if funds used to pay for electioneering ads come only from individuals. The FEC has refused to offer a clear test of what an MCFL group is—in other words, what constitutes too much candidate advocacy. It maintains that it can adequately judge each group on a case-by-case basis, which critics argue is too slow and too porous a standard. The commission even deadlocked in August 2006 on a regulation change offered by Commissioner Hans von Spakovsky that would have permitted electioneering communications from corporations and labor unions.

Even fines levied in late 2006 against MoveOn.org and the Swift Boat Veterans for Truth for actions in the 2004 elections met with little enthusiasm from those advocating aggressive campaign finance reform. The *New York Times* offered a stinging editorial rebuke of the Commission in December 2006[5]:

> Two years too late, the Federal Election Commission has gotten around to slapping token fines on a few notorious abusers of the campaign law's ban on unregulated mudslinging money.

That guarantees we will see a lot more mud being slung in 2008. The commission—ever the enabler, rarely the watchdog, of big-money politics— declined in the 2004 campaign to rein in the unlimited financing of such obviously partisan efforts as the Republicans' Swift Boat attack ads against Senator John Kerry and the Democrats' MoveOn.org assaults on President Bush. Shadowy party operatives, called 527 groups under a section of the tax code, sold the commission a bill of goods that they were mere issue advocates, not hard-edged activists crying out to be covered by the law's limits on donations.

This context was also playing out in federal court. In the summer of 2007, the Supreme Court ruled (in *FEC v. Wisconsin Right to Life*) that three ads aired in Wisconsin by the Wisconsin Right to Life group in 2004 were not electioneering communications but genuine issue speech. This was important because the ads mentioned Senator *and candidate* Russell Feingold, and BCRA had created the candidate mention bright-line test for electioneering communications. The Court argued that some exemptions should be allowed for unions, corporations, and 527s if the ad itself, despite mentioning or picturing a federal candidate, can be judged genuine issue advocacy. Although the Court judged only that the exemption can be applied based on the content of the ad itself (and not the context during which the ad aired), it opened a door for the potential weakening of the 30-day and 60-day provisions of BCRA. In the long run, clever ads from unions and corporations could completely decimate the intentions of BCRA to force election-related ads to be funded with hard money.

With such developments, the future of campaign finance regulations is uncertain. There are several possible futures. If the FEC is aggressive in regulation (and Congress acts with new legislation) that clamps down on 527s, we might see interest groups turn en masse to voter mobilization and grassroots activity. The decade of the political ad would come to a close. I doubt we will see this, however. Despite many groups choosing the ground war over the air war, the chance to reach tens of thousands simultaneously through television and radio is too good to forgo. If 527s are forced to become hard money PACs, I expect to see what we saw with parties in 2004—more hard money. Even MoveOn.org used its substantial fund-raising prowess in 2004 to raise hard and soft money. The Internet should only make being a PAC that much easier.

If, on the other hand, the FEC takes a middle ground and permits 527s to flourish, IRS disclosure data might attach a stigma to such activity. If so, 501c nonprofits (for which there is no disclosure) might become the future vehicle for issue advocacy. Again, however, evidence that disclosure stems participation seems mixed. The FEC has had disclosure for 30 years, and millions of Americans continue to contribute millions of dollars. While advocacy through 501c groups might seem attractive, the gorilla in the room is the IRS, which retains the power to revoke nonprofit status for these groups should their activity be deemed too partisan. Losing their nonprofit tax-exempt status is a huge cost for these groups. Indeed, the regulatory context on the boundaries of issue advocacy through 501c groups would have to be significantly clarified.

Having said that, in the next few years the fault line of campaign finance regulation will be on two fronts: the boundary between political and nonpolitical organizations and the standards for which candidate-mention ads are exempt from the electioneering communication rules. If we regulate activity too much, we come close to unreasonable restrictions on free speech. It is one thing to say that the line between nonmagic word issue advocacy and express advocacy is "a line in the sand drawn on a windy day," but it is quite another thing to mandate that Planned Parenthood fund pro-choice citizen education or the NRA fund ads about gun safety with hard money. How about forcing groups that sponsor public service announcements about drunk driving or churches that air ads about their congregation to fund this activity with hard dollars? Both are possible if we define anything even remotely political and said close to an election as implicit candidate advocacy.

In late 2006, one apparent unreasonable consequence concerned NASCAR driver Kirk Shelmerdine. On December 26, 2006, the FEC sent Shelmerdine a "letter of admonishment" (with no attached fines or penalties) for refusing to report a Bush/Cheney bumper-sticker he put on the back of his race car during the summer and fall of 2004. The FEC found reason to believe that the decal was an unreported independent expenditure that should have been reported to the FEC and may have been an illegal in-kind contribution to the Bush campaign. (Because Shelmerdine's car is sponsored by his racing company, the decal is associated with the corporation and not Shelmerdine as a driver.) The two-year investigation into the legality of a bumper sticker seems silly and is precisely the sort of over-enforcement that many worry about.

There are also challenging campaign finance questions concerning Internet activity. At present the FEC has chosen to leave much Internet activity unregulated. New regulations in this area became effective in May 2006 and only related to Internet ads placed on Web sites for a fee. But consider these remarks from former FEC Commissioner Bradley Smith[6]:

> The real question is: Would a link to a candidate's page be a problem? If someone sets up a home page and links to their favorite politician, is that a contribution? This is a big deal, if someone has already contributed the legal maximum, or if they're at the disclosure threshold and additional expenditures have to be disclosed under federal law.
>
> Certainly a lot of bloggers are very much out front. Do we give bloggers the press exemption? If we don't give bloggers the press exemption, we have the question of, do we extend this to online-only journals like CNET?

It is certainly possible that, as political activity on the Internet expands, future regulatory changes could impede this behavior, much to the dismay of bloggers, First Amendment activists, and regular Web surfers.

On the other hand, with a vigorous defense of speech rights close to Election Day comes the possibility for a complete dismantling of election/issue advocacy distinctions. The Supreme Court has maintained for more than a generation that regulations concerning election advocacy are acceptable if they help limit the "appearance of corruption." In that sense, very few people want the complete elimination of campaign finance restrictions. But once you defend at least some regulations on election-related speech, it becomes next to impossible to define a standard that does not potentially touch genuine issue-related speech. The candidate-mention test was designed to be that standard, but it appears open to considerable criticism. How do we manage that problem then? How do we protect issue speech if no one can agree on a definition? This problem approaches becoming an existential concern.

Indeed, much work remains to be done on clarifying and understanding the regulatory context. As such, interest groups will surely spend time learning the dimensions of the law in years to come, and part of how they act will depend on the perspectives of the regulators.

Ultimately, however, the future depends on the partisan context in Washington. So long as Washington remains polarized and each party sees majority status within reach, many interest groups will be motivated to influence the process. With an open White House in 2008 (and two contentious presidential elections still ringing in everyone's ears) and slim Democratic majorities in both houses of Congress, I expect many groups to continue their aggressive electioneering efforts. Indeed, the constraining and motivating forces of the regulatory and political context will remain relevant in years to come. As such, we can be certain there will be many more interest group choices to be made and endless changes to be studied.

Appendix: PAC Ideology Measure

Using a methodology developed by Franklin (n.d.), I leverage PAC contributions to individual federal candidates as information in estimating a PAC's liberal-conservative ideology. I created a large dataset that matches each PAC in my sample with each incumbent member of the House between 1983 and 2000. The dependent variable was whether the PAC gave to the candidate (or, in a different estimation, how much the PAC gave to the candidate). By controlling for common predictors of PAC contributions (including most importantly the ideology of the incumbent), I use the coefficient estimate on candidate ideology to estimate PAC ideology. Below, I list first the data for this estimation. Second, I describe the statistics behind the estimation. I conclude by outlining the data structure and the specific variables used.

Datasets

Federal Election Commission Data: Accessed Web site (www.fec.gov) on various dates

- Committee Master file (separate file for each election cycle, 1984–2002)—Contains information on each registered PAC and party
- Candidate Master file (separate file for each cycle, 1984–2002)—Contains information on every federal candidate
- PAC contribution file (separate file for each cycle, 1984–2002)—Records all contributions from PACs to candidates and parties

- Individual contribution file (separate file for each cycle, 1984–2002)—Records each individual contribution above $200 to each PAC, candidate, and party.

Congressional Committee data: Two files accessed from Charles Stewart's Web site on 11/6/03 (http://web.mit.edu/17.251/www/data_page.html)

- Garrison Nelson, Committees in the U.S. Congress, 1947–1992
- Charles Stewart III and Jonathan Woon. Congressional Committee Assignments, 103rd to 105th Congresses, 1993–1998

District data: Accessed from Scott Adler Web site on 11/6/03 (http://socsci .colorado.edu/~esadler/districtdatawebsite/CongressionalDistrictDatasetweb page.htm

- Adler, E. Scott. "Congressional District Data File, [98th Congress–105th Congress]." University of Colorado, Boulder, CO

DW-NOMINATE data: Accessed from Keith Poole's Web site on various dates (http://voteview.com)

Competitiveness data from October issues (in election years) of *Congressional Quarterly*

A Simple Model of PAC Donations to House Incumbents

$$\Pr(Y_{ij}=1) = f(X_j{}^{\circ}\beta + \gamma^{\circ}(V_j - \theta)^2)$$

- Y_{ij} is a dichotomous variable, equal to one if PAC$_i$ gave to Member$_j$. I also estimate this as a tobit model, where the dependent variable is the amount contributed by the PAC to the candidate (with no contribution coded as $0).
- X_j are Member-specific or contextual predictors (party, committee assignment, district characteristics, and seniority, for example).
- V_j is the Member's ideology.
- θ is the PAC ideal point.

I chose this functional form to represent a quadratic loss in the ideological distance between the Member and the PAC. Of course, we do not know θ; this is what we want to estimate. But in running the model separately for each PAC, this becomes a constant. When expanding and re-parameterizing the above equation, we get:

$$\Pr(Y_{ij}=1) = \lambda(X_j{}^{\circ}\beta + \gamma^{\circ}(V_j - \theta)^2)$$
$$\Pr(Y_{ij}=1) = \lambda(X_j{}^{\circ}\beta + V_j{}^{\circ}(-2\gamma\theta) + (V_j)^{2\circ}\gamma + \gamma\theta^2)$$

$\gamma\theta^2$ in this form is a constant, meaning it biases the intercept but not the coefficient estimates. I then run a model using member-specific and contextual predictors, incumbent ideology, and incumbent ideology squared. The coefficient on incumbent ideology is now equal to

$$(-2\gamma\theta)$$

Since I estimate the coefficient on ideology-squared, γ, directly,

$$\theta = (-2\gamma\theta)/-2\gamma$$

The Data Structure

The unit of analysis in the estimation is a PAC/Incumbent dyad, where I include each House incumbent running for re-election and each PAC included in the top 500 in each election cycle. This matching produces almost two million cases. To each dyad, I first appended information about the incumbent.

- DW-NOMINATE and NOMINATE-squared (from Poole data)
- Party; also, whether the Member was in the majority party (binary variable) (from FEC)
- Chamber seniority, measured as the number of terms served (from Charles Stewart data)
- Whether the member was in her first term (binary variable) (from Charles Stewart data)

I then included demographic data about the district (from Adler data):

- Separate variables for the number of African Americans in the district; the number of blue-collar workers in the district; the number of construction workers in the district; the number of farmers; the number of federal employees; the number of foreign-born residents; and the number of citizens employed in finance, insurance, and real estate industry
- A binary variable for whether the district contains one of country's 50 largest cities
- The median income of district
- The percent unionized workers in the state

I then added contextual data:

- The number of contributions the PAC received from individuals in that MC's state (from FEC data)

- Competitiveness of race (1=safe; 2=favored or leaning; 3=competitive) (from *CQ* data)
- To account for any large-scale contribution changes after the Republican gains in 1994 (i.e., if some PACs became more likely to support the GOP), I included a post-1994 binary variable in the models.

Finally, I added two dependent variables (from FEC data):

- Whether the PAC gave to candidate or not
- How much the PAC gave to the candidate (no contributions are coded as $0)

I then estimated two models (for each PAC) predicting whether the PAC contributed (logit) and how much the PAC contributed (tobit). As described in the chapter, I began with a sample of 1,061 PACs. I estimated ideology scores for only 927 PACs. The reduction from 1,061 to 927 resulted from some PACs giving very little to incumbent House members, which was the activity used to create the ideology scores; in these cases, there was too little information to leverage an ideology. In general, I dropped PACs (from the list of 1,061) that did not give to at least ten incumbent members of the House in any single election cycle. These PACs, although in the top 500 for total expenditures, spent the balance of their money on House challengers, presidential candidates, and in Senate races. The correlation between the logit and tobit estimates of PAC ideology was .81, and I use the estimates from the logit estimation for the analysis in Chapter 4.

Notes

Chapter 1: The Puzzle of Interest Group Electioneering

1. "Campaign Briefing," Compiled by B. Drummond Ayres Jr., *New York Times*, 10/11/2000, p. A28.

2. "Bush Basks in Southern Hospitality; Gore Battles for Vote-Rich Florida as Rest of Region Leans Toward Republican," by Ken Foskett, *Atlanta Journal-Constitution*, 10/11/2000, p. A1.

3. The data reported thus far come from reports filed with the Federal Election Commission.

4. "A Growing Addiction," Editorial, *Washington Post*, 9/4/2001, p. A18.

5. Data on soft money contributions to parties go back only to 1991, when the FEC mandated that parties report receipts to their nonfederal accounts (I expand on this in Chapter 2). While there are some data archives of political advertisements over time—namely, at the University of Oklahoma—data on the frequency of aired political advertisements go back, at the earliest, to the 1996 elections.

6. In 1974, Congress passed major campaign finance changes in the form of amendments to the tamer Federal Election Campaign Act of 1971 (FECA). I expand on this in Chapter 2.

7. This is based on Poole and Rosenthal's DW-NOMINATE scores, which places Members of Congress on a liberal-conservative dimension. The scores generally range from −1 to 1, with −1 being the extreme liberal position in the House and Senate and 1 being the extreme conservative position. According to their scaling, Jeffords' ideology as a Republican (from January 2001 to June

2001) was fairly moderate, at −0.007. The median voter in the Senate was − 0.0315. After becoming an independent, Jeffords moved to the left in the remaining 18 months of the 107th Congress, with a NOMINATE of −0.385. The median voter, however, remained fairly stable and moderate, at −0.0715. Scores can be downloaded at http://www.voteview.com.

8. "Change in Parties Would Transform Powerful Panels," by Philip Shenon, *New York Times*, 5/24/2001, p. A26.

9. "Adopting Union Tactics, Firms Dive More Deeply Into Politics," by Jonathan Weisman, *Washington Post*, 10/24/2002, p. A8.

10. Comments from the union's Web site (http://www.ble.org/) accessed on February 10, 2005. I have archived any Web pages with cited quotes.

11. http://www.nea.org, accessed on February 10, 2005.

12. Emphasis in original; http://www.clubforgrowth.org/, accessed on February 10, 2005.

13. "DeLay PAC Took Enron Funds; Records Show $50,000 Used to Set up Texas Redistricting Panel," by R.G. Ratcliffe, *Houston Chronicle*, 7/14/2004, p. A3.

14. "Debate Heated on Campaign Finance," by Thomas Edsall and Juliet Eilperin, *Washington Post*, 2/12/2002, p. A4.

15. In Franz (n.d.), I replicate CRP's soft money data collection, testing for whether scholars willing to rely on CRP's coding scheme are justified in using their data. For example, CRP includes soft money contributions from certain individuals (CEOs and spouses and children of CEOs) in the total for different groups. This approach artificially increases soft money totals for these groups. I use the base FEC data in this project, eliminating that concern.

16. There is an extensive literature that (in contrast to my analysis) examines only lobbying behavior (Milbrath 1965, Schlozman and Tierney 1986). Important questions in this literature include whether interest groups focus predominantly on legislative friends, urging their participation in key legislation (Bauer, de Sola Pool and Dexter 1964, Gormley 1998, Kingdon 1989) or whether they focus on legislative enemies, urging them to change their minds on significant issues (Austen-Smith and Wright 1994). Others study the determinants of interest group coalitions on policy debates (Hojnacki 1997).

17. "Republicans Track Politics of Lobbyists," *New York Times*, 6/10/2002, p. A18.

18. In most studies of interest group electoral politics, the universe is well defined. If studying the allocation of PAC money, for example, the universe is all PACs in the FEC committee file or some subsection therein (i.e., labor PACs; top 500 PACs; nonconnected PACs). If studying the formation of PACs, scholars often limit the universe to Fortune 500 companies (Boies 1989) or large firms (Hart 2001). The justification in these defined universes is more a matter of convenience than theory. And while Fortune 500 companies may be important in their own right, none of these studies consider whether their findings apply to organizations outside their defined universe. Some have

used lists (*Washington Representatives*, for example) of active interest groups from which to draw a sample, to which campaign activity (if there is any) is then appended (Apollonio and La Raja 2004). In this sense, the defined universe becomes all interest groups active in federal politics, and the question is why some groups choose electoral tactics of a certain type and why others do not. What this gains in theory (relative to the more restrictive universe), it loses in practicality; furthermore, this list is also a biased universe, in that it is impossible to list every active interest group. Finally, in studies of interest group lobbying tactics, the universe is usually as hard or harder to operationalize. Scholars often use the list of *Washington Representatives*, lobbying disclosure forms (Heaney 2003), and/or media coverage of groups testifying before Congress or active at the grassroots (Goldstein 1999).

Chapter 2: Election Law and Electoral Politics Between FECA and BCRA

1. "'Independent Expenditures' Magnify PAC Power; Interest Groups Pour Large Sums Into TV Ads in Support of Candidates," by Charles R. Babcock, *Washington Post*, 11/4/1988, p. A18.

2. These limits refer to multi-candidate PACs, a classification for any PAC that receives contributions from more than 50 people and makes contributions to more than five federal candidates. PACs that do not classify as multi-candidate can only contribute $1,000 to candidates, but can give $20,000 to national party committees.

3. One explanation for this decline lies in the FEC's classification of PACs. There are more than 500 PACs in the 1984 committee file that were left unclassified. Many of these appear to be nonconnected. For example, in 1984 the Save the Animals PAC and the I Love America PAC were not given any classification, but there is also no indication that they were special types of committee. In the 2002 committee file, the number of unclassified PACs tripled to about 1,800. As such, the drop noted in Figure 2.1 was likely the result of some coding omissions by the Federal Election Commission.

4. Contribution numbers are from each cycle's PAC contribution file. The FEC has archived these files back only to the 1979–1980 election cycle.

5. As a caveat, however, hard money contributions from individuals were indexed to inflation after the passage of BCRA (after being doubled from $1,000 to $2,000), while PAC contributions were not. Thus, for example, the individual hard money maximum for the 2005–2006 election was raised to $2,100, while the PAC maximum remains at $5,000.

6. "Cutting Edge in the Arts is Joining a PAC," by Alex Williams, *New York Times*, 7/4/2004, p. A1.

7. All FEC Advisory Opinions are available on the Commission's Web site.

8. It was not until the early 1990s that the FEC established a more rigid allocation criterion. See Advisory Opinion 1991–6, for example.

9. While we have comprehensive data on the amount spent by groups on hard money independent expenditures, the data on issue advocacy are quite limited longitudinally, even more so than the soft money data. The Annenberg Public Policy Center did some early work on issue advocacy in the 1996 elections (Beck et al. 1997), and the Wisconsin Advertising Project has data back to 2000 (with some limited data for 1998 and 1996) that track political advertisements in the country's top media markets. Regardless, we are limited in knowing definitively the extent to which interest groups engaged electoral politics with issue-oriented messages before this period.

10. It should also be noted that unions and for-profit corporations have always been permitted (before and after BCRA) to expressly advocate federal candidates, without limit and with candidate and party coordination, if they are communicating these messages internally to their employees or members. As such, if a labor union seeks to distribute flyers urging its members to vote for John Kerry, it can do so at any time during the campaign.

11. See "Soft Money, TV Attacks Will Go On," by Julia Malone, *Atlanta Journal-Constitution*, 9/3/2004, p. C1. The article also noted that some groups altered their tactics, ceasing issue advocacy campaigns because of the 60-day rule: "In at least one case, a group said it would stop running ads. Americans for Jobs Security, a pro-business group, has run ads in prominent congressional races and kept its donor list secret. It will shut down its TV campaign for the rest of this year."

12. The IRS defines 527s on their Web site at http://www.irs.gov/polorgs.

13. "Texan Aired 'Clean Air' Ads; Bush's Campaign Not Involved, Billionaire Says," by John Mintz, *Washington Post*, 3/4/2000, p. A6.

14. PACs and parties were exempt, as they register and report with the FEC.

15. "Democratic Groups Could Play Crucial TV Role in '04 Races," by Stuart Rothenberg, *Roll Call*, 2/2/2004. See also, "Reform Loophole," *Washington Post*, 12/2/2002, p. A20.

16. "FEC Declines to Curb Independent Fund-Raisers," by Glen Justice, *New York Times*, 5/14/2004, p. A18.

17. "Christian Coalition Ends Nonprofit Bid, Plans Big Shake-Up," by Mark Sherman, *Atlanta Journal and Constitution*, 6/11/1999, p. 3A.

18. These are from Advisory Opinions 1986-26 and 1986-37.

19. Consider also that many groups have a PAC and a 527 or 501(c) account. These differences can complicate the conceptualization of an interest group. Should Planned Parenthood's political action committee, which is used to contribute hard money, be classified a separate group than its 527, which is used to raise and spend unregulated funds for issue advocacy efforts? How does a group with a 501(c) account interact with its PAC caretakers? In response to a June 2002 press release about political ads through the first half of 2002, the Wisconsin Advertising Project received the following email from an interest group included in the study: "[Our political group] itself does buy po-

litical ads and should not be confused with [our nonprofit]. [The nonprofit] ads never mention or show candidates for public office. The ads that were calculated in your study were educational, not political. They seek to . . . inspire [Americans] to act on their beliefs. Accordingly, the inclusion of [the nonprofit] ads in your study, at least without significant clarification and distinction, was misleading." The example demonstrates the importance of at least considering these groups as distinct.

20. See also Cooper and Young (1997) and Malbin (2004).

21. Not mentioned is research on partisan polarization in the electorate. There is evidence that citizens are increasingly voting along party lines (Bartels 2000), but this trend is less important for my analysis than changes in party organization and the behavior of parties in Congress.

22. This is consistent with other pre-election measures of competitiveness. For example, Chuck Todd of the *National Journal* ranks House and Senate races in each election cycle. In 1998, he added a component of his ranking scale that addressed potential party control impacts of different race outcomes. It is instructive that, prior to this cycle, he and his associates found this component to be unnecessary.

23. The quotes from the previous two paragraphs are taken from *CQ*'s pre-election forecast report. Specifically, 10/13/1984, pp. 2500–2502; 10/13/1990, pp. 3279–3283; 10/19/1996, pp. 2954–2954; and 9/23/2000, pp. 2182–2185.

24. For newspapers, I searched through the day of the election. For AP and ABC transcripts, I searched up through the day before the election.

25. Quoted in "Feud Between GOP, PACs Stings Candidates," *Congressional Quarterly*, 9/3/1988, pp. 2447–2450.

26. "Who's Afraid of George Soros," by David Tell, *Weekly Standard*, 3/08/2004.

27. Corrado (2005)'s chapter on the history of campaign finance laws is the best and most concise review I have encountered on the subject.

28. "Major Campaign Reforms Take Effect," *New York Times*, 1/2/1975, p. 27.

29. In addition to FECA amendments, Congress also passed the Revenue Act in 1971, which created public financing of presidential campaigns. In 2000, it amended the Internal Revenue Code, requiring Section 527 organizations to disclose their contributions and expenditures to the IRS (as was mentioned earlier).

30. "An Extraordinary Victory," *New York Times*, 3/21/2002, p. A36.

31. "Hope for Campaign Reform," *Denver Post*, 2/15/2002, p. B6.

Chapter 3: A Theory of Emergent and Changing Interest Group Tactics

1. The importance of a success calculation was also evident after the 1996 elections. David Broder and Ruth Marcus wrote in 1997: "There is no

agreement on how effective the issue ads were. The Business-Industry Political Action Committee (BIPAC), an umbrella group whose political counsel is widely heeded, said in a July report that 'labor may have miscalculated' and that, had the unions spent as much on traditional get-out-the-vote activities as they did on issue ads, 'perhaps control of Congress, at least control of the House, might have shifted back to the Democrats"; "Wielding Third Force in Politics; Sky's the Limit in Issue Advocacy," by David Broder and Ruth Marcus, *Washington Post*, 9/20/1997, p. A1.

2. Wright (1985) distinguishes them as type I and type II strategies. See also Jacobson and Kernell (1983). I could also add the goal of issue salience. Certainly, the goal of some electoral behavior (issue advocacy campaigns, for example) might be to put issues or policy proposals on the agenda. I'm less interested in this goal, in that it is more easily classified as a lobbying tactic and not one necessarily directed at one candidate (Kollman 1998). Indeed, most evidence indicates that if an advertisement mentions or pictures a politician, it is usually interpreted by viewers as designed to affect election outcomes.

3. There is no consensus, however, on whether access strategies are successful. There is an extensive literature on the relationship between roll call votes and PAC contributions, with some finding effects and others finding null results. Smith (1995) reviews this literature and argues that contributions are likely to affect roll calls under certain circumstances; when the issue is not salient with the national electorate, for example. See Baumgartner and Leech (1998) for a critique of the literature. Alternatively, there has been more empirical success in showing that contributions affect levels of member of Congress participation (Hall and Wayman 1990) and committee voting (Wright 1990). I am not concerned in this research with testing the effectiveness of tactical choices.

4. To be sure, this second goal of elections can be pursued in a variety of ways, but it is harder and less likely to succeed. Election outcomes are no easy thing to affect (Goldstein and Freedman 2000, Green and Krasno 1988, Jacobson 2004), and interest groups have scarce resources.

5. Sorauf (1975, pp. 22–23) asks a similar question for political parties: should we understand them as independent or dependent variables in party systems? He argues the latter: "Probably the most nearly precise way to summarize the relationship between political parties and the course of political development in general during the last hundred years and more is to say that the role of parties and party systems has changed to one of adaptation and adjustment rather than one of innovation."

6. See also Wayman (1985).

7. Union leader, name withheld; interview with author by phone—April 3, 2003.

8. See also Eismeier and Pollock (1988) and Jacobson (2004, p. 72).

9. Document accessed from a Web archival search on relevant campaign

finance cases. The electronic version is no longer online, but a hard copy is available from the author on request.

10. Page 38 in *McConnell v. FEC*; emphasis added.

11. Endnote 47 in *McConnell v. FEC.*

12. Accessed from campaign finance materials at http://www.law.stanford .edu/publications/projects/campaignfinance/collection/

13. "Candidates Expect Another Fall of 'Issue Advocacy' Spots," by Ruth Marcus, *Washington Post*, 6/30/1998.

14. "Issue Ads Crowd Airwaves Before 2000 Election," by Jim Drinkard, *USA Today*, 11/29/1999, p. A11.

15. Name withheld; interview with author, Washington, DC—March 19, 2003.

16. Accessed from campaign finance materials at http://www.law.stanford .edu/publications/projects/campaignfinance/collection/

17. From the NRA's Institute for Legislative Action Web site, http://www .nraila.org/

18. Name withheld; interview with author, Washington, DC—March 21, 2003.

19. "Even With Campaign Finance Law, Money Talks Louder Than Ever," by Glen Justice, *New York Times*, 11/8/2004, p. A16.

20. Name withheld; interview with author, Washington, DC—March 19, 2003.

21. "Issue Ads Crowd Airwaves Before 2000 Election," by Jim Drinkard, *USA Today*, 11/29/1999, p. A11.

22. "A Shadow Party in Hot Pursuit of Soft Money," *Boston Globe*, April 10, 2004, p. A11.

23. According to the *Washington Post* in August 2003: "One of the [527s], Progress for America, is operating from the downtown offices of a company run by Tony Feather. He was the political director of the Bush-Cheney 2000 campaign and remains a close ally of Karl Rove, President Bush's top political aide. Democrats are busy, too. Three former high-ranking aides of Clinton—Harold Ickes, Doug Sosnik and John D. Podesta—are working to set up a Democratic soft-money operation with the goal of running pro-Democratic 'issue ads.' The three are part of the informal brain trust of Democratic National Committee Chairman Terence McAuliffe."—8/24/03, p. A1.

24. "Big Gifts to Parties MIA in '04; 'Soft Money' Limits Have Caused Wealthy Donors to Hold Back," *Columbus Dispatch*, August 8, 2004, p. 1B.

Chapter 4: Putting PACs in (Political) Context(s)

1. "Bush Campaign-Reform Plan Takes Aim at Incumbents," *Congressional Quarterly*, 7/1/1989, pp. 1648–1649.

2. Letter to the Editor, *New York Times*, 9/28/1986.

3. In comparing the list of included and excluded PACs, my sample has

a slightly higher proportion of corporate, labor, and trade union PACs when compared to excluded committees. More specifically, of the excluded PACs, 40 percent were corporate-sponsored, 7 percent were labor committees, and 16.7 percent were trade association PACs. My sample has 47.6 percent corporate, 8 percent labor, and 20.6 percent trade association. In contrast, 13.2 percent of the excluded PACs are nonconnected compared to 11.7 percent in my sample.

4. These are ideal because they are coded in the same way over time and because they are available for a number of election cycles. There are other ratings of competitiveness, including Charlie Cook's political report, but these are harder to track over time (especially back to the early 1980s). In addition, *CQ*'s ratings are pre-election classifications (usually in October of the election year). It should be noted that there are two other *CQ* classifications—races that lean Republican or Democrat, and races that favor the Republican or Democrat. Leaning races are the second most competitive, while favored races are the second most safe. I exclude these races in this analysis and compare only contributions in the most competitive and the safest races.

5. Note, the safe seat model is for incumbents only and the competitive model combines incumbents and challengers. Also, I reran these models for just contributions and for independent expenditures, and the results are similar across these runs. Also, because the dependent variables are censored at zero (you cannot spend negative dollars), I estimated all models in this section using tobit. A potential criticism of this approach lies in assuming that one substantive process explains contribution decisions (Grier, Munger and Roberts 1994). More likely, two decisions characterize a contribution process—whether to give and how much to give. This is true especially when PAC/member dyads are the unit of analysis, but may not be as true when looking at aggregate electoral activity at the level of the PAC.

6. There are a number of other PAC types not included in the models, namely cooperatives, corporations without stock, and unclassified PACs. This exclusion is necessary for statistical estimation; the results will show how each of the included PAC categories is different from the excluded categories.

7. Because a PAC can be included up to 10 times (one for each election cycle), it is possible for the D.C measure to change. In other words, if a PAC moves its office to D.C. after a few cycles, the variable will change from 0 to 1 and vice versa.

8. I take the natural log to account for a diminishing return of each added dollar in the extreme.

9. The House numbers for all 10 cycles, starting in 1984, are −27, −33, −30, −33, −16, −2, 21, 13, 10, and 7. The Senate numbers, from 1984 until 2002, are −3, 0, −3, −3, −6, −2, 5, 4, −2, and 5.

10. Note that the N for the safe seat House model is only 6,694 (as opposed to 7,441 in all other models). I had to exclude 1998 from the safe seat House analysis because in that year the *Congressional Quarterly* only listed

races that were competitive and leaning. They did not distinguish among all other races that were favored or safe.

11. As with the previous analysis, all values are adjusted for inflation to represent their value in 2002.

12. Of course, one caveat of this approach is that I ignore important variation within each category. For example, PACs very far to the left of the Democratic median should behave differently than PACs just barely more liberal than the median Democrat. I also estimated the models below using the full range of PAC ideology. That is, Democratic PACs are coded as such if they were more extreme than the median, but their value was their ideology; vice versa for GOP PACs. The substantive results under this conceptualization remain the same.

13. I tested but do not report one other time effect in separate models. I interacted the labor and corporation dummies with the balance of power measure. The balance of power°labor works in the same direction as the Democratic PAC°balance measure (in both the House and Senate), but the corporation interaction is insignificant in both models.

14. Union leader, name withheld; interview with author by phone—March 21, 2003

15. I estimate all models in this section using Ordinary Least Squares, and I report robust standard errors. There is evidence of heteroskedasticity in these models, which is the reason for the robust SEs. I plotted the residuals against the independent variables, finding greater variance for PACs with high expenditures, for years with a tighter balance of power, and for PACs included in the sample a high number of times. There appear to be no extreme residuals (one or two cases that cause higher variance), indicating that the heteroskedasticity is driven by greater variance in these variables overall. This is something we might expect (i.e., PACs that spend more should have more variance than PACs that spend comparatively less), and with robust standard errors we can be more confident in the results.

Chapter 5: Understanding Soft Money

1. "Blue Jeans and Big Bucks," by Marjorie Williams. *Washington Post*, 5/26/2000, p. A35.

2. "Editorial," by Marty Meehan and John McCain, *Washington Post*, 7/12/2001, p. A.27

3. "Sore Loser in the Senate," *San Diego Union-Tribune*, 4/1/2001, p. G5.

4. "If Soft Money Goes, Then So Does Free Speech." by Joel Gora and Peter Wallison, *New York Times*, 3/17/2001, p. A11.

5. Document accessed from a Web archival search on relevant campaign finance cases. The electronic version is no longer online, but a hard copy is available from the author on request.

6. There are a few challenges in managing the data. In almost all cases the FEC records contributions from individuals as LAST NAME, FIRST NAME, with a comma in between the last and first names. In contrast, almost all nonindividual contributors have no comma. As a first cut through the data, I separated each contributor with a comma in the string field from contributors with no comma. I created a dummy variable that assigned a 0 to the former and 1 to the latter. I then looked through all comma-based entries to identify nonindividuals (for example, law firms with multiple partner names separated by a comma), changing the code from 0 to 1. I saved all nonindividual contributors into a new file, creating a separate file for each cycle. (See Clawson, Neustadl and Weller 1998, for an earlier discussion of these issues.) In Franz (n.d.), I compare my data cleaning procedure with a previously cleaned set of soft money data, stored at the Center for Responsive Politics (CRP). For the most part, I can replicate their soft money totals; I rely on my independent coding so as to include data back to 1992—CRP has free downloadable data available back only to 1998.

7. Another challenge concerned labor groups. If a particular labor union has multiple branches, each with its own PAC (i.e., Teamsters Local 14), I chose not to link the local PAC to either the larger union or a different Local in the soft money contributor file. For example, if I randomly selected a Local Teamsters Union PAC, but the soft money database does not list this Local, only the Teamsters generally or even a different Local, I did not list this as a match.

8. "Worried Over Soft Money, G.O.P. Readies Major Gala," by Philip Shenon, *Atlanta Journal-Constitution*, 6/20/2001, p. A16.

9. It is important to note that I exclude Washington, D.C., from the analysis. The Capitol is truly not comparable with the other states. It has no Senate elections and the presidential race is never competitive, not to mention that the district is extremely small but generates a huge amount of soft money.

10. Because of the lagged measure, January of the off-year is dropped from the models, meaning the month variable ranges only from 2–22. When I include post-Election Day through December of the on-year as the lagged measure for the first month of the next off-year (i.e., November and December of 1998 as the lag for January 1999), the results do not change.

11. Because there is no easy-to-access state-level presidential competitiveness score, as with *CQ* for Senate races, I chose this less than perfect post-election standard as a way to parallel the coding across the three presidential elections covered by this analysis. Also, I did not code for House competitiveness because the number of districts in each state varies, which complicates the conceptualization of a state-level measure.

12. The set-up means that every month of the year and every state are included in the data multiple times (Maine in January 2000, Maine in February 2000, Maine in March 2000, etc). Standard statistical estimation is not appropriate since so many repeated observations make separating out unique effects of causal variables much more difficult. To compensate, I run a statistical tech-

nique called a cross-sectional time series regression with fixed-effects for states. This allows me to control for omitted variables that differ between cases but are constant over time (demographic factors based on census data, for example). Because of this set-up, state-level demographic data are not included in the estimation. In the mid-term model, however, I include a variable for the number of electoral votes in the state. This variable taps not only the size of the state but, as a proxy, also the resource base. I also do not control for other factors that might increase fund-raising in a specific state—for example, whether the party had a fund-raiser. My suspicion is that most fund-raisers are held in Washington, D.C., as with the example at the beginning of the chapter. I could also include variables that track when there are important policy votes in Congress, when Congress is out of session, and when the President visits certain states.

13. "AFLAC Big on 'Soft Money'; Giant Firm in Columbus Leans to GOP," by George Edmonson, *Atlanta Journal-Constitution*, 6/23/2001, p. A9.

14. There were 508 such groups in 1992; 571 in 1994; 1,186 in 1996; 929 in 1998; 1,478 in 2000; and 1,268 in 2002.

15. To identify a contributor's issue area, I relied on a number of online resources such as "Associations Unlimited" (www.galenet.com), LexisNexis, Google, and existing online soft money databases (the Center for Responsive Politics, at www.opensecrets.org).

16. There is evidence of heteroskedasticity in this model, and some labor and banks are clear outliers. I ran the model without these outliers, and substantive results hold.

Chapter 6: Following 527s and Watching Issue Advocacy

1. "Candidates Expect Another Fall of 'Issue Advocacy' Spots," by Ruth Marcus, *Washington Post*, 6/30/1998.

2. "The 527 Factor: It's Big in State Races, Too," by Staci D. Kramer, *Christian Science Monitor*, 9/23/2004, p. 3.

3. The Wisconsin Advertising Project tracked the top 75 media markets in 2000 and the top 100 markets in 2002 and 2004. For ease of comparison, I look only at the top 75 media markets in all three elections. The data are described in more detail in Goldstein and Freedman (1999, 2000), and I report the results of inter-reliability tests on the 2000 data in Franz, Freedman, Goldstein, and Ridout (2007).

4. There is already some empirical evidence of this in the 2000 election (Goldstein and Freedman 2001).

5. I exclude races not covered by CMAG-tracked markets and races covered by CMAG but where no ads aired. This latter decision might bias the results, as there could be some competitive races in urban areas where it is too costly to air ads. When I include the 25 additional markets in 2002 and 2004, the substantive results do not change.

6. "Pelosi Prediction: 'I Am Going to Be Speaker' in '05; House's Top Dem Confident of Return to Majority Party," by Edward Epstein, *San Francisco Chronicle*, 7/16/2004, p. A16

7. "Recircling the Democrats' Wagons," *New York Times*, 11/9/2004, p. A22.

8. "A Stronger GOP Dusts Off Long-Delayed Agenda; Wins Open Door to Arctic Drilling, Social Security Overhaul and Other Plans," by Lawrence M. O'Rourke, *Sacramento Bee*, 11/04/2004, p. A10.

9. I downloaded the data from the IRS Web site on February 14, 2005. The IRS updates its records every Sunday. By waiting more than three months after the end of the 2004 campaign I was able to include any data from post-election reports.

10. In addition, the downloadable data are not split by year or election cycle, but are instead combined into one text file. Further still, every form is put into the same large text file. Both issues create two major problems. First, when you download the data you must separate out each form type. Second, if you want to update your existing IRS files by adding data from the last few months (or even last few weeks), you have to download the entire dataset and select the latest data.

11. http://www.rga.org/—accessed on 4/20/2005.

12. There is an initial caveat. Most importantly, we do not have systematic data on contributions to these 527s before 2003 and 2004 (as stated there is some limited evidence from 2002); therefore, we cannot directly test whether contributors increased or switched their donations from nonfederal party committees to these 527s—which would be a natural experiment of behavior before and after BCRA. We can only test whether donors in 2004 were also party donors pre-BCRA.

13. There is a final category of "other" codes that might not apply to any of the above categories or that might fit into more than one. For example, when a 527 lists mail or postage as its expenditure purpose, it is unclear whether those costs are related to the standard operations of a committee or whether they refer to costs incurred for larger, direct mailing activity. Therefore, I included only those codes that fit easily into the four categories.

14. Some of this 527's activity was highlighted in the national media. See "W.Va. Supreme Court Justice Defeated in Rancorous Contest," by Carol Morello, *Washington Post*, 11/4/2004, p. A15.

15. "Dirt, Mud and Smear: Politics as Usual This Year," by O. Ricardo Pimental, *Milwaukee Journal Sentinel*, 9/19/2004, p. J1.

Chapter 7: Tracking the Regulatory Context

1. "Who's Afraid of George Soros," by David Tell, *Weekly Standard*, 3/08/2004.

2. We have no reason to believe that candidates and parties do not consider the constraining effects of campaign finance law; so I include them in the analysis as well.

3. This is similar to AO 2004-31, in which Russ Darrow—a candidate for Senate in the 2004 Wisconsin Republican primary—asked if advertisements for his car dealerships should be considered "electioneering communications" under BCRA. He hoped not, and the FEC ruled that they were not.

4. Because I coded all AOs on up to five codes, it was possible for the AO to deal with both. I excluded AOs from 1977 to 1982 because I have only limited FEC data during that time on candidates, parties, and interest groups.

5. I estimate the models using a poisson. I tested for whether the negative binomial is more appropriate, but found little evidence of over-dispersion. The matching fund model is a logit, as there was only one month where the FEC considered more than one of these requests. In addition, I report robust standard errors. I also tested for clustering effects by year and month, and for whether there are panel effects for each month. In all tests, the substantive results remain the same.

6. I did not track whether the AOs specifically mentioned the recent regulations. There would be measurement error in doing so, as the letters I coded do not mention every aspect of the petitioner's request.

7. I also tested for whether the number of months to the next election has an effect, which it does not, and for whether the make-up of the FEC (how long since a new commissioner was appointed and how many commissioners were appointed by a Republican president) affects the number of requests made. I found no significant effects of these variables as well.

8. I re-estimated each model including regulatory change variables for unrelated regulation changes. For example, I included the fund-raising regulation variables in the electioneering model to confirm that these changes have no effect on the frequency of electioneering requests. The coefficients on these variables were insignificant.

9. I calculated these probabilities for a month with a mean number of other opinions, in an election after 1994, when the GOP controlled the Senate but before the passage of BCRA, and in the month of February.

10. "Agency That Referees Elections Protects Parties First," by Jim Drinkard, *USA Today*, 11/12/2002, p. 1A.

11. Thomas and Noble quotes accessed from documents on www.FEC .gov.

12. "Chipping Away at Campaign Reform," by David Broder, *Washington Post*, 9/1/2005, p. A29.

13. "Political Ads Test the Limits; 'Issues Advocacy' Growing Despite Partisanship Concerns," by Ruth Marcus, *Washington Post*, 4/8/1996, p. A1.

14. "Harder Than Soft Money," *American Prospect* (Online Edition), 1/1/1998—Accessed on 1/19/2007.

Chapter 8: Conclusion

1. I downloaded the entire script from http://communicationsoffice .tripod.com, which maintains an archive of all West Wing scripts. Accessed on 4/12/05.

2. Editorial, *The Washington Post*, 3/29/2006, p.A19.

3. "Democrats Get Late Donations From Business," by Jeff Zeleny and Aron Pilhofer, *The New York Times*, 10/28/2006, p.A1.

4. "Unregulated Groups Wield Millions To Sway Voters," by Stephanie Simon, *Los Angeles Times*, 10/30/2006, p.A1.

5. "And This Just In on Elections," *The New York Times*, 12/16/2006, p.A16.

6. CNET News.com, accessed on 3/5/05.

Bibliography

Aldrich, John. 1995. *Why Parties?* Chicago: University of Chicago Press.

Aldrich, John and David Rohde. 2000a. "The Consequences of Party Organization in the House: The Role of the Majority and Minority Parties in Conditional Party Government," in *Polarized Politics: Congress and the President in a Partisan Era*, ed. Jon Bond and Richard Fleisher. Washington, D.C.: Congressional Quarterly Press.

Aldrich, John and David Rohde. 2000b. "The Republican Revolution and the House Appropriations Committee." *Journal of Politics* 62(1):1–33.

Alexander, Herbert. 1972. *Money in Politics*. Washington, D.C.: Public Affairs Press.

Ansolabehere, Stephen, John de Figueiredo and James Snyder. 2003. "Why Is There So Little Money in U.S. Politics?" *Journal of Economic Perspectives* 17(1):105–130.

Ansolabehere, Stephen and James Snyder. 2000. "Soft Money, Hard Money, Strong Parties." *Columbia Law Review* 100(3):598–619.

Ansolabehere, Stephen, James Snyder Jr. and Charles Stewart. 2001. "Candidate Positioning in U.S. House Elections." *American Journal of Political Science* 45(1):136–159.

Apollonio, D.E. and Raymond La Raja. 2002. "Interest Group Contribution Strategies With Soft Money." Paper Presented at the Annual Convention of the Midwest Political Science Association, Chicago, Illinois.

Apollonio, D.E. and Raymond La Raja. 2004. "Who Gave Soft Money? The Effect of Interest Group Resources on Political Contributions." *The Journal of Politics* 66(4):1134–1154.

Archer, Robin. 1998. "Unions, Courts, and Parties: Judicial Repression and Labor Politics in Late Nineteenth-Century America." *Politics and Society* 26(3): 391–422.

Armstrong, Jerome and Markos Moulitsas Zuniga. 2006. *Crashing the Gate: Netroots, Grassroots, and the Rise of People-Powered Politics*. White River Junction, VT: Chelsea Green Publishing Company.

Astley, W. Graham and Charles Fombrun. 1983. "Collective Strategy: Social Ecology of Organizational Environments." *Academy of Management Review* 8(4): 576–587.

Austen-Smith, David. 1995. "Campaign Contributions and Access." *American Political Science Review* 89(3): 566–581.

Austen-Smith, David and John Wright. 1994. "Counteractive Lobbying." *American Journal of Political Science* 38(1): 25–44.

Baer, Denise and David Bositis. 1993. *Politics and Linkage in a Democratic Society*. New York: Prentice Hall College Division.

Bartels, Larry. 2000. "Partisanship and Voting Behavior, 1952–1996." *American Journal of Political Science* 44(1):35–50.

Bauer, Raymond, Ithiel de Sola Pool and Lewis Dexter. 1964. *American Business and Public Policy*. New York: Atherton Press.

Baumgartner, Frank and Beth Leech. 1998. *Basic Interests*. Princeton, NJ: Princeton University Press.

Beck, Deborah, Paul Taylor, Jeffrey Stanger and Douglas Rivlin. 1997. *Issue Advocacy Advertising During the 1996 Campaign*. Philadelphia: University of Pennsylvania Annenberg Public Policy Center.

Bibby, John. 1998. "Partisan Organizations, 1946–1996," in *Partisan Approaches to Postwar American Politics*, ed. Byron Shafer. New York: Chatham House Publishers.

Boies, John. 1989. "Money, Business, and the State: Material Interests, Fortune 500 Corporations, and the Size of Political Action Committees." *American Sociological Review* 54(5): 821–833.

Bond, Jon and Richard Fleisher. 2000. *Polarized Politics: Congress and the President in a Partisan Era*. Washington, D.C.: Congressional Quarterly Press.

Bradford, W. David and Andrew Kleit. 2006. "Evaluating the Welfare Effects of Drug Advertising: Consumer Behavior Indicates Broadcast Drug Ads Have Positive Health Benefits." Cato Institute.

Breaux Symposium. 2002. *Parties, PACs, and Persuasion*. Baton Rouge, LA: Louisiana State University Reilly Center for Media and Public Affairs.

Bruno, Jerry and Jeff Greenfield. 1971. *Advance Man*. New York: Bantam Books.

Clawson, Dan, Alan Neustadl and Mark Weller. 1998. *Dollars and Votes: How Business Campaign Contributions Subvert Democracy*. Philadelphia: Temple University Press.

Clemens, Elisabeth. 1997. *The People's Lobby*. Chicago: University of Chicago Press.

Clinton, William. 2004. *My Life*. New York: Knopf.

Coleman, John. 1996. *Party Decline in America: Policy, Politics, and the Fiscal State*. Princeton, NJ: Princeton University Press.

Coleman, John. 1997. "The Decline and Resurgence of Congressional Party Conflict." *Journal of Politics* 59(1): 165–184.

Cooper, Joseph and Garry Young. 1997. "Partisanship, Bipartisanship, and Cross-partisanship in Congress Since the New Deal," in *Congress Reconsidered* (6th Edition), ed. Lawrence Dodd and Bruce Oppenheimer. Washington, D.C.: Congressional Quarterly Press.

Cooper, Joseph and Garry Young. 2002. "Party and Preference in Congressional Decision Making: Roll Call Voting in the U.S. House of Representatives, 1889–1997," in *Political Change in Congress: New Directions in Studying the History of the U.S. Congress*, ed. Mathew McCubbins and David Brady. Stanford: Stanford University Press.

Corrado, Anthony. 2005. "Money and Politics: A History of Federal Campaign Finance Law," in *The New Campaign Finance Sourcebook*, ed. Anthony Corrado, Thomas Mann, Daniel Ortiz, and Trevor Potter. Washington, D.C.: Brookings Institute.

Corrado, Anthony, Thomas Mann and Trevor Potter. 2003. *Inside the Campaign Finance Battle: Court Testimony on the New Reforms*. Washington, D.C.: Brookings Institution Press.

Cox, Gary and Eric Magar. 1999. "How Much is Majority Status in the U.S. Congress Worth?" *American Political Science Review* 93(2): 299–309.

Crotty, W.J. and Gary Jacobson. 1980. *Party Decline in America*. Boston: Little Brown.

Cyert, Richard and James March. 1963. *A Behavioral Theory of the Firm*. Englewood Cliffs, NJ: Prentice-Hall.

Davis, F.L. 1992. "Sophistication in Corporate PAC Contributions: Demobilizing the Opposition." *American Politics Quarterly* 20(4): 381–410.

Dominguez, Casey and Kathryn Pearson. 2005. "Big Dollars, But How Much Change? A Comparison of Soft Money Donors Pre- and Post-BCRA." Paper Prepared for Presentation at the Annual Meeting of the Midwest Political Science Association, Chicago.

Drew, Elizabeth. 1983. *Politics and Money: The New Road to Corruption*. New York: Macmillan.

Dwyre, Diana. 1996. "Spinning Straw Into Gold: Soft Money and U.S. House Elections." *Legislative Studies Quarterly* 21(3): 409–423.

Dwyre, Diana. 2002. "Campaigning Outside the Law: Interest Group Issue Advocacy," in *Interest Group Politics* (6th Edition), ed. Allan Cigler and Burdett Loomis. Washington, D.C.: Congressional Quarterly Press.

Dwyre, Diana and Robin Kolodny. 2002. "Throwing Out the Rule Book: Party Financing of the 2000 Elections," in *Financing the 2000 Elections*, ed. David Magleby. Washington, D.C.: Brookings Institutions Press.

Eismeier, Theodore J. and Philip H. Pollock. 1985. "An Organizational Analysis of Political Action Committees." *Political Behavior* 7(2): 192–216.

Eismeier, Theodore J. and Philip H. Pollock. 1988. *Business, Money, and the Rise of Corporate PACs in American Elections*. New York: Quorum Books.

Elliot, Lee Ann. 1980. "Political Action Committees—Precincts of the '80s." *Arizona Law Review* 22(2): 539–549.

Endersby, James W. and Michael C. Munger. 1992. "The Impact of Legislator Attributes on Union PAC Campaign Contributions." *Journal of Labor Research* 12(4): 79–97.

Epstein, Edwin. 1980a. "Business and Labor Under the Federal Election Campaign Act of 1971," in *Parties, Interest Groups, and Campaign Finance Laws*, ed. Michael Malbin. Washington, D.C.: American Enterprise Institute.

Epstein, Edwin. 1980b. "The PAC Phenomenon: An Overview." *Arizona Law Review* 22(2): 355–372.

Evans, Diana. 1988. "Oil PACs and Aggressive Contribution Strategies." *The Journal of Politics* 50(4):1047–1056.

Fiorina, Morris. 1980. "The Decline of Collective Responsibility in American Politics." *Daedalus* 109(3): 25–45.

Francia, Peter. 2006. *The Future of Organized Labor in American Politics*. New York: Columbia University Press.

Franklin, Charles. n.d. "Estimating PAC Ideology Location and Sensitivity." Unpublished Paper.

Franz, Michael M. n.d. "Comparing the OpenSecrets Soft Money Database with FEC Reports." Unpublished Paper.

Franz, Michael, Paul Freedman, Kenneth Goldstein, and Travis Ridout. 2007. *Campaign Advertising and American Democracy* Philadelphia: Temple University Press.

Gaddie, Ronald Keith. 1995. "Investing in the Future: Economic Political Action Committee Contributions to Open-Seat House Candidates." *American Politics Quarterly* 23(3): 339–354.

Gaddie, Ronald Keith and James L. Regens. 1997. "Economic Interest Group Allocations in Open Seat Senate Elections." *American Politics Quarterly* 25(3): 347–362.

Goldstein, Kenneth. 1999. *Interest Groups, Lobbying, and Participation in America*. New York: Cambridge University Press.

Goldstein, Kenneth and Paul Freedman. 2001. "Lessons Learned: Political Advertising in the 2000 Elections." *Political Communication*. 19(1): 5–28.

Goldstein, Kenneth and Paul Freedman. 1999. "Measuring Media Exposure and the Effects of Negative Campaign Ads." *American Journal of Political Science* 43(4): 1189–1208.

Goldstein, Kenneth and Paul Freedman. 2000. "New Evidence for New Arguments." *Journal of Politics*. 62(4): 1087–1108.

Gopoian, J. David. 1984. "What Makes PACs Tick? An Analysis of the Allocation Patterns of Economic Interest Groups." *American Journal of Political Science* 28(2): 259–281.

Gormley, William. 1998. "Witnesses for a Revolution." *American Politics Quarterly* 26(2): 174–195.

Gray, Virginia and David Lowery. 1997. "Re-conceptualizing PAC Formation: It's Not a Collective Action Problem and It May Be an Arms Race." *American Politics Quarterly* 25(3): 319–346.

Green, Donald Phillip and Jonathan Krasno. 1988. "Salvation for the Spendthrift Incumbent: Re-estimating the Effects of Campaign Spending in House Elections." *American Journal of Political Science* 32(4): 884–907.

Green, Mark. 2002. *Selling Out: How Big Corporate Money Buys Elections, Rams Through Legislation, and Betrays Our Democracy*. New York: ReganBooks.

Greene, Steve and Eric Heberlig. 2005. "The Impact of BCRA in the 2004 North Carolina Senate Election." Paper Presented at the Annual Convention of the Midwest Political Science Association, Chicago.

Grenzke, Janet. 1989. "Candidate Attributes and PAC Contributions." *Western Political Science Quarterly* 42(2): 245–264.

Grier, Kevin B. and Michael C. Munger. 1991. "Committee Assignments, Constituency Interests, and Campaign Contributions." *Economic Inquiry* 29(1): 24–43.

Grier, Kevin B. and Michael C. Munger. 1993. "Comparing Interest Group PAC Contributions to House and Senate Incumbents, 1980-1986." *Journal of Politics* 55(3): 615–643.

Grier, Kevin B., Michael C. Munger and Brian Roberts. 1994. "The Determinants of Industry Political Activity, 1978–1986." *American Political Science Review* 88(4): 911–926.

Groseclose, Tim and Jeffrey Milyo. 2005. "A Measure of Media Bias." *Quarterly Journal of Economics* 120(4): 1191–1237.

Hall, Richard and Frank Wayman. 1990. "Buying Time: Moneyed Interests and the Mobilization of Bias in Congressional Committees." *American Political Science Review* 90(4): 797–820.

Hansen, John Mark. 1991. *Gaining Access: Congress and the Farm Lobby, 1918–1991*. Chicago: University of Chicago Press.

Hansen, Wendy, Neil Mitchell and Jeffrey Drope. 2005. "The Logic of Private and Collective Action." *American Journal of Political Science* 49(1): 150–167.

Hart, David. 2001. "Why Do Some Firms Give? Why Do Some Firms Give A Lot? High-Tech PACs, 1977–1996." *Journal of Politics* 63(4): 1230–1249.

Harvey, Anna. 1996. "The Political Consequences of Suffrage Exclusion: Organizations, Institutions, and the Electoral Mobilization of Women." *Social Science History* 20(1): 97–132.

Heaney, Michael. 2003. "Coalitions and Interest Group Influence Over Health Care Policy." Paper Presented at the Annual Convention of the American Political Science Association, Philadelphia.

Heard, Alexander. 1960. *The Costs of Democracy*. Chapel Hill, NC: University of North Carolina Press.

Heclo, Hugh. 1978. "Issue Networks and the Executive Establishment," in *The New American Political System*, ed. Anthony King. Washington, D.C.: American Enterprise Institute.

Herndon, James. 1982. "Access, Record, and Competition as Influences on Interest Group Contributions to Congressional Campaigns." *The Journal of Politics* 44(4): 996–1019.

Herrera, Richard and Michael Yawn. 1999. "The Emergence of the Personal Vote." *Journal of Politics* 61(1): 136–150.

Herrnson, Paul. 1986. "Do Parties Make a Difference? The Role of Party Organizations in Congressional Elections." *The Journal of Politics* 48(3): 589–615.

Herrnson, Paul. 1998a. "Interest Groups, PACs, and Campaigns," in *The Interest Group Connection: Electioneering, Lobbying, and Policymaking in Washington*, ed. Paul Herrnson, Ronald G. Shaiko and Clyde Wilcox. Chatham, NJ: Chatham House Publishers.

Herrnson, Paul. 1998b. "Parties and Interest Groups in Post-Reform Congressional Elections," in *Interest Group Politics* (5th Edition), ed. Allan Cigler and Burdett Loomis. Washington, D.C.: Congressional Quarterly Press.

Herrnson, Paul and Kelly Patterson. 2002. "Financing the 2000 Congressional Elections," in *Financing the 2000 Election*, ed. David Magleby. Washington, D.C.: Brookings Institution Press.

Hojnacki, Marie. 1997. "Interest Groups' Decisions to Join Alliances or Work Alone." *American Journal of Political Science* 41(1): 61–87.

Hojnacki, Marie and David Kimball. 1998. "Organized Interests and the Decision Whom to Lobby." *American Political Science Review* 92(4): 775–790.

Holbrook, Thomas. 1996. *Do Campaigns Matter?* London: Sage Publications.

Holloway, Harry. 1979. "Interest Groups in the Post-Partisan Era: The Political Machine of the AFL-CIO." *Political Science Quarterly* 94(1): 117–133.

Hrebenar, Ronald J. and Ruth Scott. 1997. *Interest Group Politics in America*. New York: M.E. Sharpe.

Jackson, Brooks. 1990a. *Broken Promise: Why the Federal Election Commission Failed*. New York: Priority Press.

Jackson, Brooks. 1990b. *Honest Graft: Big Money and the American Political Process*. Washington, D.C.: Farragut Publishing Company.

Jacobson, Gary. 2004. *The Politics of Congressional Elections*. New York: Longman.

Jacobson, Gary and Samuel Kernell. 1983. *Strategy and Choice in Congressional Elections*. New Haven: Yale University Press.

Kahn, Kim Fridkin and Patrick Kenney. 2004. *No Holds Barred: Negativity in U.S. Senate Campaigns*. Upper Saddle River, NJ: Pearson.

Kau, James, Donald Keenan and Paul Rubin. 1982. "A General Equilibrium

Model of Congressional Voting." *Quarterly Journal of Economics* 97(2): 271–293.

Kingdon, John. 1989. *Congressman's Voting Decisions*. Ann Arbor: University of Michigan Press.

Kingdon, John. 1994. "Agendas, Ideas, and Policy Change," in *New Perspectives on American Politics*, ed. Lawrence Dodd and Calvin Jilson. Washington, D.C.: Congressional Quarterly Press.

Kollman, Ken. 1998. *Outside Lobbying: Public Opinion and Interest Group Strategies*. Princeton, NJ: Princeton University Press.

Kolodny, Robin and Justin Gollob. 2005. "The Impact of BCRA in the 2004 Pennsylvania 13th Congressional District Election." Paper Presented at the Annual Convention of the Midwest Political Science Association, Chicago.

Lochner, Todd and Bruce Cain. 1999. "Equity and Efficacy in the Enforcement of Campaign Finance Laws." *Texas Law Review* 77(7): 1891–1942.

Lowery, David and Virginia Gray. 1995. "The Population Ecology of Gucci Gulch, or the Natural Regulation of Interest Group Numbers in the American States." *American Journal of Political Science* 39(1): 1–29.

Lowi, Theodore, Benjamin Ginsberg and Kenneth Shepsle. 2006. *American Government: Freedom and Power* (Brief 2006 Edition). New York: W.W. Norton and Company.

Magleby, David. 2001. *Getting Inside the Outside Campaign*. Provo,UT: Brigham Young University Center for the Study of Elections and Democracy.

Magleby, David. 2002. *Financing the 2000 Elections*. Washington, D.C.: Brookings Institutions Press.

Magleby, David. 2003. *The Other Campaign*. New York: Rowman and Littlefield Publishers, Inc.

Maisel, Sandy. 2002. *The Parties Respond*. Boulder, CO: Westview Press.

Malbin, Michael. 1980. "Of Mountains and Molehills: PACs, Campaigns, and Public Policy," in *Parties, Interest Groups, and Campaign Finance Laws*, ed. Michael Malbin. Washington, D.C.: American Enterprise Institute for Public Policy Research.

Malbin, Michael. 2004. "Political Parties Under Post-McConnell Bipartisan Campaign Reform Act." *Election Law Journal* 3(2): 177–191.

Malbin, Michael, Clyde Wilcox, Mark Rozell and Richard Skinner. 2002. "New Interest Group Strategies – A Preview of Post McCain-Feingold Politics?" Washington, D.C.: Campaign Finance Institute (CFI) Interest Group Project.

Mann, Thomas. 2003. "Linking Knowledge and Action: Political Science and Campaign Finance Reform." *Perspectives on Politics* 1(1): 69–84.

Martin, Cathie Jo. 1995. "Nature or Nurture? Sources of Firm Preference for National Health Reform." *American Political Science Review* 89(4): 898–914.

Masters, Marick and Gerald Keim. 1985. "Determinants of PAC Participation Among Large Corporations." *Journal of Politics* 47(4): 1158–1173.

Mayhew, David. 1974. "Congressional Elections: The Case of the Vanishing Marginals." *Polity* 6(3): 295–317.

Mayhew, David. 1986. *Placing Parties in American Politics*. Princeton, NJ: Princeton University Press.

McCarty, Nolan and Lawrence Rothenberg. 1993. "The Strategic Decisions of Political Action Committees." Paper Presented at the Annual Convention of the American Political Science Association, Washington, D.C.

McCarty, Nolan and Lawrence Rothenberg. 2000. "Coalitional Maintenance: Politicians, Parties, and Organized Groups." *American Politics Quarterly* 28(3): 291–308.

McConnell, Mitch. 2004. "The Future is Now." *Election Law Journal* 3(2):123–125.

Milbrath, Lester. 1965. *The Washington Lobbyists*. Chicago: Rand McNally and Company.

Mintrom, Michael and Sandra Vergari. 1998. "Policy Networks and Innovation Diffusion: The Case of State Education Reforms." *Journal of Politics* 60(1): 126–148.

Morehouse, Sarah McCally. 1981. *State Politics, Parties and Policy*. New York: Holt, Rinehart, and Winston.

Morris, Dick. 1997. *Behind the Oval Office*. New York: Random House.

Nelson, Candice. 1998. "The Money Chase: Partisanship, Committee Leadership Change, and PAC Contributions in the House of Representatives," in *The Interest Group Connection: Electioneering, Lobbying, and Policymaking in Washington*, ed. Paul Herrnson, Ronald G. Shaiko and Clyde Wilcox. Chatham, NJ: Chatham House Publishers.

Parker, David. 2005. "Resources Rule" Unpublished Dissertation, University of Wisconsin- Madison.

Parker, David and John Coleman. 2004. "Pay to Play: Parties, Interests, and Money in Federal Elections," in *The Medium and the Message: Television Advertising and American Elections*, ed. Kenneth Goldstein and Patricia Strach. Englewood Cliffs, NJ: Prentice Hall.

Petracca, Mark, ed. 1992. *The Politics of Interests: Interest Groups Transformed*. Boulder, CO.: Westview Press.

Petrocik, John R. 1996. "Issue Ownership in Presidential Elections, with a 1980 Case Study." *American Journal of Political Science* 40(3): 825–850.

Pomper, Gerald. 1977. "The Decline of the Party in American Elections." *Political Science Quarterly* 92(1): 21–41.

Poole, Keith T. and Howard Rosenthal. 1997. *Congress: A Political-Economic History of Roll Call Voting*. New York: Oxford University Press

Poole, Keith and Thomas Romer. 1985. "Patterns of Political Action Committee Contributions to the 1980 Campaigns for the United States House of Representatives." *Public Choice* 47(1): 63–111.

Poole, Keith, Thomas Romer and H. Rosenthal. 1987. "The Revealed Preferences of Political Action Committees." *American Economic Review* 77(2): 298–302.

Potter, Trevor. 2005. "The Current State of Campaign Finance Laws," in *The New Campaign Finance Sourcebook*, ed. Anthony Corrado, Thomas Mann, Daniel Ortiz and Trevor Potter. Washington, D.C.: Brookings Institute.

Reiter, Howard. 1993. *Parties and Elections in Corporate America*. New York: Longman.

Rogers, Everett. 1983. *Diffusions of Innovations*. New York: The Free Press.

Romer, Thomas and James Snyder. 1994. "An Empirical Investigation of the Dynamics of PAC Contributions." *American Journal of Political Science* 38(3): 745–769.

Rossiter, Clinton. 1961. *The Federalist Papers*. New York: New American Library.

Rozell, Mark and Clyde Wilcox. 1999. *Interest Groups in American Campaigns*. Washington, D.C.: CG Press.

Sabato, Larry. 1984. *PAC Power*. New York: Norton.

Sahr, Robert. 2004. "Using Inflation-Adjusted Dollars in Analyzing Political Developments." *PS: Political Science and Politics* 37(2): 273–284.

Saltzman, Gregory. 1987. "Congressional Voting on Labor Issues: The Role of PACs." *Industrial and Labor Relations Review* 40(2): 163–179.

Schattschneider, E.E. 1942. *Party Government*. New York: Greenwood Publishing Group.

Schlozman, Kay Lehman. 1984. "What Accent the Heavenly Chorus." *Journal of Politics* 46(4): 1006–1032.

Schlozman, Kay Lehman and John Tierney. 1986. *Organized Interests and American Democracy*. New York: Harper and Row.

Skinner, Richard. 2005. "Do 527's Add Up to a Party? Thinking About the "Shadows" of Politics," *The Forum* 3(3), Article 5. Available at: http://www.bepress.com/forum/vol3/iss3/art5

Smith, Bradley. 2001. *Unfree Speech: The Folly of Campaign Finance Reform*. Princeton, NJ: Princeton University Press.

Smith, Bradley and Stephen Hoersting. 2002. "A Toothless Anaconda: Innovation, Impotence and Over-enforcement at the Federal Election Commission." *Election Law Journal* 1(2): 145–171.

Smith, Richard. 1995. "Interest Group Influence in the U.S. Congress." *Legislative Studies Quarterly* 20(1) :89–139.

Sorauf, Frank J. 1975. *Party Politics in America*. Boston: Little Brown.

Sorauf, Frank. 1996. "Political Action Committees," in *Campaign Finance Reform: A Sourcebook*, ed. Anthony Corrado, Thomas Mann, Daniel Ortiz, Trevor Potter and Frank Sorauf. Washington, D.C.: Brookings Institute.

Sorauf, Frank J. and Scott Wilson. 1994. "Political Parties and Campaign Finance: Adaption and Accommodation Toward a Changing Role," in *The Parties Respond*, ed. Sandy Maisel. Boulder, CO: Westview Press.

Suarez, Sandra. 2000. *Does Business Learn? Tax Breaks, Uncertainty, and Political Strategies*. Ann Arbor: University of Michigan Press.

Taylor, Andrew. 2003. "Conditional Party Government and Campaign Contributions: Insights From the Tobacco and Alcoholic Beverage Industries." *American Journal of Political Science* 47 (2): 293–3004.

Walker, Jack. 1991. *Mobilizing Interests in America*. Ann Arbor: University of Michigan Press.

Wattenberg, Martin. 1984. *The Decline of American Political Parties, 1952–1980*. Cambridge, MA: Harvard University Press.

Wayman, Frank. 1985. "Arms Control and Strategic Arms Voting in the U.S. Senate: Patterns of Change, 1967-1983." *The Journal of Conflict Resolution* 29(2): 225–251.

Weissman, Steve and Ruth Hassan. 2005. "BCRA and the 527 Groups," in *The Election After Reform: Money, Politics and the Bipartisan Campaign Reform Act*, ed. Michael J. Malbin. Rowman and Littlefield.

Welch, William. 1980. "The Allocation of Political Monies: Economic Interest Groups." *Public Choice* 35(1): 97–120.

Wilson, Graham. 1981. *Interest Groups in the United States*. Oxford: Clarendon Press.

Wilson, James Q. 1995. *Political Organizations*. Princeton, NJ: Princeton University Press.

Wright, John. 1985. "PACs, Contributions, and Roll Call: An Organizational Perspective." *American Political Science Review* 79(2): 400–414.

Wright, John. 1989. "PAC Contributions, Lobbying, and Representation." *Journal of Politics* 51(3): 713–729.

Wright, John. 1990. "Contributions, Lobbying, and Committee Voting in the U.S. House of Representatives." *American Political Science Review* 84(2): 417–438.

Zaller, John. 1996. "The Myth of Massive Media Impact Revisited," in *Political Persuasion and Attitude Change*, ed. Michael J. Malbin. Diana C. Mutz and Paul M. Sniderman and Richard A. Brody. Ann Arbor: University of Michigan Press.

Index

Weiss, Daniel, 65
Weissman, Steve, 130–131
West Wing, The, 172, 181
Whirlpool Corporation, 153
Wilson, Scott, 86
Wirth, Timothy, 63
Wisconsin Advertising Project, 11,
 119–120, 196n9, 196n19, 203n3
Wisconsin Right to Life v. FEC, 185

Women's Alliance for Israel PAC,
 18
Woon, Jonathan, 190
Wright, John, 68, 198n2
WV Media, 138

Young Democrats of America, 130

Zuniga, Markos Moulitsas, 178

Michael M. Franz is Assistant Professor of Government and Legal Studies at Bowdoin College. His research interests include political advertising, interest groups politics, campaign finance reform, and mass media. He has published articles in *The American Journal of Political Science, Political Communication, Political Analysis, Political Behavior*, and *The Journal of Politics*. In 2007, he was awarded the American Political Science Association's E.E. Schattschneider Award for the best doctoral dissertation in the field of American government. He is also the co-author of *Campaign Advertising and American Democracy* (Temple).